AFRICAN AMERICAN
VIEWS OF THE JAPANESE

SUNY Series, Global Conflict and Peace Education
Betty Reardon, Editor

AFRICAN AMERICAN VIEWS OF THE JAPANESE

Solidarity or Sedition?

REGINALD KEARNEY

STATE UNIVERSITY OF NEW YORK PRESS

Published by
State University of New York Press, Albany

© 1998 State University of New York

All rights reserved

Printed in the United States of America

For information, address State University of New York
Press, State University Plaza, Albany, N.Y., 12246

Production by E. Moore
Marketing by Fran Keneston

Library of Congress Cataloging-in-Publication Data

Kearney, Reginald, 1938–
    African American views of the Japanese : solidarity or sedition /
Reginald Kearney.
        p.   cm. — (SUNY series, global conflict and peace education)
    Based on author's thesis (Ph.D.—Kent State University).
    Includes bibliographical references and index.
    ISBN 0-7914-3911-9 (hardcover : alk. paper). — ISBN 0-7914-3912-7
(pbk. : alk. paper)
        1. Afro-Americans—Relations with Japanese. 2. United States-
-Race relations. I. Title. II. Series.
    E185.615.K36 1998
    305.8'00973—dc21   97-44963
                                                                          CIP

10 9 8 7 6 5 4 3 2 1

To the memory of Sara and Sandy,
my first mentors

CONTENTS

⊗⊗⊗⊗⊗

EDITOR'S PREFACE

One of the most heralded developments of the "Post-Cold War" Era has been the "emergence of global civil society." While it is true that transnational citizens' movements, as attested by the awarding of the 1997 Nobel Prize for Peace to the campaign to outlaw land mines, is more visible, vigorous, and effective than ever before, such transnational relationships among citizens have far deeper historical roots. This book deals with one such relationship which is of special significance to the present global system, to the relationship between the United States and Japan, and to Americans' understanding of their own history.

The global system today is plagued by ethnic tensions that often erupt into armed violence or escalate into international crises. The instigators of these crises may be playing the traditional and lethal games for political power, but for many, if not most, of those who bear the arms, the issue is identity and dignity, the motivation for many epic human struggles. Understanding the profound and undeniable needs of all peoples to realize their own unique identities and to experience their fundamental human dignity in their identities is essential to coping with those concepts. Further, to understand that a unique identity does not necessarily stand as an obstacle to the realization of a national political or even universal human identity is even more important. Moreover, important to the point of becoming an essential prerequisite for peace is recognizing that the denial of identity and dignity can lead to severe and often violence conflict and, as we have experienced, war. These very contemporary issues are imbedded in the history Reginald Kearney recounts in *African American Views of the Japanese*, a new perspective on World War II.

The war between the United States and Japan was the product of multiple causes, including the power game, but it was experienced as a clash of cultures, exacerbated on both sides by racial prejudices. As made clear by Kearney's account, it is easy to see that these tensions and competitions would have profound effects on Americans still suffering from the various deprivations and discriminations imposed by the racism that has characterized this country since its inception. The affinities they felt for other "people of color" presaged the solidarity efforts of many in all the colonized and exploited nations of the world.

Today there is much discussion of U.S.-Japanese relations, mainly focused on the issues of cooperation and conflict produced by the relationship of two "world powers," two competitive allies. However, there is little attention paid to the collaboration between American and Japanese citizens on various issues, from greenhouse gas emissions to the "Mutual Security" arrangement and the Status of Forces Agreements. Much of this cooperation reflects a common challenge to their respective governments and to policies from which they dissent. Disagreement with the majority position in both societies poses the issue of loyalty. What those collaborating in a common opposition to national policy see as solidarity raises questions of loyalty in the minds of the establishments of their respective countries. When the opposed policies relate to national security, the questions of loyalty can become suspicious, even accusations, of sedition. This book invites us to reflect on such issues, the problems and the possibilities of this form of transnational citizen cooperation in which citizens challenge their own states.

African American View of the Japanese thus reveals experiences which help us to understand previously unconsidered aspects of global civil society and provides us with information to guide us through the development of a more effective global citizens' movement. These are important lessons for all world citizens. It has, as well, special lessons for American and Japanese citizens, instructing them in a chapter of their own common history that has been largely ignored. There is a great interest among Japanese in the American civil rights movement, some interest in black history, but little knowledge of these black American-Japanese affinities of the past. That there is interest in filling this void is attested by the positive response this book received when it was published in Japanese in 1995.

Yet, of all those who have much to learn from Kearney's research, it is American citizens who most need to attend to the lessons it provides. It demonstrates many aspects of black history that American society seems yet to have realized: that there has been all along a sharp political awareness of mainstream politics and foreign policy and the implications for blacks among the black citizenry; that a wide range of political diversity is far more characteristic of black America than the monolithic and stereotypical view from which mainstream politics is formed; and what is most significant, that certain recent "citizen diplomacy" on the part of some black leaders did not represent the view of all blacks nor was it for black citizens an unprecedented venture into "transnational politics."

Reginald Kearney's work is a welcome addition to this series. It sheds significant new light on the roots and possibilities of global cooperation as well as of global conflict. It provides important lessons for that sphere of peace education concerned about issues of identity, voice, and marginalization. This is a work that should be central to black studies, the study of U.S.-Japanese relations, and certainly to peace studies.

BETTY REARDON
SERIES EDITOR

※※※※

PREFACE

In September 1989, American newspapers reported that former Prime Minister Yasuhiro Nakasone had said that the presence of African Americans, Puerto Ricans, and Mexicans was responsible for a decline in American intelligence levels. Subsequently, two other high-level members of Japan's ruling party received notoriety for equally disparaging remarks about African Americans. Then there were disclosures about the discriminatory business practices of Japanese companies operating in the United States, use of stereotypical Sambo images, and treatment of immigrant laborers and indigenous minorities in Japan. Even the flap over an alleged remark by Salevaa Atisone, the huge Hawaiian-born sumo wrestler, was reported in the *New York Times*. Better known in Japan as Konishiki, Atisone denied saying that his failure to gain promotion to the highest rank of *yokozuna* was because he was non-Japanese.[1] This series of revelations hit black America like an earthquake followed by a string of aftershocks. As a result of this series of shocks, a great many African Americans were ready to believe that all Japanese are racists, that Japan is a land of racism.

African Americans who reached such a conclusion probably would be surprised to learn that it puts them at odds with some of their greatest and most militant heroes. My own interest in the views and attitudes that black Americans held regarding the Japanese began as a result of conversations with my father when I was a high school student.

My father, who was a truck driver most of his adult life, returned from the war in the Pacific with skills that should have qualified him for work in the public utilities company in Hackensack, New Jersey. When he applied, the company policy was not to hire "you people." Getting and keeping jobs or trying to get into the truckers union was often a source of frustration and anger. Disillusionment and anger caused him to say things that I, in my naivete, thought heretical: America was not a land of freedom and equality; Negroes had no flag, no chance to advance, no rights that a white man would respect. I remember asking him if he had ever heard of Thomas Jefferson, the Declaration of Independence, or the American ideal that all men are created equal. Arguments that would be identified with Malcolm X in the 1960s, I first heard a decade earlier sitting at our kitchen table.

Sometimes my father would talk about military life as he experienced it. One Saturday, in the heat of discussion, he said that he had no particular ideological or patriotic reason for fighting against the Japanese. Black soldiers, he told me, had been put in a position by the government where it was a matter of kill or be killed; the primeval instinct to survive was important not ideology. All he wanted to do was make it back to his family. Despite his memories of air raids and bomb attacks, he said that he was not particularly interested in fighting against the Japanese soldiers because, as he put it, they were colored people like us.

These discussions around the kitchen table made enough of an impression on me that I wanted to know if others shared the attitudes of my father regarding the Japanese. What I found was that if Sandy Kearney's views were heresy it was a heresy shared by tens of thousands in the African American community. Actually, a great many African Americans, of different philosophies, social and economic circumstances, and educational attainments shared and may even have influenced my father's views of the Japanese. What perceptions have African Americans had of the Japanese? The answer to this question constitutes the substance of this study.

Besides the practical consideration that there is a paucity of primary source materials on the subject, there are two other important reasons why the interest African Americans had in Japan remained so long a secret: first, generally speaking, African Americans have not been seen as having views regarding international matters significantly different from those of white Americans.[2] Second, African Americans themselves helped perpetuate the myth that, save perhaps during the Revolutionary and Civil Wars, when they offered their talents to whichever side extended the better promise of freedom, they have not had divided loyalties during their country's times of trial.

This study, to a considerable degree, relies on the black press as a primary source. As G. James Fleming, the former editor and college professor who analyzed the role of the black press for the Gunnar Myrdal study, *The American Dilemma*, pointed out, "Negro opinion—at least among the more alert and articulate groups—can be ascertained and studied in the Negro press." The black press was most valuable because of its unique role in the black community as "An Organ for the Negro Protest." Fleming made three points that were particularly important. The black press, more than any other institution, "created the Negro group as a social and psychological reality to the individual Negro." By this he meant that individual African Americans, through sharing "the sufferings, grievances, and pretensions of the millions of Negroes" reported in the black press, came to have a group identity that reached "far outside the narrow local community," creating "a feeling of strength and solidarity." Second, Fleming considered the black press to be "the chief agency of group control." It told individuals how they should think and feel as Negro Americans, he says. By so doing, Fleming contended, the black press "creates a tremendous power of suggestion by implying that all other Negroes think and feel in this manner." Third, he argued that the black press was primarily the instrument of the upper and middle classes. It was their doings and sayings that were recorded there. They set the tone. In addition, the upper and middle classes used the press to spread their opinions to the lower classes.[3]

Fleming noticed that the black press took pride in the attainments of the Japanese. He suggested that expressing pride in the Japanese for their "strikingly quick adaptation to western ways" was one way the black press compensated for the reality of its own existence in a white-dominated world. All the problems of Japan, Haiti, or India became the problems of Negroes because the black press found, cultivated, and adopted "all the other 'darker peoples of the world.'"[4] As impressive as the rate of modernization was, black intellectuals were more fascinated with the extraordinary image of a nonwhite nation that had earned the respect and prestige of a great power.

At the turn of the century, the United States, on the basis of its Pacific holdings, was ranked among those nations that presumed a special responsibility toward those whom they regarded as the more benighted races. During this same period, Japan, an Oriental nation, stood on the threshold of world power status. Clearly, African Americans were as likely as their fellow citizens to ponder the meaning of the changing alignment , it must be said that finding items concerning Japan in black newspapers was like panning for gold in a sea of distress over lynchings, disfranchisement, segregation, intimidation, and denial. On the one hand, this attests to the peripheral nature of black interest in Japan and foreign matters generally. On the other hand, however, the pattern of interest ebbs and flows in accordance with blacks' perception of the quality of life in the United States.

Unlike whites, when African Americans looked at foreign affairs they were more particularly inclined to seek implications for a reordering of racial hegemony. Having borne the burdens of white racism, African Americans could not agree that the proper relationship among the races was one in which white stood above black, yellow, red, or brown.

To understand the extent to which Japan and Japanese culture intruded into the black stream of consciousness, the black press is the richest source. Periodically, short items touched on political, economic, diplomatic, military, social, or cultural aspects of Japanese society. Editorials or columns devoted to Japan, however, usually appeared when diplomacy or international events made Japan a focal point of Occidental attention. From the arrival of the first Japanese diplomatic mission to the United States in 1860, leaders in the black community tried to interpret Japan's impact on world affairs and the race question.[5] In the pages of the black press, one may read views expressed by the foremost intellectuals, leaders, and image makers of black America. A partial list, beginning with the leading light of the nineteenth century, Frederick Douglass, would include notables, such as, W. E. B. Du Bois, Booker T. Washington, Mary Church Terrell, John Edward Bruce, James Weldon Johnson, T. Thomas Fortune, Joel A. Rogers, George Schuyler, Marcus Garvey, Dean Kelly Miller, Walter White, Roy Wilkens, Ida Wells Barnett, Adam Clayton Powell Jr., and A. Philip Randolph. Of the people mentioned, only Powell and Randolph were consistently negative in their assessments of the Japanese government and its policies.

In my survey of the black press, except for the period 1900 to 1904, I have chosen to value editorials and columns above straight news stories. These were expository and didactic regarding what Japan meant to black America and what African Americans should think about Japan. An extended news story—such as the coverage of the Russo-Japanese War in the *Savannah Tribune*—sometimes indicated a topic that should be of interest to African Americans. From the straight news story, readers would not learn how the event would, could, or might be important to blacks. The writers of front page news might avoid telling readers how they were supposed to feel about what they read. I have chosen to weigh more heavily the opinionated articles and columns that attempted to interpret and explain the significance of events.

Black intellectuals, who differed sharply from one another regarding domestic goals and strategies for black advancement, were in basic agreement that Japan's achievements on the world scene were good for peoples of color everywhere. The positions of Du Bois and Washington have been represented as a split between "conservatives and radicals." The differences between Du Bois and Garvey finally reduced discussion to a series of charges, counter-charges, and name-calling. Still, they were unanimous in seeing Japan as a positive force in the struggle for racial equality and advancement.

The possibility that Japanese might pose an economic threat sometimes sparked expressions of hostility and ambivalence among African Americans. But that was unusual. The *Chicago Defender*, for example, was unmatched in its support and advocacy of the migration of Southern rural African Americans to the cities of the North; its editorials railed against the "invasion" of European immigrants on economic grounds. Yet, the *Defender* opposed discriminating against the Japanese, claiming at different times, "most of our domestic troubles are due to lawless acts of foreigners who come from other countries than Japan or China" and "there is no just reason for singling out the Japanese as the goat in framing immigration laws."[6]

Another important source for this study is the use of certain government documents, foremost of which are investigative files of the Federal Bureau of Investigation, obtained under the Freedom of Information Act. These FBI materials, which include reports from police, military intelligence, and other investigative agencies, although they must be used most judiciously, are invaluable for the information on the radical fringe of the black community in the 1930s and 1940s. In addition to the data drawn from informants and agents, there are transcripts of recordings of the meetings and interrogations of the suspects. These allow insight into the depth of these people's frustration and despair; they tell of the dreams and fantastic schemes that attest to the extreme alienation of a significant segment in the black community. The views of these people are important to the topic of this paper because these street people not only spoke to the average citizen of the black community, they, in large measure, were *the* average citizen. They worked as laborers, stockyard and social workers, painters, and performers of odd jobs. Ralph Green Best, spiritual leader of the Ethiopian Pacific movement, claimed to be an ordained minister of the New York Colored National Spiritualist Organization. Lester Holness, the group's secretary, had lived in and gone to college in California. James Thornhill, formerly had been a member of the Universal Negro Improvement Association with Jordan.

Some of these people were downwardly mobile. William and Maude Gordon had owned a delicatessen in Chicago for nine years before going out of business. Robert Jordan claimed to have had his own business for seventeen years, an automobile paint shop and used car lot. Information about these people would have been lost without the interest of the FBI since they rarely earned space in the black press. When they did attract the attention of the media, white or black, it was usually condemnatory in nature. In spite of this, the views of these extremist groups add an important dimension to this study. Their inclusion produces a rich mix of personalities and philosophies that contribute to the mosaic that constitutes an African American view of the Japanese.

Although the files of the FBI hold information otherwise unavailable, the biggest drawback to using them is the length of time required to comply with a request. Although the FOIA requires federal agencies to determine whether to release requested records within ten days, with an additional ten day extension allowance, the waiting list for FBI documents is now about three or four years. Currently, I am waiting for a file requested in December 1993. A tremendous backlog has been created by the increased number of requests made under the Freedom of Information and Privacy Acts. Many thousands of requests and millions of pages, I have been told, have strained the resources of the FOIPA section. When I first asked for information under the FOIPA, I received a letter from the director, Clarence Kelly, telling me that it would cost $13,000 dollars. I revised the request and got much less than what I wanted, and it cost a lot less. Today, the FOIPA is alleged to be more "requester" friendly. But historical scholarship is not a priority area of concern. According to a guideline issued by the Justice Department's Office of Information and Privacy, beyond a threat to life or safety and loss of substantial due process rights, requesters must wait patiently because a decision to take a FOIA request out of turn entails delay for others. Simple fairness demands such.

My original request, filed when I was still a Ph.D. candidate at Kent State University, sought all records about alleged Negro-Japanese subversive activities. That request was never completely fulfilled. Twenty years later I learned that copies of my letter had been placed in files that never were made available to me. Thus, I know that this is hardly the definitive story. But I hope the reader will find that it contributes something of importance to the mosaic of American history.

FBI files of Martin Luther King Jr., Jesse Jackson, John Lennon, and other celebrated personalities have been released and can be read on the Internet. In my view, records dating back to the 1930s and 1940s ought to reside in the National Archives where they would be more accessible to scholars. I see no real justification for guarding them further.

⣝⣝⣝⣝

ACKNOWLEDGMENTS

Every historian who discovers some esoteric new information probably feels that his or her find deserves a wide audience, and I am no different. If you are reading this, it means that I have completed an odyssey worthy of Homer. When first setting out on my uncharted journey, I was much like a miner panning for gold, happy to find an occasional nugget to spur me on just a bit longer.

Historians like to talk of the fortuitous circumstances, and it is certainly appropriate to do so here. I shall be ever grateful to Betty Reardon for judging my study worthy of inclusion in her series *Global Conflict and Peace Education*. I know no one else who globe trots as incessantly as she does, but she slowed down long enough to teach and become a colleague at the Kanda University of International Studies in Chiba, Japan. The powers that be must have been smiling on me; I had all but given up hope of an American audience for my study. The circumstances that put me in Japan at the same time, I suppose, were rather fortuitous as well. I have not the words to express my heartfelt thanks.

Since this book began as a dissertation, my greatest debt is owed to the members of my committee. Friends of my father used to call him "Bulldog." Whenever they met me, I became "Little

Bulldog." August Meier, the late Elliott Rudwick, Henry Leonard, and James Lewis made me earn the appellation at Kent State University. Under their tutelage, I learned as much humility as scholarship and am better for it. I confess to having had a penchant for what I thought of as rhetorical flourish. To the extent that it is less reflected in my writing, I owe thanks to Leonard. With regard to content, Lewis challenged my assumptions, my facts, and me with meticulous care.

My greatest indebtedness is to Meier, a friend of long standing, who acted as my dissertation advisor and taskmaster. In writing the afterword to Meier's book *A White Scholar and the Black Community, 1945–1965*, John Bracey wrote, "One does hear that Meier is a harsh taskmaster, a ruthless editor of manuscripts, an unstinting critic." I can attest to the first of these. Like my high school coach used to admonish us to eat, sleep, think football, Meier preached that there were no extenuating circumstances where the pursuit of scholarship was concerned. This was a lesson I learned imperfectly, but I loved the challenge.

When I accepted a position at Morgan State College, my undergraduate alma mater, and began trying to balance the rigors of teaching with the responsibilities that go with helping to raise two sons, I postponed the priority of research and writing. Rather than golden nuggets, Mervyn Daniel and Tom Cripps became the spurs prodding me to finish my dissertation. Cripps endured several versions of my draft, and I benefited each time. When he thought computer skills would facilitate my work, he told me that I was one of the last Neanderthals. It was not until much later that I learned that he banged on an old Smith Corona long after I did.

The following friends and colleagues have contributed to this book through the support that they have given me at different stages: Mitsuo Akamatsu, George Akita, Arna Bontemps, Lena Boyd-Brown, Elaine Breslaw, Sulayman Clark, Charles Countess, Ana De Miguel, Roland Edmonds, Elaine Edmonds, Clifton Ford, Hiromi Furukawa, Cornell Greene, Tim Greene, Sozo Honda, John Hudgins, James Hudson, Charles Johnson, Calvin Kuniyuki, Joe Overton, JoAnn Robinson, Barbara Stephenson, Jennifer Stephenson, Kati Stephenson, Rosalyn Terborg-Penn, Roland Williams, Robert Thompson, Carol Wagner, and Sam Wagner.

I appreciate the services rendered by the staffs at various libraries. Most especially, I thank Margaret Koyne and Elaine Tsubota of Soper Library of Morgan State University for many hours of fulfilling requests, but more for their pleasant attitudes, which made going to the reference or microform centers less a chore. I am grateful to the widow of James Weldon Johnson for permission to use materials from the James Weldon Johnson Memorial Collection on deposit at the Beineke Library of Yale University. I thank the staffs of the following repositories for professional and courteous service: the Schomburg Collection of the New York Public Library; the Enoch Pratt Free Library of Baltimore; the National Archives; the National Record Center in Suitland, Maryland; the Library of Congress; the National Diet Library; and the Diplomatic Record Office of the Ministry of Foreign Affairs in Tokyo.

During the course of my research, I benefited from a modest grant from the Faculty Research Committee at Morgan State University, and a Japan Foundation Language Fellowship to study at the Inter-University Center for Japanese Language Studies provided me a chance to follow some research leads as well.

My indebtedness to Ryoko is without bounds. Yoshiharu and Tetsuro, I thank just for being.

※※※※※

INTRODUCTION

When war broke out between the United States and Japan on December 7, 1941, a few African Americans preferred to hail the Japanese as potential liberators rather than view them as enemies. During the previous three decades a minor theme of African American protest had identified the Japanese as another "colored people" who had struggled successfully in a white-dominated world against the myth that whites were inherently superior to nonwhites. This radical fringe, spawned of the frustration and despair within the black ghettos of America, refused to allow the outbreak of war between their homeland and Japan to deter them from their infatuation with the Japanese people.

As early as 1905, William Edward Burghhardt Du Bois, "the dean of the protest advocate leaders during the first half of the twentieth century," "the senior intellectual militant of his people," had told black America that the "Negro problem" was but a local variation of a world-wide pattern of racism. Du Bois and other black intellectuals pointed at the Japanese as an example of people who demonstrated the fallacy of white assertions that people of color were innately incompetent or inferior. For more than thirty years, Du Bois had helped project an image of Japan as an ally in the struggle for racial equality.[1] This image of Japan had wide appeal among African Americans of different social and economic circumstances.

The tenacity of that appeal was revealed in the 1930s with the emergence of Robert Leonard Jordan, an obscure Harlem hustler and street corner orator, and groups such as the Ethiopian Pacific Movement, which he headed. The members of this group were unabashedly pro-Japanese. Before and after Japanese naval forces attacked Pearl Harbor, Jordan and his followers declared themselves opposed to conscription and counselled all who would listen to resist military service in an army that would be deployed against Japan.

Although both Du Bois and Jordan were convinced that the war in the Pacific was due, in large measure, to Japan's demanding equity with the other great powers and Anglo-American unwillingness to concede coequal status, Jordan was the one who became so alienated from the American racial system that he chose to charge full ahead—damn the consequences—steady on a course of pro-Japanese advocacy. The black and white press both widely denounced him as the "Black Hitler of Harlem"; the government indicted, convicted, and sentenced him to ten years in prison. Were the differences between Jordan and Du Bois symptomatic of greater division within the ranks of black Americans regarding Japan?

The African American community, generally speaking, first embraced the Japanese as people of color during the Russo-Japanese War. At times like this, when Japanese were embroiled in crisis, blacks paid them more notice. In periods of normalcy or when African Americans were too preoccupied with their own problems, interest in Japan was more muted. In general, African Americans tended to look at the people of Japan from two points of view: Japanese were the people who disproved all those myths which perpetuated the notion that colored peoples were unable to compete on a par with whites; they were a people whose circumstances were analogous to those of blacks. Prior to Japan's attack on Pearl Harbor, I think that I can say without overstating the case, a great many, perhaps most, African Americans had only positive impressions of the Japanese and their achievements.[2]

After Pearl Harbor, all but the most radical diehards retreated from previous unequivocal backing of the East Asian power and helped to create a serious division of opinion among African Americans regarding Japan as an enemy of the United States. Most African Americans came to support the war effort of the United

States, some more enthusiastically than others. An extreme element opposed the war effort and publicly flaunted their pro-Japanese sympathies.

Although it denounced the pro-Japanese element in the African American community as merely a "lunatic fringe," the U.S. government regarded these numerically insignificant people as potential threats to the successful prosecution of the war and a danger to the continued well-being of the nation. As a result of surveys conducted by the Office of War Information (OWI) and because of agitation by the African American press, the government monitored the mood of black America in order to head off possible subversive activity in response to the extreme utterances of black radicals. OWI surveys conducted in New York City indicated that nearly one-half of the sample believed they would be no worse off under Japanese rule. It is significant that the result reflected the views of middle-class African Americans as told to black interviewers. Lower-class folks, suspicious of government surrogates probing their views of the Japanese, remained taciturn.[3]

Fearful of the deleterious effect a few rotten apples might have within the black body politic, certain government officials opted to work with the more moderate elements in the African American community. Social scientists working at OWI were so inclined. Agents of the Federal Bureau of Investigation, however, demonstrated concern about the possible efficacy of Japanese agitation among blacks more than two decades before Pearl Harbor. As early as 1917, agents of the FBI responsible for countertintelligence began to compile files on "Negro subversion." To some extent this occurred in response to a few blacks who made no effort to keep secret their infatuation with Japan. In 1919 a letter signed "Negroes of Birmingham" declared that in the next war Negroes would join the side of the Japanese. In the same year, the FBI began to make a list of "suspected organizations."[4]

With the rise of Marcus Garvey as the preeminent mass leader of the 1920s, the potential for Japanese influence among African Americans seemed more ominous. Garvey's broad appeal among those at the lowest end of the social, economic, and political scale and his conspicuous embrace of the Japanese convinced J. Edgar Hoover, director of the FBI, and other government and military figures that angry blacks represented a potential danger to the security of the United States.

Although the government was able to imprison Garvey for mail fraud and subsequently deported him back to Jamaica, his message regarding the Japanese as important to the rise of black people remained a consistent theme in the rhetoric of former followers and admirers. Dispersed like so much kindling in major cities about the country, the remnants of Garvey's movement in the 1930s attracted the intensified scrutiny of America's national security apparatus.

By the time of World War II, the government feared that the Japanese would make a concerted effort to exploit the pent up anger and frustration that permeated the black ghettos of America. According to one intelligence report, the Japanese, from the time of the furor over anti-alien land laws, tried to stir up blacks with the admonition that they must stick together in resisting the injustices of whites. The same report indicated that all Japanese consulates in the United States were under orders to survey the situation of blacks in order to ascertain their susceptibility to overtures. By 1941 the Japanese had plans for using African Americans to carry out subversive and espionage activities, American intelligence sources maintained.[5]

Sources within OWI believed that the Japanese had a potently persuasive argument with which they might have tried "to drive the racial wedge deeper in hope of inciting the Negro minority to Civil War." In a critique of Japanese propaganda efforts, a report of the Foreign Broadcast Intelligence Service (FBIS) pointed out Japan's increasing tendency to vigorously champion the cause of African Americans. The treatment of African Americans, it stated, was epitomized as a specific example of the exploitation and oppression of colored peoples by Anglo-Saxons.[6]

According to this report of FBIS, the Japanese had broadened the question of race from being merely a yellow versus white issue to the view that all of the colored peoples of the world stood against the English and Americans. In their propaganda, the Japanese attacked America's Achilles heel and lashed out at three points of particular vulnerability: the treatment of African Americans in the military, the efforts to keep African Americans in their "place," and discrimination in industry. The Japanese also noted that some whites wanted to deport African Americans to West Africa.[7]

Ultimately, the Japanese influenced American government policy and race relations. In the face of the perceived threat posed by Japanese propagandists, certain government officials, who were ready to acknowledge that the issue of race was America's Achilles heel, took a variety of steps in their effort to counteract and nullify any possible combination of African Americans and Japanese working against the interests of the country. Spearheaded by social scientists in the employ of OWI, some officials advocated making the kinds of liberal reforms which would address the real grievances of the moderates within the African American community. These officials were critical of, and worked to modify, the attitudes and actions of the more conservative government agencies, most particularly, the FBI and the military.

The more enlightened officials were most interested in reversing policies and practices that were especially odious to African Americans. In order to lift the morale of blacks, these agents agreed that the government needed to end the navy's policy of employing African Americans strictly in menial servant positions, end the marine's lily-white policy, end the army's policy of segregation and limited promotion of African Americans to officer ranks, and end the government's discriminatory policy of employment and promotion. Officials in OWI also favored enforcement powers for the Federal Employment Practices Commission, black representation on the War Labor Board, and nondiscrimination in low-cost and defense housing. In addition, OWI personnel urged action to allow the occupation of the Sojourner Truth Homes, a Detroit project, and asked to have a statement issued declaring that the government did not condone the riots that erupted as a result of white opposition. OWI wanted to go further. They suggested that the president demonstrate his commitment to improve the status of African Americans with an appointment to his staff as administrative assistant or secretary. They envisioned that as a position to be filled by someone who could serve as the president's advisor on matters relating to black participation in the war.[8]

Some OWI officials believed it was necessary to work at changing white attitudes regarding African Americans. In a broad attempt to reach a diverse and at times mutually hostile audience, these liberal-minded members of OWI decided to employ the most potent device for mass propagandizing then available. One memo referred to the American motion picture as "probably the most universally influential mass communication medium in the world." Hoping to marshal the "great unrealized potential force as an active aid to the prosecution of the war, OWI opened its Office of the Bureau of Motion Pictures in Hollywood.[9]

Carlton Moss, the production manager of the Council on Negro Culture, a New York–based operation, suggested how motion pictures might be employed specifically to reduce white animosity toward African Americans and encourage among blacks a sense of involvement. Moss was aghast at finding how prevalent pro-Japanese sentiment was in the barber shops, on the street corners, and in other places in Harlem where people congregated and discussed the war. Moss wrote to Archibald MacLeish, librarian of Congress and director of the Office of Facts and Figures, the predecessor of OWI, complaining about the government's obvious lack of a program to address the problem of pro-Japanese sympathies among African Americans. Believing that the government had to campaign actively for African American support, Moss offered a vehicle that he thought would rekindle their sparks of patriotism. He was convinced his dramatic pageant *Salute to Negro Troops*, a dramatization of the historical role African Americans played in America's wars, would achieve this. A corollary theme of Moss's production was the suggestion that "a Hitler-Japan-Mussolini victory" would bring about a loss of hard-won freedoms.[10]

Moss thought that his dramatic production would aid in getting African Americans to support fully the government's mobilization for war by serving as "a stimulus to unity and morale." He invited OWI to send a representative to view the play during its one-week stint at Harlem's famous Apollo Theatre. The thrust of the production, he promised, would be two-pronged: it would draw attention to the evils that continued to hinder the Negro's full integration into the life of America, and it would point "the way to a better day."[11]

Moss's anxiety over the government's lack of a program for wedding African Americans to the United States mobilization program arose from his belief that "the opposition," particularly the Japanese, had successfully planted the seeds of discord. He recounted some of the arguments that he overheard: "Japan is the friend of the colored races"; "What Japan is doing should be an inspiration to the darker races"; "Japan is showing the world that the darker races can't be kicked around"; "Japan is only fighting China because China sold out to the white race"; "Japan is ashamed of [Negroes] because we haven't done right by the darker races"; and "Japan don't want the United States, she just wants to run the whites out."[12]

When his pageant was finally made into the movie *Negro Soldier*, under the auspices of the U.S. Army, Moss, in the role of pastor-narrator, included but one line addressing his dread of the Japanese. In that single line, the minister denied that there was any truth to the notion that Japan was "the savior of the colored races."[13]

Spencer Williams, another African American producer of

films, also attempted to deny that a kindred spirit occurred between his community and the Japanese. Williams made all-black movies that were supposed to be the answer to Hollywood's inability to treat African Americans in a serious manner. But Williams's movie, *Marching On*, was nowhere near the same creative class as the Hollywood-slick *Negro Soldier*.

Marching On was a melodramatic movie with monodimensional characters and a threadbare plot. The protagonist, Rodney Tucker, was the only character who questioned America's motives for going to war against Japan, but not too convincingly. The film ends with Tucker capturing a clandestine Japanese spy ring sending radio messages from a cave in the Arizona desert. Williams wanted his film to convey to African Americans his sense of alarm. He was convinced that the United States, up against a powerful and wily enemy, faced its greatest crisis in history. Furthermore, he believed that if African Americans did not put their shoulders to the wheel, something bad might befall the country. Whether because of the poor quality of the film or the lack of empathy for the message, clearly, African Americans audiences shunned *Marching On* and allowed it to pass hardly noticed onto the trash pile of cinematography.[14]

African Americans went in droves, however, to see the Hollywood production *Behind the Rising Sun*, a movie OWI officials tagged a "serious interpretation of the enemy." Supposedly based on the notes of a reporter who had spent thirteen years in Japan, this motion picture featured stars such as Robert Ryan, Tom Neal, J. Carrol Naish, Gloria Holden, and Margo. Publicists advertised it as the first realistic look at "the Japanese mentality." This movie, they claimed, revealed "the hidden motives behind the attack on Pearl Harbor" and disclosed "Japan's mad dream of world conquest."[15]

Sparing few invectives, Hollywood publicists wrote leads such as the following: "The bowing, hissing monkey men of the Island Empire lay brutal hands on Gloria Holden" and "mothers, wives and daughters at the mercy of the lust-mad conquerors." The advertisers promised to reveal "prisoners mutilated and mangled, helpless victims clad in dred 'black kimonas [sic],'" "babes torn from their helpless mothers' arms to die horribly on a bayonet point," and "opium fed to starving, war-crazed Chinese children!" By means of this undisguised racist appeal, these Hollywood heroes hoped *Behind the Rising Sun* would stir the passions of patriotism until every red-blooded American man upon seeing the actors masquerading as Japanese on the screen would become "mad enough to want to smash them with [their] bare fists!"[16]

When *Behind the Rising Sun* opened for a two-week engagement at the Lincoln Theatre in Washington, D.C., Baltimore's Afro-American newspaper noted that it was "said to be one of the most significant films of the year." In its second week at the Lincoln the movie was still breaking all attendance records and a manager of the theatre remarked that he was unaware that African Americans were so violently anti-Japanese. Ralph Matthews, a columnist at the *Afro*, believed the manager misunderstood the real appeal of the movie for African American patrons. Matthews confessed that he himself found it "gratifying to see for once a picture in which the lordly white man got a taste of his own medicine."[17]

Matthews seriously doubted that other African Americans dreamed of putting other nonwhites "in their place" or wanted to punish a colored people for having the audacity to think that they were as good as whites. This, he believed, was the thrust of the movie, and he was persuaded that what blacks got from the movie was different and at odds with that which whites took away with them. Clearly, Matthews understood that white and black audiences interpreted racial themes very differently. While they might have deplored the "carnal atrocities" and "beastiality" attributed to the Japanese soldier, African Americans saw that as little different from atrocities southern whites perpetrated against blacks of the South. "We," Matthews declared, "also deplore the beastiality of Dixie lynchers and we see no reason why we should die to eradicate one, while the other is permitted to carry on." Matthews' pledge of allegiance to the United States was conditional: "We will gladly help Uncle Sam punish the Jap[anese] if he will show some inclination to protect us from his beasts at home. This is the price tag we put on our blood in the Far East. The best propaganda America can spread against the Japanese is equality and tolerance at home. One reader of the *Afro*, George Calloway, of Bristol, Tennessee, in a letter to the editor, called Matthews' critique "the most down-to-earth truth that has been published by the *Afro*."[18]

Surveys conducted by OWI supported Matthews' analysis. One survey of African American opinion in New York City found that nearly two-fifths of the people interviewed felt that it was more important to make democracy work at home than to beat Germany and Japan. Nearly half the same sample voiced a belief that they would probably be no worse off under Japanese rule and that they were in a society where prejudice and discrimination were rampant.[19]

The African American elite, by its portrayal of the Japanese as fellow colored people who struggled against white oppression, in large measure helped shape the view of the Japanese held by nonelite African Americans. Once awakened to see the Japanese in the role of race champions, some of these nonelite African Americans, even in the wake of Pearl Harbor, were disinclined to abandon their perception of Japan as a positive influence on the racial question. Whether through utter despair or bravado, some of these nonelite types, whether northern urban ghetto dwellers or southern tenant farmers, when compared with those who settled for an inch of progress were less inhibited about voicing positions that left them open to charges of sedition. Yet, members of the black middle class shared with the lower classes the view that the Japanese enemy was a factor that made a difference in the way the war would affect the racial situation in this country. Thus, people who were regarded as leaders by officials in government were unable to promise with certainty African American cohesiveness regarding the question of their support in the war with Japan.

Data compiled over two decades by various investigative agencies alerted officials of the federal government to the probability that the twin themes that the Japanese preached—that colored peoples shared a common brotherhood and that they suffered a common oppression—fell upon receptive ears among the various strata of African American society. The government had documented the activities of certain Japanese who moved with ease among African Americans, two of whom were Naka Nakane, also known as Major Satakata Takahashi, and Yasuichi Hikida. The government's own reports showed that the Japanese had appeal across a broad spectrum of the African American community. Officials at OWI understood what few white Americans suspected: from time to time, African Americans have been interested in developments overseas, but that interest might not necessarily mirror that of whites and might even be at odds with the views of most white Americans. Fearing that African American empathy for Japanese endangered the national security, some liberal elements within the national government reached out to moderate black leaders while trying to work within the bureaucracy to redress some of the real and most blatant grievances of African Americans.

This coalition of liberal bureaucrats and moderate African American leadership, partially in response to the negative stimulus provided by a radical fringe, sought to change policies and fought to eliminate the negative attitudes regarding African Americans held by most white Americans, within the government and without. Thus it may be said that the views and attitudes that African Americans had of the Japanese, in some measure, contributed to a change of racial attitudes and patterns in the United States of America.

PART I

❈❈❈❈

FIRST IMPRESSIONS

ONE

❧❧❧❧

EARLY VIEWS
OF THE JAPANESE

B etween 1900 and 1904, African Americans and their press began to take notice of Japan and some of the issues that affected developments in that country. At first, their views of the Japanese were comparable to those of whites; they too made allusions to the uniqueness, strangeness, or ridiculousness of the Japanese as a people and a culture; then, African Americans showed interest in Japanese conduct in China, especially after Japan's decisive victory in the Sino-Japanese War; and finally, they expressed apprehension that the Japanese would arrive in America as competitors in the labor market.

Before 1904, references to Japan in the black media, like those in the white media, were usually comments on the progress or exoticism of the Japanese, but with time the black editors, reporters, and other shapers of opinion began to comment on the Japanese more from a racial angle. Most early references to Japan were presented as boilerplate. Drawing upon the same sources, sharing common attitudes about non-Americans, African American newspaper editors and reporters, when they bothered to look at the culturally remote Japanese, looked through an American cultural prism, not necessarily a black one.

Early writers were drawn to what they perceived to be the

arcane cultural traditions of the Japanese. Habitual readers of the tidbits about Japan learned many interesting facts along with a fair amount of fiction. They learned that the land of the rising sun was a place founded by "gentle spirits" and that its ruler could trace his imperial pedigree back 2,500 years. It was a country where even sumo wrestlers had lineages more than three centuries long; where bonsai—the cultivation of dwarfed trees—was an art form; where houses were built without the use of nails. In Japan, African American readers learned, fire fighters tattooed their bodies, wives blackened their teeth, and parents put name-and-address labels on their children. Japanese ate pickled plums, made paper toys, and poured cascades of water on the heads of lying boys. The Japanese sold crickets in cages, went fishing not with worms but with diving birds, shod their horses with straw, and ate fish raw. The Japanese cuisine included delicacies such as lily roots and bamboo shoots.[1]

In some regards, the Japanese not only appeared to do things differently from Westerners, but also seemed to do them just the reverse. Carpenters pulled planes toward themselves; readers of books read from right to left and footnotes were placed at the top of pages; at funerals the mourners wore white; and the best room in a home was at the rear of the house.[2]

Some aspects of Japanese culture seemed worthy of emulation. An article which appeared in the *Indianapolis World* touted the mode of living in Japan as especially conducive to good health. In hygiene and preventive medicine, the writer contended, the Japanese were in advance of other nations because of the "national and historic habit of living in the fresh air and sunshine." While Western homes suffered from poor ventilation and impure air, Japanese houses were at all times open to wind and sun. The commentator observed that both the structures of the houses and personal habits of cleanliness contributed to the good health of the Japanese. In this regard, the observer declared that the Japanese were "the most cleanly of body of all peoples." Moreover, the reporter claimed that in Tokyo alone there were approximately eight hundred public baths that were frequented by a clientele that partook in daily, and sometimes twice daily, ablutions.[3]

At other times, Japanese cultural differences invited the kind of ridicule revealed in a bit of doggerel that appeared in a Portland, Oregon newspaper:

I am a jolly, jolly, little Jap,
Hear my little shoes go clap, clap, clap;

When I go to school I leave them at the door,
Then down I sit on a mat on the floor,
I use these chopsticks when its time to dine,
A silk gown I wear when I'm dressed up fine.

On another occasion, the same newspaper described sleeping practices in different parts of the world. In the piece, the writer reported
that the Japanese slept on "matting" laid on the floor and used a
"stiff uncomfortable headrest." This, he decided, was a "bed of tor-
ture." As condescending as the scribe was regarding the Japanese
style of sleeping, he saved his most negative assessment for
Africans. "Of all people the easiest to suit in the way of sleeping
quarters are Negroes. An African Negro, like a wild animal, can
curl up anywhere," he reported.[4] Carrying an undoubtedly biased
evaluation of Japanese and African cultural practices such as this
showed a producer of an African American newspaper could share
with his white counterparts certain attitudes when looking at peoples of other cultures. Clearly, to the degree that this reportage
reflected the shared attitudes of its readers, attitudes and utterances
of African Americans regarding other ethnic groups might be as
insensitive as any white person's.

African Americans seemed to be more impressed by evidence
of Japan's progress toward modernization than its culture. They
were aware that the Japanese succeeded in the transformation of a
pre-industrial nation into a modern state through the application of
self-help, group solidarity, and determined leadership, a formula
that most African Americans saw as necessary for their own
advancement. The readers of the black press could envy the record
of Japanese progress: in a mere half century, Japanese leaders fash-
ioned a powerful and respected nation from what had been a feu-
dally fragmented and technologically deficient country. This cadre
of leaders led in the adaptation of Western industrial technology,
expansion of a modern communication system, and development
of the strategic industries required of a modern military power.
When they dipped into the fountain of Western knowledge, the
Japanese infused what had been regarded as the ways of the West
with an indigenous vitality born of a oneness of purpose and made
Japan a flood plain of perpetual forward motion. As the world,
sometimes begrudgingly, rarely wholeheartedly, acknowledged
Japanese attainments, Calvin Chase, editor of the *Washington Bee*,
seemed particularly impressed with Japan's focus on education as a
vehicle in the great leap up from "barbarism." The *Chicago Broad*

Ax also marveled at Japanese educational achievements, but still poked fun at "ludicrous mistakes" such as the shoemaker's sign that read, "Shoes maid and men dead hear."[5]

Sometimes black writers thought of the Japanese as a superlative people. In Oregon, a state where there were not great numbers of either African Americans or Japanese, a writer for the *Portland New Age* characterized Japan as "the hardiest nation on earth" and described Admiral Heihachiro Togo, "Japan's fighting admiral," as "the typical Japanese." This typical Japanese, according to the writer, was "short, almost stout, rather reserved . . . cool, keen, alert and determined." He was a rather reticent man who was content to allow his accomplishments to speak for themselves. The *Kansas City Rising Son* credited Japan's success to an ability to wed "the power of originality of the English to the practical intuition of the German." The *Indianapolis World* referred to the Japanese as imitators, but "very clever imitators" who only imitated "proper things."[6]

In Indianapolis, black readers learned that the Japanese set a high standard of citizenship and civic responsibility. One of the great lessons that Japan taught, in the estimation of the *World*, was that a country propelled by "the self-sacrificing patriotism of its citizens possessed a tremendous power." In the opinion of this newspaper, Americans and their government needed to appreciate the view that duties of citizenship must be fulfilled without thought of immediate personal gain. The *World* saw the subordination of personal reward to national interests as behavior typical of the Japanese. The *Indianapolis Freeman*, one of the leading newspapers of its day, shared this view. It told its readers that the notion of self-sacrifice was so strong among them that the Japanese yearned to surrender their lives in the service of their emperor and that families gladly offered up their husbands, fathers, brothers, and sons. The *Indianapolis World* corroborated this with a report of a Japanese mother who committed suicide so that she would not be the reason her only son would be prevented from joining the army.[7]

Among the black newspapers of the period, the *Chicago Ax*, in terms of the number of references to Japan, was unmatched in its attention to the Japanese. Julius F. Taylor, its editor and publisher, seemed intrigued by the image of Japan's leadership as the very personification of progress. Emperor Mutsuhito was described as a monarch who had humanized a hoary institution which once required subjects to grovel in the dirt as a demonstration of their awe before a kind of demigod. Quoting a Japanese newspaper, the

Broad Ax told its readers that the emperor of Japan was an ideal prototype of the constitutional monarch; he was "just a plain individual" who had little regard for the ostentatious display of "barbaric splendor. " Complementing the model monarch, Empress Manako felt and expressed concern for the woes and afflictions of the downtrodden, the *Broad Ax* noted.[8]

Although the attention paid Japan was uneven, African American reporters, as they observed Japan's involvement in international politics, increasingly began to reveal a racial angle in their writings about the Japanese. Issues such as the participation of Japan in the expeditionary force sent to quell the so-called Boxer uprisings in China, the alliance with Great Britain, even transgressions against the Koreans and Chinese received but scant attention and practically no editorial commentary. What references there were generally occurred as sidebars.

When the black press did choose to address such issues at more length, it was usually in order to pursue some racial angle. Commenting on the plight of China in 1900, the *Broad Ax* depicted China as the "richest of all fields for conquest" over which all the powers of Europe and Japan clamored "after the choicest bits." Yet, as they looked abroad and analyzed the maneuverings of the imperialist powers in China, black journalists concluded that the Japanese were less predatory, even empathetic toward the Chinese. When the Japanese army led in the capture of Tientsin (Tianjin), a city southeast of Peking (Beijing), the *Indianapolis World* reported that there were Chinese who, at the time of the city's surrender, offered the soldiers of Japan cakes, fruits, and tea as a gesture of appreciation for the exemplary conduct of those troops. The *Savannah Tribune*, citing as its source the Associated Press correspondent in Yokohama, reported that in Japan there was increasingly "a revolution of sentiment in favor of China." According to the dispatch, this expression of sympathy which originated among the general population swelled to such proportions that the government was forced to take cognizance of it and aligned itself with those powers advocating "the most moderate terms possible in the negotiations with the Chinese court."[9]

Some African Americans, on the basis of such incidents, surmised that a natural affinity existed between the Japanese and the Chinese. The *Portland New Age* was certain that the Japanese sincerely desired the fostering of friendly relations with China. Claiming that missionary incursions into China were "tantamount to filibustering expeditions," the *Savannah Tribune* suggested, "The

Japanese are naturally asking what they would have done under similar provocation."[10]

Not all African Americans were uncritical of Japanese imperialism in China because they believed a natural affinity occurred between the East Asian neighbors. Some African Americans because of their own basic contempt for the Chinese tended to view Japanese predation as an improvement over what the Chinese might achieve themselves. Besides, if bullying neighbors gained Japan recognition as an imperial powerhouse, a great many found that acceptable as proof that a colored nation could operate at the level of the leading nations in the world. The attitude that African Americans had regarding Chinese was partially rooted in the traditional American anti-Chinese bias. Their disdain, however, became particularly acute when African Americans measured the cultural heirs of Confucious against the accomplishments of their more modernized island neighbor. The *Denver Statesman* contrasted "filthy Peking" and the frightfully unsanitary conditions of China's capital to the "gayety of Japan" with its tea houses, gardens, and polite and cheerful citizens. To go from Japan to China, according to the *Statesman*, was comparable to a descent into "Avernus," a mythical reference to hell. One black educator described the difference between China and Japan to be "as marked as though an ocean and two continents were between them." In the experiences of the Chinese and Japanese, according to this particular writer, could be seen "the inclinations and disinclinations of people springing from a common stock and the same proclivities." A president of the National Association of Colored Women cited China as "one of the brilliant examples of impeded progress."[11]

One black observer credited the Japanese with bringing a new zest to the Orient. According to this view, the "magic touch" of the Japanese spurred East Asia "into new life." Thanks to Japanese initiatives, the writer enthused, there was "a drowsy stir, a rubbing of sleepy eyes, a shaking off of ancient lethargy" which ultimately would result in a "great awakening" of "new hopes of freedom from Western dominance."[12] The belief that Japan would lead peoples of color from under the yoke of white imperialism was the key reason African Americans were so tolerant of Japan's transgressions against China's sovereignty. They were convinced that Japan's efforts were positive in three respects: they meant the diminution, if not the outright expulsion, of white influence in East Asia; a less exclusive grouping of imperial powers opened the possibility for developing the potential of other heretofore repressed colored nations; and a Sino-Japanese coalition might become the forerunner of a greater combination of non-white peoples. China, in this view, only had to learn from Japan to bring about the renovation necessary to move "the sleeping tiger" into the ranks of the greatest modern nations. Control of China by the Japanese, in the minds of some, was a prerequisite to Japan's completing its self-appointed task of "directing the destinies of the Orient." The Japanese, some observers pointed out, were setting up schools in which young Chinese students were "exalted and imbued with new Japanese ideas."[13]

The idea of a Japan leading a fight against the white imperialism movement had appeal among African Americans. Even a conservative follower of Booker T. Washington looked upon Japan's rise as "A Colored Man's Dream." When Japan imposed its Twenty-one Demands, a clear abuse of China's sovereignty, the *Baltimore American Ledger* merely reported that China had agreed to accept officers of the Japanese army to train Chinese troops and other Japanese experts to help reorganize financial and police affairs. The *Broad Ax* chose to interpret this to mean that China was "preparing to become a fighting nation."[14]

If they failed to comprehend Japan's offenses against the Chinese, African Americans understood, all too well, European transgression against the Japanese. Both the *Portland New Age* and the *St. Paul-Minneapolis Afro-American Advance* commented on the "apparent reluctance of Germany and Russia to consent to a Japanese commander" for the expeditionary force in China. The *Advance* thought that despite the military successes on behalf of the international community, Japan still had "to win the confidence of the powers and avoid acts likely to generate suspicion." William H. Logan, an enlisted man of the ninth United States Cavalry, treated the readers of the *Savannah Tribune* to an African American's firsthand impression after seeing soldiers of "every [major] nation of the world" while on duty in Beijing. While stationed in the Philippines, he wrote a letter to the editor expressing his opinion that "the colored race have [*sic*] many of them bested." He told of an incident in which European and Japanese soldiers were supposed to carry out a coordinated assault. The maneuver must have been less than successful, for Logan wrote that the Japanese soldiers found "many gold bricks" among the Allied forces. By this, Logan clearly meant that the European troops failed to fulfill their responsibilities in the operation.[15]

While there was relatively little editorializing about the

Japanese prior to the Russo-Japanese War, an issue which did evoke some editorial commentaries was immigration. These commentaries were at times hostile. There were three fundamental reasons for expressions of hostility toward the Japanese: African Americans sometimes shared the general anti-Asian prejudice common to Americans; they inherited a degree of insecurity being black in a white society, and occasionally the Japanese made antiblack remarks that invited retaliation. When the Japanese began to come to the United States in appreciable numbers, African Americans increasingly felt threatened and expressed feelings of anger toward the new Orientals who loomed larger as potential competitors likely to enter the marketplace of unskilled and agricultural labor. The hysterically inflated, jingoistic rumors of "coolies" flooding into the country were bound to unnerve black workers even more than white ones. Since about 90 percent of the black labor was unskilled at the time, the bottom-runged African Americans were most likely to meet the new Asian threat face-to-face.

In large measure, much of the negative comment of African Americans reflected their anxiety over their own status in this country. Howard S. Taylor, a writer for the *Chicago Broad Ax*, feared that the pending struggle between Americans and Asians would be intense because the Oriental was accustomed "to living upon mere fragments of the slightest and cheapest character" while the colored man aspired to live as whites did. Another writer who was candidly biased against both Japanese and Chinese, labeled them "obstacles to Negro progress." Nicholas H. Campbell, a sailor in the U.S. Navy, described Asians as "unclean in their habits," but, he claimed, they concealed it with "oriental duplicity." In his mind, the Asian interlopers were two heads of the same menace. Campbell complained that as soon as East Asians learned some English they received preference in advancement, while more was expected of Negroes. By "more," Campbell meant that African Americans were expected to be "polite and submissive." Clearly, he was more anxious about the status of African Americans in the navy than he was concerned with the welfare of Asians.[16]

The fear of job competition from Asians, at times, generated in the black press as well as the white media fantastic statistics about supposedly "swarming millions of Asiatic coolies." Before the anti-Japanese movement grew full-blown on the Pacific Coast, Howard S. Taylor, writing for the *Broad Ax* and echoing the *crie de coeur* used during the persecution of the Chinese, asked, "Must the Japanese go too?" Then on the front page he urged readers to cast their votes for William Jennings Bryan and Adlai E. Stevenson precisely because the Democratic party was "opposed to having cooley subjects, cooley labor, and cooley immigrants."[17]

This same newspaper, however, also could express sympathy with the position that Japan needed an "outlet" for its surplus population. Although it expressed relief that the Japanese government had taken action to restrict the emigration of laborers to the United States, the *Broad Ax* hoped that this action would offset what it perceived to be the "danger of a demand on Congress for a Japanese exclusion law."[18]

Although the *Broad Ax* saw the likelihood of an exclusion law aimed at the Japanese as a potential danger, Ernest Hogan, a celebrated ragtime composer, singer, playwright, and actor, saw it as an opportunity for the introduction of black American agricultural workers into the sugar fields of Hawaii. The audacity of the Japanese in the defense of their perceived rights caused considerable consternation among white planters. During one labor dispute, Japanese workers imprisoned the whites who opposed their strike. Another time, plantation managers complained that they had yielded "everything asked for" only to find the laborers still unsatisfied. Planters were most aggrieved, however, because they believed that they were being denied some of the best sugar fields in Hawaii partially due to land acquisitions by Japanese.[19]

Hogan saw Hawaii as a place where white people and black could achieve a more mutually beneficial relationship than was possible within the continental United States. He was prepared to work toward getting black workers for white planters in the islands. White planters in Hawaii when compared to their southern counterparts seemed more forward-looking, Hogan thought. If his efforts proved successful, Hawaiian sugar planters would acquire a docile labor force and African American agricultural workers would acquire a compatible work environment. Hogan claimed that there was considerable sentiment among sugar growers for bringing African Americans to the islands to replace the Japanese if Negroes in sufficient numbers could be induced to make the move. This was "a splendid opportunity for the betterment of the condition of the American Negro," Hogan argued. Hawaii, he believed, offered African Americans a change of scenery, good wages, excellent treatment, and a chance to "stand as men among men."[20]

An enthusiastic supporter of Hogan's scheme was George Knox, publisher and editor of the *Indianapolis Freeman*, one of the top black newspapers of its day. Labeling Hogan's scheme "fairly

Utopian," the *Freeman* concluded that the transplantation of black agricultural workers into Hawaii was an idea to be "looked upon with much favor." "With the inducements held out," the *Freeman* surmised, "Mr. Hogan will have no trouble at all in securing thousands who will gladly try that country." A physician who wrote a regular column for the *Freeman* added the "push factor." "The Negro," he advised, "cannot injure himself by going to Hawaii to work on sugar plantations" inasmuch as he "does the very same work in Louisiana and gets lynched there to [sic]."[21]

Hogan's scheme even found some support among strategic thinkers in the War Department. They asked T. Thomas Fortune, journalist and longtime editor of the militant *New York Age*, the leading black newspaper of the period, to investigate the feasibility of replacing Japanese, Chinese, Portuguese, and Puerto Ricans in Hawaii with black field hands from Georgia and Mississippi. In 1902, Fortune concluded that while African Americans lacked the "persistence, frugality, and ethnic adhesiveness" of the Orientals, they were superior to both Chinese and Japanese when it came to "intellect, morality, and industrial force."[22]

One important voice raised in opposition to Fortune's mission to Hawaii (and the Philippines) belonged to William Monroe Trotter. The fiery editor of the *Boston Guardian* denounced it as "political chicanery" and accused Fortune of being the "dupe of Senator [John T.] Morgan of Alabama, who had urged the project on the War Department." Trotter believed that the real stumbling block to colonizing the Hawaiian islands with African Americans was that the Negro had had "too long a taste of independence" and was "not as docile or abject as the coolie."[23]

Although he used the term "coolie," Trotter made a point of informing his readers that he did not include the Japanese within its meaning: the Japanese were "not half so backward as we are accustomed to think." What particularly impressed him was their "readiness to resent a slur on race at any and all times." This, he thought, ought "to serve as a lesson to all non-Caucasian people."[24]

Trotter's observation was substantiated by reports about the Japanese fighting in places ranging from Hawaii to British Columbia. The Japanese were involved in strikes and disputes over labor conditions, fishing rights, and seal hunting. Periodic mention of the possible arrival of this class of competitor in the domestic help industry, as pullman car porters, or as agricultural workers reminded African Americans that trends in immigration might have some bearing on their future well-being.

However, economic issues were not crucial in shaping African American attitudes toward the Japanese. The demographic reality prevented any serious economic friction. In the regions where the Japanese were most conspicuous—in Hawaii and on the Pacific Coast—the numbers of African Americans were most negligible. Often the criticisms of the Japanese found in the black press had nothing to do with economic issues. They were just as likely to be about self-interest or even jealousy. Certainly, African Americans thought it unfair that Japanese might be accommodated at hotels from which African Americans were barred or were accorded other privileges denied Negroes. Occasionally, African Americans became angry because some Japanese person made a disparaging remark. Such affronts, naturally, elicited retaliatory barbs from African Americans. The *Washington Bee* became quite agitated when an envoy of Japan was quoted as having said that the American Negro was inferior and should be treated as such.[25]

When a Japanese student allegedly refused to sit next to a black woman at the Park Theater in Indianapolis, the incident prompted the *World* to characterize it as "an instance when the 'yellow peril' was afraid of the 'black peril.'" When the World's Fair was held in St. Louis, Missouri, in 1904, some of the black ladies of the city requested permission to invite Japanese and Chinese to their homes, parties, and balls. A member of Japan's World's Fair commission declined the invitation by means of a letter to the editor of the white-owned *St. Louis Post Dispatch*. The commissioner, claiming to speak on behalf of the refined and educated Japanese who were visiting the fair, explained that they preferred to associate exclusively with white people and hoped Negroes would leave them alone.[26]

At least one reader of the black press understood and sympathized with the position of the impolitic fair commissioner. James S. Stemons, a resident of Philadelphia but a reader of the *New York Age*, felt compelled to put the St. Louis incident in context. He believed it was unnecessary to upbraid or criticize the position of the Japanese; on the contrary, Stemons rebuked the black ladies of St. Louis for extending the invitation. In Stemons' opinion, these women had committed an indiscretion which humiliated the entire race. This action of the women, coming at a time when anti-Negro sentiments were abnormally high, he contended, had forced "a people who had always maintained a friendly attitude toward African Americans" to array themselves against Negroes. As far as he was concerned, the Japanese were merely trying to avoid the ostracism

that would result from association with African Americans. Stemons did not fault them.[27]

Stemons' appraisal touched a sore point and hit upon a reason
those born black in America found it most difficult to relate to
other nonwhites in unambiguous ways: African Americans were
ambivalent about themselves. The Japanese, in his view, were little
different from fair-skinned Negroes who shunned darker members
of the race or denied their ancestry in their efforts to escape "the
odium which ignorance and bigotry attaches to the Negro race."[28]

Better than Stemons, however, the women of St. Louis seemed
to understand that, for African Americans who suffered from the
lack of a self-image in America, cheering for the Japanese had therapeutic value. Japan was acknowledged as one among the world
powers. Among the colored peoples of the time, the Japanese stood
forth as the best and the brightest. Before the world they had
demonstrated that they could play at what had been thought of as
an exclusively white man's game—international power politics—
and win.

The manner in which some African Americans tried to identify with the Japanese reflected the psychic lift they achieved
through Japanese accomplishments. The *Indianapolis Freeman*
described the Japanese as "people whose skins are dark almost to
blackness." The *Colored American Magazine* depicted them as
"sleepy-eyed-looking, black-haired men with non-Caucasian com-
plexions." A black minister from Troy, New York, the Reverend
James Boddy, in a letter to the *New York Age*, went further and
extolled "the Asian Negroes . . . the most progressive Asian wing of
the Negro race, the Japanese." Boddy, a graduate of Lincoln University, the Princeton Theological Seminary, and Albany Medical College, cited several ethnographic studies, including one by the
Smithsonian Institution, as his authoritive sources.[29]

In black communities about the country, the popularity of the
"Asian Negroes" seemed to shape and encourage Japanese themes
in a whole range of activities, gift giving, and entertainment. Black
socialites held a great many "Japanese" activities in order to raise
money for churches, orphanages, homes for the elderly, assorted
social events, and special projects. While their white counterparts
might have held "Martha Washington teas," African Americans
from Boston to Chicago to Savannah listed Japanese bazaars, Japanese socials, Japanese drills, or Japanese teas among the coming
events of the social world. The Japanese functions easily were more
popular than the occasional Egyptian, Chinese, or Gypsy theme.

Groups such as the Wide Awakes, the Women's Home and Foreign Missionary Club of the FBB Church, the West End Quintette, the Young Adelphia Aid and Social Club, the Crispus Attucks, Love and Charity, the Silver Cross Circle, the junior branch of King's Daughters of the AME Zion Church, and the Phyllis Wheatley Woman's Club all used Japanese themes for their fund raisers. These affairs were quite elaborate and sometimes lasted for ten days or more. They seemed uniformly profitable as social and financial projects. The programs commonly included music, dancing, and refreshments. The halls were decorated with Japanese-inspired accoutrements, and ladies wore Japanese "costumes." Of course, these activities were usually church related, and at times even interdenominational. In Savannah, Georgia, for example, the St. Philips Episcopal Church teamed up with the First African Baptist Church for an all-day rally. Participants were divided into two teams, either "the Japs" or "the Russians." A total of $460 was collected, not including the table collection of $28.[30]

The proliferation of such activities among African Americans strongly suggests that these themes grew out of their intellectual identification with the Japanese. It even influenced fashions. The *Kansas City Rising Son* reported that ivory toilet sets, which had been replaced in popularity by first silver-backed and then gold-backed ones, after many years, were again popular. The piece concluded that the trend occurred because of "the interest we feel in the Japanese at this moment."[31]

Culturally, too, a Japanese theme had broad appeal in the black community. When the black citizens of Indianapolis decided to put on the opera *The Mikado* for the benefit of the St. Philips Episcopal Mission building fund, the event was acclaimed as "one of the most successful from the standpoint of merit and attendance ever given by the colored people of the city." People from Marion, Muncie, Anderson, and Evansville joined "the city's representative colored people" in making the event a success. Tickets for the opera were to go on sale at eight o'clock on a Monday morning at Pink's drug store, but an irritated music lover complained that she and several other ladies had arrived before the appointed time only to find that others had queued up from midnight of the previous night, and 75 percent of the tickets already had been sold.[32]

The interest in Japan even influenced the kinds of gifts that were given on special occasions. When the Chicago couple, Joseph S. Tandy and his wife, celebrated their twentieth wedding anniversary, among the long list of presents from friends and relatives were a Nipponware berry set, a Moriwagi ornamenatal vase, a Japanese chocolate set, a Japanese chocolate pot, a Japanese plaque, Japanese cups and saucers, two Japanese teapots, and one dozen Japanese bread-and-butter dishes.[33]

The Japanese touched the black community in a variety of ways. They flavored the taste in fashions, and aromas of sandlewood and flowers enriched the social atmosphere. Members of a baseball team called themselves the "Japs." The Beach Institute in Savannah, Georgia, began its commencement exercises in May 1905 with a Japanese march titled "Kimona [sic] Girl." The Bethel church in Chicago had had a Mr. Kimura as a guest speaker and concluded that he was "an ardent lover of the gospel."[34]

The attention African Americans paid the Japanese was more than a mirror of the general American middle-class interest in Japan during that time. African Americans seemed to appreciate the Japanese more the more white interest soured. In their attempts to offset negative self-images, a by-product of living in a hostile white society, African Americans' identification with the Japanese offered the same kind of solace as identification with Africa—a broader, more global frame of reference. It actually offered a more satisfying connection since it put them in harness with proven winners. It placed African Americans in a context in which people of color determined their own destinies, built their own institutions, and drew upon their own heritage. It provided more of a basis for criticism of the conventional wisdom of white people.

As Marcus Garvey would in a later period, the Japanese allowed African Americans to turn the white value system upside down. An issue which sorely upset African Americans was the notion among whites that marriage across racial lines or interracial sexual activity menaced the "purity" of their race. A castelike feature of the American racial system was the idea, comparable to the Hindu concept of 'pollution', that a relationship between nonequals was always to the detriment of the supposedly "superior" race. The upper element was made impure or polluted, but the lower could never be made clean; thus, the offspring of such a union in America invariably was considered black. When an obscure white actress and a nephew of J. Pierpont Morgan married Japanese, African Americans had two chances to speculate as to which partners would be considered inferior in Japan. From time to time, white Europeans and Americans sometimes accused the Japanese of being "swell-headed" and even condescending toward non-Japanese, meaning whites.[35]

On another level, the Japanese provided grist for those who bridled under a white assertion that one of the racial characteristics of black people was a peculiar animallike body odor. The *Washington Bee* summed up the white attitude: whites believed that the odor emanating from Negroes was "the reverse of pleasant" and "almost unbearable" in hot weather. With undisguised satisfaction, the *Bee* reported that a Japanese doctor found that there was nothing so malodorous as "the pungent and penetrating emana proceeding from the western nations," especially where there were "traces of garlic, cheese, and evidence of overabundant dietary habits." Although the doctor was saying that cultural and dietary habits determine body odor, this message might have been lost on those pleased to read expert testimony that colored olfactory organs found the scent of white people offensive. Even while liking what the Japanese doctor said, the reporter at the *Washington Bee* was himself rather condescending in explaining the reason for the doctor's expertise. "Primitive races" had a keener sense of smell than "civilized races," and since the Japanese experience with civilization was of such short duration, the qualities of a "people living in a state of nature" might not be completely lost to them, he reasoned.[36]

At the beginning of this century, African Americans had but little interest in Japan. Comments made by them were often ambivalent, sometimes negative. This was less so when African American reporters, editors, journalists, and other members of the elite viewed the position of Japan in the world as analogous to their own circumstances within America society. It took a distant war between the Japanese and the Russians to sharpen the African American focus on Japan.

TWO

~~~~~

REACTIONS TO THE RUSSO-JAPANESE WAR

W hen the Russians and the Japanese, after much jockeying for hegemony in East Asia, went to war, the opinion makers and agenda setters of African America, like their white counterparts, searched for meaning in the distant conflagration that pitted a modernized nonwhite nation against one of the powers of Europe. The *St. Louis Palladium*, in a subtitle, designated the Russo-Japanese War "Probably Most Important Historical Event of Twentieth Century."[1] Whether not all Americans agreed with this evaluation, both African Americans and whites saw the Japanese as threatening to push white people from their pedestals of privilege, a notion repugnant to most whites but welcomed by most African Americans. For African Americans, this prospect represented a major turning point in race relations; consequently, this war was an international event in which African Americans were vitally interested. During this period, they honed their image of the Japanese as a colored people, as a people able to overthrow white supremacy.

In a time when black intellectuals, leaders, and journalists were divided into conservative and radical camps, African American thinkers achieved surprising unanimity in their estimates of the significance of Japan's rise to power. Whether they supported

Booker T. Washington's program of accommodation, industrial education, and economic enhancement or Du Bois' advocacy of protest,
political agitation, and academic advancement, many among the
African American intelligentsia concurred that Japan had ushered
in a new era, that not only had Russia been crushed, but the claims
of the superiority of whites over nonwhites had been forever
destroyed, and the Japanese stood as examples of the dormant
power of "other dark and accursed races."[2]

Du Bois, from this period, championed Japan as the best hope
for saving the nonwhite world from enslavement to Europe. Washington's most effective critic credited the Japanese for having broken the "foolish modern magic of the word 'white.'" He foresaw a
time when the "brown and black races" would follow the lead of
Japan. This, in his view, was the real meaning of the so-called "yellow peril" which menaced white hegemony in the world. Du Bois'
appraisal that the defeat of Russia by Japan awakened among
whites "a fear of colored revolt against white exploitation" was still
unchanged in 1940 when he wrote his autobiography.[3]

Media controlled by Washington, the nation's most powerful
black political broker, articulated the theme of white demise and
black rise as stridently as did Du Bois. Commenting on Japan's
prowess at Port Arthur, Mukden, the battle at Tsushima Straits,
and the Portsmouth Conference, the *Colored American* declared
the "yellow peril" to be no more than the fear that Japan would
arouse Asia to the point that the Asians would throw off the yoke
of Europe. What was most important about Japanese activities, in
the somewhat exaggerated view of the *Colored American*, was that
Japan had set Asia and Africa to thinking. If Anglo-Saxons lauded
Japan, it said, it was a "reluctant praise" which did not dispel the
fear that white people were soon to be displaced by "a newer and
more brilliant light." David McJon, a contributor to *Alexander's
Magazine*, another Washington-supported journal, saw the Japanese
victory over Russia as the "miracle of modern times," coming as it
did within thirty-seven years of Japan's emergence as a modernized
state.[4]

Other African Americans as well predicted the unleashing of
dormant nationalism among colored peoples and prophesied that
the day was not far off when the Japanese would raise the cry "Asia
for the Asiatics!" Several African American intellectuals saw these
events as the precursors to the time when similar cries would echo
across the vast continent of mother Africa. According to the *New
York Age*, the way was being prepared for African peoples to assert

themselves. The Russo-Japanese War had heralded a new epoch in which the "backward races" would no longer be thwarted by the Euro-American imperialists. The *Age* anticipated the era of the "black peril" that time when "the reawakened African Americans will reclaim the African continent from the usurpation and exploitation of Europeans."

Mary Church Terrell, multilingual educator, lecturer, and advocate of civil and political rights for African Americans and women, traveled about the country amplifying the view that Japan had buried the myth of racial superiority. Even if the Japanese had lost the war against the Russians, she contended, they still would have been able to take consolation in knowing "that they had riddled the world's pet theory with reference to the inferiority of dark nations to death." The lessons to be learned by "a heavily handicapped, painfully persecuted people" were plain. Terrell observed, "There are colossa [*sic*] and Sleeping Giants to torment and terrify us, so long as we quail before them at a distance, but . . . which will disappear and vanish . . . as soon as we meet them face to face." When she spoke in St. Louis, Missouri, the *St. Louis Palladium* cited the "glowing points" made regarding the "Japanese-Russian War" as constituting "one of the best lectures that the people of the city had the pleasure of listening to."[5]

With regard to the domestic racial scene, Mary Church Terrell eschewed dogmatism, seeing the merit both in the programs of Washington and in the protestations of Du Bois. She was an active member of the National Association for the Advancement of Colored People and the vice-president of the Washington branch, while her spouse, Judge Robert H. Terrell, enjoyed the patronage of Booker T. Washington.[6]

African Americans preferred to view the war from a racial perspective. Mary Church Terrell suggested that the "miniature brown nation with its undersized brown men" functioned as surrogates for African Americans. "The black boys were not there," she pointed out, "but the yellows were out in number." Archibald Grimke looked upon the Japanese as instruments of God visited upon "an overweeningly prideful people." From the pages of the *New York Age*, he exhorted the "little brown iconoclasts":

Go . . . ye little brown men, conquering and to
conquer. Sheath not your terrible sword, lay not aside
yet your bloody scourge. Ye shall overthrow. . . . Ye have
thrown Russia down, ye are destined to throw down others

than Russia in their pride, in their lust for power,
to bring down to the dust the mighty of the earth.[7]

Before the war, Grimke, seeing himself as a "Russophile," claimed
to admire Japan but reserved "something very much like affection"
for Russia. He acknowledged that during the war he had undergone
a transformation which proceeded from "a sneaking predilection
for Russia" at the beginning of the conflict to a position where he
was "pro-Japanese in sympathy and prayed for Japanese success."[8]

Some of the black opinion makers saw in the Japanese characteristics usually associated with African Americans. The Japanese soldier, in the view of the *Washington Bee*, personified a mix of
conservatism and militancy; they were exemplars of a self-help philosophy; they stood as examples of how to be humble without being
humbled. Even among "a habitually docile people," according to
the *Bee*, there could be kindled "the old samurai spirit" which produced warriors who were undaunted in the face of death. A poem
which appeared in the *Chicago Broad Ax* illustrated how the Japanese soldier could be poetic even in displaying his disdain for death.
The poem, written in blood, was found on the headband of a fallen
soldier:

> Forever shall we guard the august
> standard of our sovereign prince,
> Even though these, our lives of earth
> Should vanish with the dews of the morrow.

According to the *Bee*, the Japanese soldier was even childlike when
not engaged in combat but, once so engaged, anything but childlike.
The Japanese soldier portrayed in the Washington newspaper had a
spiritual resilience that was complemented by a lifestyle that made
deprivation a virtue. The *Bee* told its readers that soldiers of the
Mikado could make do with only three hours of sleep; cost the state
about nine cents a day; traveled lightly; and could carry enough fish
and rice to make themselves independent of the commissary trains
which were indispensable to other armies.

The *Washington Bee* tried to project an image of the Japanese
soldier as a person of impeccable character whether in uniform or
out. Nothing better illustrates this effort than when it reported that
a peculiarity of the imperial Japanese soldier was that when he was
not soldiering he would be found probably drinking tea or hanging
about old book shops, but he could "never be found drunk."[9] Since

abstinence from strong drink was not a virtue of the samurai past, there is little reason to believe that Japanese soldiers became teetotalers during the war.

Some African Americans were impressed that the Japanese were exceedingly public spirited. The imperial soldiers seemed to redefine personal sacrifice and patriotism as gifts to their gods and country. One writer for the *New York Age* saw this as their unique contribution, a passion born not from some furious fanaticism or vapid emotionalism but of cold intellect. Japanese patriotism, he explained, was "stolid, undemonstrative even incomprehensible to the occidental mind." Yet it could inspire its devotees "to rush to the embraces of assured death . . . with the utmost sang-froid." According to the writer, this spirit was within all Japanese, from the emperor to the humblest soldier, from the empress to the lowliest peasant girl.[10]

The ultimate expression of Japanese sacrifice, self-immolation by means of ritual disembowelment, both horrified and mesmerized African Americans, as it had other Westerners. This phenomenon helped African Americans to assimilate an image of the Japanese as a people who had a "sublime fearlessness of death," who believed it "more glorious to die than to live," and who, when duty summoned, were even "happy to die."[11]

When they looked at the quality of leadership available to the Japanese in their war with the Russians, African Americans were very much impressed: the men who led the military forces of Japan against one of the great powers of Europe had only recently been converted from medieval armor, bows and arrows, and samurai swords. The profiles of Japanese heroes that appeared in African American newspapers projected images of resolute and effective leaders. The *Colored American Magazine* and *Indianapolis Freeman* both ranked Admiral Heihachiro Togo and General Iwao Oyama alongside Booker T. Washington as recognized masters in their respective fields. Togo's defeat of the Russian Baltic fleet ranked with the sinking of the Spanish Armada in the annals of naval history, and Oyama's victory at Mukden was one of the greatest of the war. So Togo was to naval science and Oyama was to military strategy what Washington was to industrial education, the two newspapers claimed.[12]

From the broadened frame of reference that the Japanese provided, some people who were dissatisfied with the rate of progress African Americans were experiencing attempted to evaluate the caliber of leadership available to the black community, and, contrasted with the Japanese, black leaders were found to be wanting. The leaders of the black communities, by comparison to the Japanese, were hardly "up to snuff." The *Chicago Broad Ax*, in an obvious reference to Washington, complained that "so-called leaders" ran about "with their hats under their arms" looking for "some white person to toss them a few dollars." The passage of time did little to moderate the *Ax*'s harsh assessment of black leadership. Almost a decade later, still using the Japanese as its measure of quality, the *Broad Ax* denounced "black educated leaders" as "a consummate band of bootlicks, cowards and sycophants." The lesser black folk were dismissed as "moral and intellectual cowards" who lacked "the moral courage to resent a wrong" and accepted "every Jim-Crow accommodation offered." By contrast, the *Broad Ax* readily pointed out, "The Jap resents with all of his soul, with all of his might, every wrong done him because of his race, his color or his condition."[13]

Contrasting the image of the Japanese as a cohesive people with their own circumstances, some African Americans criticized their leaders for failure to unify them. The *Washington Bee* was critical of what it called "false leadership." Its criticism was sparked by a report about a Japanese diplomat who allegedly made a negative comment about America's perpetual underclass. Unflattering comments by foreigners, according to the *Bee*, were inspired by "the so-called educated negro" who "befouls his own nest." The *Broad Ax* agreed with the *Bee* that the lack of unity was a distinguishing and problematic feature of interrelationships among African Americans. "There is no race so divided against itself," the *Broad Ax* lamented. The *Bee*, alluding to an enduring conflict, attributed such divisiveness to the leadership class's desire to be white. The *Bee*, not too tactfully, proposed that "the bleached Negro first say what he wants and then the others will know what to do." The *Kansas City Rising Son* zeroed in on the too many ministers of the gospel who failed to measure up to the standard of intelligence and enlightenment required of leaders. The *Rising Son* ran its negative critique of black leadership alongside an article titled "Japanese Quick to Learn." The *Indianapolis Freeman*, focusing its attention on the South, earlier had denounced "the 'white folks' Negroes of Alabama and other southern states" as a "detestable lot."[14]

If some African Americans were dissatisfied with their leadership, some of the leaders were not enthusiastic about their "followership." The *Indianapolis World* blamed the black masses for the American racial situation:

Unfortunately, the great body of the race . . . is like a vast sluggish mass of uncooled lava over a large section of the country, burying some portions and affecting the whole . . . beneath its surface smoulder fires which may at any time burst forth unexpectedly. . . . It is this mass increasing from beneath, not from above, which constitutes the Negro question.[15]

Booker T. Washington, during an address in Brooklyn, New York, before an audience which included a prominent member of the Japanese Diet, complained about the "loafers seen about saloons and railroad stations" who gave the entire race a bad name.

Having seen parallels in the characteristics and experiences of the Japanese and their own, African Americans easily assimilated the imagery of Japan as an underdog in its clash with the Russian colossus. Biblical imagery heightened the impact of the Japanese victory within the black community by reducing complex international issues to an idiom common to American African Americans. Archibald Grimke, predisposed to use the biblical metaphor, wrote, "Yellow David has smitten white Goliath." Juxtaposing "little Japan" against "one of the largest, most courageous, and bravest" of European powers made Japan the odds-on favorite underdog. The Atlanta-based *Voice of the Negro* magazine, using the analogy of a spider and fly, rooted for the fly. In one article the contrast was presented hyperbolically with the "white giants of Muscovy" postured on the one side and the "brown pigmies of Dai Nippon" on the other.[16] The empathy African Americans displayed toward the Japanese was consistent with their traditional penchant for identifying with "Br'er Rabbit" over "Br'er Fox," the hare over the hound, and the tortoise over the hare.

Contrasted with the empathy expressed for the Japanese, Russians were treated derisively; this slant must have delighted the broad audiences that it surely reached. African Americans made Russians the subjects of the kind of "put-down" that comprised the ammunition for the pithy, rapid, staccato repartee heard incessantly in the smoke shops, poolhalls, and barbershops of urban black America. Because black newspapers often were read aloud and shared with those unable to read, these short remarks facilitated the sharing of news greatly beyond contemporary circulation figures. Some of the very good ones were circulated nationally. One titled "The Russian Bath," which the *Portland New Age* extracted from the Philadelphia press, also appeared in the *Chicago Broad Ax*. It was a fictitious conversation between "Ragson Tatters" and

"Weary Willie." Ragson begins, "Gee! I hope dem Japs jumps in an' licks de stuffin' out de Russians." Willie guessed they were "pretty decent people," and he was told, "Yeh; dey don't make no trouble fur nobody; dey ain't got no bath named after 'em." The *New Age* and *Indianapolis World* both reported about a Russian admiral who, in a diving suit, was "going down to review the fleet." In the former it was presented as a postcard, and in the latter, a cartoon.[17]

A number of these gibes appeared in the *Indianapolis World*. When a Russian magazine complained that England and the United States were behind Japan, the *World* responded: "Oh! we don't know we're not nearly so far behind Japan as Russia is." In reply to the assertion that the Japanese were using "wireless telegraphy" during the bombardment of Port Arthur, the repartee was that the Russians would be better off if the Japanese used "fireless shells" as well. When a Russian newspaper suggested that Port Arthur's name be changed to Russian, the *World* replied, "Too late; if it is changed it will be to 'Corkosumato,' or something Japaneasy like that." The *World* hinted at the frustration that must have overwhelmed many Russians, writing, "The Japs are damming the Yalu River. So are the Russians but the Russian spelling is different." When it was reported that a Russian had invented a device to suppress the noise of canons, the *World* taunted, "The Japanese gunners seem most successful in silencing the Russian guns." On the same page it was mentioned that the Japanese fleet had disappeared from Port Arthur. The notice continued that the Russian fleet had done likewise "but it may easily be found with the proper kind of dredges."[18]

Other newspapers took their shots as well. One gibe that reversed the theme of Japanese as underdogs and depicted them as indestructible ended with the statement that the Russians welcomed anything that would relieve "the monotony of defeat." According to the *Indianapolis Freeman*, "Russia's war vessels are not what they are cracked up to be." Then the *Freeman* concludes with the statement: "The Japs feel that they are there for the purpose of being cracked up."[19] When the fictional character, Ragson Tatters hoped that the Japanese would "lick de stuffin out de Russians," he probably spoke for a broad consensus in black America.

In their more serious discussions of Japan and the Japanese, African Americans tried to understand and explain the reasons for Japan's particular philosophical and spiritual character. Among those African Americans who were moved and educated enough to argue their views in the black press, there was sharp disagreement over whether the Japanese spirit was the result of indigenous forces or indebted to contact with Western influences. In their debate these people hinted at possible courses of action as they tried to fathom the extent to which Japanese success derived from straddling and benefiting from two cultures.

Charles Taylor, an attorney in Providence, Rhode Island, in a letter to the editor of the *Broad Ax*, concluded that Japan's success was due to the absence of Christian or any other significant religious influence. Referring to the Asian power as "free-thought Japan" and "free thought Atheistic Japan," he saw the absence of a religious encumbrance as a source of strength and hoped African Americans would learn this lesson and become "the Japanese of the new world"; he referred to the members of the Ninth and Tenth Cavalry as "the Japanese of the American army." George Frazier Miller, rector of St. Augustine's Church in Brooklyn, New York, and an activist in Monroe Trotter's National Equal Rights League, felt compelled to reply to Taylor's letter. Miller argued that the "remarkable progress and dazzling prowess" demonstrated by the Japanese were by-products of the introduction of Western thought and customs by Christian missionaries.[20]

Some African Americans joined with whites, both Americans and Europeans, in viewing what in a later period would be termed "cultural pluralism" as evidence of the imperfect assimilation of Western ways by the Japanese. The *Washington Bee* commented on the etiquette of Japanese males toward their spouses; it varied according to whether the wife was wearing the traditional kimono or European-style dresses. It also pointed out that Japanese men might don Western-style clothes during business hours but preferred the kimono when at home relaxing.[21]

Although prepared to admit that the Japanese had learned from the West, another group of African Americans agreed with Taylor that Christianity was a negligible factor in Japan's emergence as a modern state, but they disagreed with his contention that no religion was important to the Japanese. The *Kansas City Rising Son* maintained that Japan actually had benefited from a renaissance of Shinto and a revival of Buddhism as the Japanese strove to preserve a more indigenous attitude toward faith and morals. One writer aptly noted that Japan was "at the core Asiatic" and any borrowing from the West was small compared to what was retained of the traditional cultural and institutional forms. Regardless of the lessons learned from the West, the Japanese, in the words of the *New York Age*, "made a contribution from their own character" and excelled "in all the qualities which Occidental peoples have piqued themselves on as indubitable signs of fitness to rule."[22]

Beyond administrative or organizational fitness, a number of African Americans were impressed with the physical strength of individual Japanese. A member of the Tenth United States Cavalry credited the fortitude with which Japanese endured the hardships of war to superior athletic training. "Somehow," one writer for the *Portland New Age* mused, "one gets an idea notwithstanding their small stature the Japs would make pretty good football players." Some writers believed that even the physical culture of the Japanese was a product of native genius. Several writers commented on jujitsu, the style of hand-to-hand combat that allows a small individual to render a larger opponent senseless. The invention of jujitsu, which seemed ideally suited to the Japanese, appeared to bear out the assertion of one writer who argued that the Japanese exhibited the "power of originality" usually associated with the English and the "practical intuition" of the German.[23]

Existing in the reality of a racially segregated society in which they were the mudsill, African Americans followed the exploits of the Japanese and speculated on their meaning for the future of race relations; this was cathartic. Japanese victories provided African Americans with a vicarious satisfaction. The Mikado's minions would turn around the "backward races"; they would school the ignorant and stir the inert.[24] The antagonism displayed toward the Russians underscored the degree to which African Americans interpreted the war as a prelude to an adjustment of racial hegemony.

Had the Russians been fighting any power other than the Japanese, African American intellectuals, conceivably, would have worked to line up support on behalf of Russia; they had diplomatic ties with Russia. Archibald Grimke and Richard Theodore Greener came to know the Russians as no other African Americans and only a few whites in America did, both having served as consular agents in Vladivostok. Had Grimke and Greener's views been circulated widely within the African American community, perhaps an African American position in support of Russia largely on sentimental grounds would have been possible. Grimke, writing in the *New York Age*, outlined some of the reasons he thought African Americans might cheer the Russian state had Japan not been its adversary:Aleksandr Pushkin, one of the greatest geniuses of Russian literature, was black; the family of the tsar's servants, who were decked out in gold-threaded liveries, were Negroes; the Russians had abolished serfdom as this country ended slavery; and during the Civil War, when the British threatened intervention on the side of the Confederacy, the tsar, as a diplomatic counterfoil, sent his Pacific squadron to San Francisco and part of his Baltic fleet to New York.[25]

Greener, whose six-year tenure at Vladivostok encompassed the Russo-Japanese War, in 1900 wrote about the "very pleasant and agreeable" official and social life at his post. The first black graduate of Harvard College told how he respected Russia "as one admires a strong man—one who knows his strength and can keep it in leash until time comes to use it." Furthermore, Greener observed, Russia "boasts of citizens of all races and conditions and protects them at home as well as abroad." With regard to certain negative aspects of Russian society, he noted that although Russia might have persecuted and ostracized some of its native born citizens, they were never those "who willing accepted her religion and civilization with their nativity."[26]

By 1905 the Japanese government was "very much gratified with certain service which American Consul Richard Theodore Greener had rendered the Japanese at Vladavostok [sic]." Greener in his official capacity had rendered valuable services on behalf of the Japanese. Before war erupted between Japan and Russia, as a lawyer, Greener defended two Japanese nationals on trial for seal poaching and got their sentences reduced. He arranged the repatriation of the Japanese consular staff and six hundred other Japanese subjects shortly after the war began. Once Japanese diplomats returned to Japan, Greener assisted refugees, cared for Japanese interests in Siberia, visited prisoners of war, arranged for the burial of Japanese dead, and maintained a line of communication with Nagasaki.

During a period of anti-Japanese rioting, the African American diplomat took time to visit Japanese ships on a daily basis to keep them informed of the situation. Greener seemed to take pride in letters and accounts that lauded his care and attention to the Japanese. He felt that he had performed every duty required of him "to the satisfaction of the Japanese Government."[27]

Both Grimke and Greener experienced similar changes of attitude regarding the Russians because of the war with Japan. Other African Americans, lacking the intimate contact with Russia, found it even easier to choose the side of Japan: they could point to the persecution of Jews and slavic minorities as analogous to the racial system in America. The *Washington Bee* was quick to suggest that the sympathies of black folks ought to be with the Japanese, equating the Russian soldiers with Southern white men and a Russian triumph with a victory for color prejudice.[28]

Grimke succinctly summed up what he perceived to be the general black attitude toward the Russo-Japanese War. "The interest and sympathy of the colored people of America," he asserted, "went with Japan from the beginning." In the minds of the masses, he explained, the issue was a question of race; they saw a race of brown men at war with a race of white men, and the former seemed more akin. A war that stemmed from competing imperialism in Manchuria and Korea was interpreted by African Americans as arising out of Japan's interest in calling a halt to white brutality and oppression.

African Americans of the period might have had a well-deserved reputation for compassion; but, rather than,remorse at reading of the great tolls suffered by the Russians, African Americans, Grimke claimed, were filled with joy, pride, and exultation over the military achievements of the Japanese. Grimke confessed his own jubilation at seeing the plight of Russians in East Asia. "Across the seas, across the continents, across the ages," he enthused, the samurai had come as "the avenger of God." The samurai's sword was the instrument of God that would not be stayed "until liberty and justice descend from on high . . . to make men, brown men and white men and black men brothers again."[29]

African Americans could easily justify their support for Japan on a number of grounds. Some believed that Asia constituted Japan's natural sphere of influence and blamed Russia for disrupting the peace of the world. The editor of the *Indianapolis World* charged that the Russians instigated the war by means of an aggressive anti-Korean policy that menaced Japan. Ignoring whatever claims to sovereignty Korea might have had, the *World* concurred with a position taken by the *Portland New Age* that, as far as Korea was concerned, Japan was "clearly in the right" and had reason to resent Russian policies there. African American critics held that policies of the Russians forced Japan into the war. A Chicago reader of the *Indianapolis Freeman*, Peter Gibson Finch, in a letter to the editor, expressed his view that the war was inevitable and Russia had only "played the diplomacy game as long as she could hoodwink Japan." The *World*, branding the tsar "the greatest land robber in the world," charged that his idea of peaceful coexistence was when "the lion shall lie down with the lamb, but the lamb must be inside the lion."[30]

Another critic saw the issue as Japan's fight for the right to life and expansion versus Russia's lust for ill-gained goods "like a robber lusts for his stolen property." Joseph G. Bryant, a writer for the

Colored American, pointed specifically to the collective action of France, Germany, and Russia, which forced Japan to relinquish concessions won from the Chinese in the wake of the Sino-Japanese War in 1895 as the genesis for the Russo-Japanese War. "From that year the humiliated and wronged nation began to prepare for the present conflict," Bryant correctly surmised. The fundamental cause for the war, in his opinion, was the contemptuous attitude of the Russians toward the Japanese. The attitudes of the white Russians toward the Japanese were comparable to the attitudes of white Americans toward Negroes, or so it seemed to Bryant. He thought that the Russians should have known that the temperament and character of the "progressive and sensitive little brown men" would not permit them to suffer long the "gross injustice which compelled the relinquishment of rights in Manchuria." Bryant attributed what he termed the "lamentable mistake" of the Russians to a "habit common to the Caucasian character." Due to a "hubristic sense of racial superiority," he maintained, the Russians underestimated the intelligence and ability of nonwhite races.[31] In Manchuria, the soldiers of Japan demonstrated before the world a superlative competence in military strategy and tactics, logistics, engineering, and courage, areas which heretofore had been billed "for whites only." Colored people fulfilling command functions caught the attention of African Americans. Headlines of the *Savannah Tribune*, which were typical, such as "Japs Win Again," "Russians Fleeing," "800 Russians Drowned," or "Japs Win Great Battle" were the stuff of which dreams were born and fantasies nourished.[32]

At the beginning of the war, the president of the United States was included among those who initially rooted for Japan, choosing to see the Oriental power as a likely counterbalance to Russia's dominance of East Asia. As one Japanese success followed after another in an astoundingly rapid fashion, however, Theodore Roosevelt and the conservative constituency that he represented developed reservations and reevaluated their previous enthusiasm at seeing Japan's display of military might. The little Oriental gentlemen, in the eyes of racial chauvinists, had begun to assume sinister proportions when measured against the goal of preserving the hegemony of white civilization. Therefore, Roosevelt offered to act as mediator in order to bring the debacle to an end.

The reactions of African American shapers of opinion were varied. Many of them, of course, praised effusively Roosevelt's efforts to bring about peace. An honorable peace, for some of those who marveled at the exploits of the little brown men, had to be one which reflected Japan's superiority. Whether or not the Japanese got everything that they were due, whether the president acted more as a peacemaker or a white man, African Americans wanted to know.The varying interpretations of these matters acted as a wedge separating black opinion.

New York's *Age* was among those newspapers that applauded Roosevelt as a "peacemaker" for his role in bringing the belligerents to the negotiating table at Portsmouth, New Hampshire, during the summer of 1905. Rehabilitating partly discarded "principles of peace," the *Age* exclaimed, Roosevelt had used "every particle of his great influence" in a supreme effort to bring about a "just and lasting peace." When the negotiations were completed and the treaty accepted by the representatives of Russia and Japan, the *Indianapolis Freeman* acclaimed Roosevelt's mediation efforts the "most signal victory ever achieved by any single individual in history."[33]

From the pulpits around the nation, Christian leaders joined in rendering Roosevelt praise. Booker T. Washington commemorated the diplomatic triumph with a "Roosevelt Day" and had the president as the featured speaker. An editorial writer for the *Indianapolis World* wrote eloquently of Roosevelt's role: "No event since the angel sang 'peace' to the earth's millions has moved the heart of the world as his intervention between Russia and Japan." The writer hoped that Roosevelt's remarks at Tuskegee signaled America's new influence as "arbiter of peace between North and South, black and white." The *Age*, more directly, even as it expressed pride in the diplomatic achievement of its national leader, beseeched him to continue his exertions in equally humanitarian and righteous causes, an obvious reference to America's unresolved racial dilemma.[34]

Some African Americans were critical of Roosevelt because they believed his motivation was rooted in a racial perspective and he acted to save a fellow member of the fraternal order of white rulers from further humiliation. Charles Taylor, the Rhode Island attorney, accused the president of "premature interference" in the negotiations as a result of undue pro-Russian influence in Washington. Had military postures been reversed, Taylor argued, Roosevelt would have been less anxious to bring a halt to the war. A writer for the *Colored American* excoriated the president: "In war, America sided with victory and right; in peace she sided with wrong and defeat, simply because they hung about the necks of those whose skin is pale." The *Broad Ax* complained that the president had spent too much time trying to settle "the rumpus between Russia and Japan" while he "utterly failed to raise his little finger to abolish 'discrimination' against African Americans."[35]

Traditional interpretations of Roosevelt's reasons for consenting to mediate the peace negotiations between Russia and Japan include his admiration for the Japanese, his distrust of the Russians, his concern for China's territorial integrity, his fear that the Philippines were an Achilles heel. Historians tend to agree that Theodore Roosevelt wanted ultimately a balance of power in East Asia and the maintenance of an "Open Door policy," meaning American commercial access to the region regardless of what other power wielded de facto hegemony.

In a period when exaggerated theories of racial superiority proliferated, it is amazing how historians generally have ignored racism as a possible factor in Roosevelt's decision to mediate the Russo-Japanese conflict. Two students of Roosevelt's racist views have shown that, in spite of his much publicized dinner invitation to Booker T. Washington; his appointment of Dr. William D. Crum as revenue collector in Charleston, South Carolina; and his closing of a post office when the town of Indianola, Mississippi, forced the resignation of Minnie Cox and refused to reinstate her, Roosevelt was motivated by an abiding belief in the innate difference of racial groups. According to Seth M. Scheiner, this constant belief dominated "Roosevelt's philosophy of man and society." Where he took actions that seemingly deviated from that philosophy it was due to his perception of political necessity. But in the final analysis, he was committed to the notion expressed at a Lincoln Day dinner in 1905: "Race purity must be maintained." George Sinkler, in his study of the racial attitudes of ten American presidents, pointed out that Theodore Roosevelt was inclined to be expansive in spreading his protective mantle when he believed white civilization was threatened by nonwhites: "Roosevelt did not want to see the crushing of a white, though slavic, Russia by a powerful but alien and yellow Japan."[36] When the magnitude of Japan's success was considered, Roosevelt thought it important that he accept the Russian assertion that Russia stood as the great bulwark against the menace of the Oriental hordes, that, in essence, Russia was fighting on behalf of white civilization. Thus, he tipped the scales in favor of race and the notion of innate differences.

The Japanese government sent its plenipotentiaries to Portsmouth with objectives categorized as absolutely indispensable, relatively and minimally important. Among its first items, the Japanese government wanted acknowledgment of its suzerainty over Korea, withdrawal of Russian troops from Manchuria within a specified time, and cession of the Liaotung Peninsula and Trans-Siberian Railway. These were considered absolutely vital to achieving Japan's war aims and guaranteeing its security. The second set of items included Russia's payment of an indemnity, acquisition of Russian vessels stranded in neutral ports at the end of the war, cession of Sakhalin Island, and fishing rights along the coast of the maritime provinces. These were to be secured insofar as circumstances permitted. The third set, which included limitation of Russian naval strength in East Asia and the defortification of Vladivostok, were little more than bargaining chips.[37] The representatives of Japan won all of those points listed under "absolutely indispensable" and most of those designated "relatively important." The issues of indemnity and territory, in the public mind, loomed larger than the government intended. Riots, the imposition of martial law in Tokyo, and reports of dissatisfaction among troops in Manchuria were all indications of widespread Japanese disenchantment with the terms of the Portsmouth peace.

Some African Americans were perplexed by conduct that the *Age* termed "regrettable." *Alexander's Magazine,* published by Charles Alexander in Boston with support from Booker T. Washington, expressed the opinion that Japan had been victorious in peace as in war. The *Colored American* understood that indemnity was a subsidiary issue and that the Japanese had won their major goals.[38]

African Americans, of course, could not match the despair felt by ordinary citizens of Japan who rioted in the streets, but many made it clear that they, too, believed Japan had been cheated of its just deserts. The *Indianapolis Freeman,* which had commented favorably on Roosevelt's role, agreed that the Portsmouth treaty gave less than Japan had a right to expect or deserved. It was the sense of the *Freeman* that Japan lost at the conference table in Portsmouth gains rightfully earned on the battlefield. The tone of the *St. Louis Palladium* was especially irate: "Japan conceded . . . she withdrew . . . she gave up . . . she receded . . . she abandoned. . . ." The *Palladium* sought consolation in the thought that, while Russia might have gotten the diplomatic victory, the Japanese could lay claim to the moral victory.[39]

While the view that Japan should have pushed its diplomatic objectives further even at the risk of continued warfare was com-

patible with the mass opinion in Japan, it demonstrated an ignorance of Japan's military situation. Although the Japanese had won
a number of spectacular victories, Japan's financial and military situation had reached the point where a protracted war would more
likely have benefited Russia. Despite what African Americans and
ordinary Japanese citizens might have believed, the Japanese government had no choice but to conclude peace. It found it increasingly difficult to float new foreign loans, and the military outlook
began to turn increasingly bleak. The victories of the Japanese had
been achieved at great cost. The leadership ethos that put officers
at the head of their troops reduced the officer corps until most of
the regular officers were either corpses or casualties. This largely
left reserve officers to lead the imperial army. However, the Russian forces were three times as strong as the Japanese. The Russian
troops were crack forces newly arrived from Europe. Morale among
the Russians was improved while that of the Japanese deterio-
rated.⁴⁰ Clearly, the Japanese government understood that it was to
its advantage that the war ended when it did.

Once the war ended, African Americans, too, looked for and
focused on the positive benefits that were to be derived from the
great conflagration. Many believed that China, Korea, Manchuria,
and, psychologically speaking, even Negro America benefited.
From the vantage point of the *Indianapolis World*, by Japan's ascendancy to dominance in East Asia, China would get relief from the
exactions of the Russians, Korea would regain "comparative freedom" and be developed by "a nation of sympathetic tastes," and
Manchuria would become "freer than before European intrusion."
The *Colored American* agreed that China would benefit from
Japan's new status in East Asia. Referring to the Chinese as formerly "battered and persecuted," the African American magazine
concluded that they now had an "ally, friend, if needs be,
defender."⁴¹

White Americans too speculated about the possibility of such
an alignment, but the prospect of such Asian unity left them
unnerved. This was made clear at the end of the conference in
Portsmouth when a grand banquet was given in honor of the Russian delegation. The publisher of *Harper's* blatantly tried to calm a
collective anxiety with the peroration "From the Great White
Nation of the West to the Great White Nation of the East."⁴² This
toast of mutual reassurance underscored the image of a coalition of
white nations banding together in order to gang up on Japan.

African Americans derived their own sense of assurance from

viewing the Japanese victory as having direct relevance to the future advancement and improvement of conditions within black America. A reader of the *Indianapolis Freeman* tried to draw a direct parallel between the program of Booker T. Washington and the policies of the Japanese government. Referring to the Triple Intervention, Adelbert H. Roberts of Chicago wrote, "When Russia robbed Japan of the fruits of victory . . . , the little island empire could not force Russia to duty by protests and demands." Roberts described the Japanese as people who had mastered what Roosevelt suggested; they had learned to "speak softly" until they were "prepared in every way to carry a big stick." In the South, in Roberts' view, the Negro had been "Russianized" and African Americans were unable to prevent the "trespassing upon our rights." Designating him "the black Mikado of our race," Roberts claimed that Washington was in the process of "Japanizing his people." In other words, Roberts believed Washington's program of accommodation was a rite of passage in preparation for the time when African Americans would be able to make demands from a position of strength.[43]

Most African Americans, however, unlike Roberts, were more inclined to focus on the militancy of the Japanese as the reason for their victory over the Russians. The tone of the *Seattle Republican* was simple and representative, "White supremacy is getting a terrible black eye in and about Manchuria and Mukden." The pugilistic terminology of the *Indianapolis Freeman* chose to emphasize the pugnacious, not an accommodating attitude of the Japanese: "The brown men continue to thrash the white men in the east. In fact, Russia has been so badly and so continuously licked by the Japanese that they are about to throw up the sponge entirely and admit themselves vanquished. Perhaps the colored races are at last to have their innings and disprove the long-asserted claim of white superiority.[44]

One example of the extent to which African Americans were willing to identify with the Japanese can be seen in Indianapolis where the three black newspapers ran an editorial from the white daily which alleged that "Negro or negrito blood . . . is authoritively regarded as the dominant strain in the Japanese."[45]

By the end of the Russo-Japanese War, the Japanese, on the basis of their victory, enjoyed a new status in the eyes of the African Americans, for they had generated a hope that a new era was at hand: white supremacy was dead, and color was no longer relevant in assessing a people's worth. On the basis of Roosevelt's entry as mediator in the peace negotiations, some African Americans anticipated a new liberalism, which might make the president more amenable to taking a direct hand in racial matters at home. Therefore, Japan's victory over Russia in areas of Inner Asia was a cause for optimism in black America.

When war first broke out, it had been less clear to African Americans that Japan had such a grandiose role: the first editorials in the black newspapers had been cautious, divided, and more than a little concerned about Japan's chances of surviving, much less winning against one of the leading powers of Europe. The *Topeka Star Ledger* cited the outbreak of war between Russia and Japan as one of the disasters of the year. The editor of the *Portland New Age* expressed concern for Korea's well-being. He characterized Korea as a "disinterested spectator" in the same way "a crippled rat over which two terriers are fighting is a disinterested spectator of the dog fight."[46]

Yet the *New Age* expressed both admiration and concern for Japan. The writer applauded the display of "pluck, dedication and courage" of the Japanese at Port Arthur and labeled their posture "one of righteousness." At the same time, however, he expressed fear that in a long-continued war there could be little doubt as to the final victor. The Japanese, with a combination of patriotism, daring, luck, and fairly good ships, might harass Russian naval forces for a time, but, once embattled on land, the *New Age* concluded that there could be no doubt that Russia's preponderant power would prevail. The *Indianapolis World* summed up the situation simply: it was "suicidal folly" that Japan would "think that she could whip Russia single-handed."[47]

Several key African American intellectuals and journalists chose to see the war as a metaphor suggesting that white hegemony would be undercut and black status enhanced. If one darker race could defeat one white nation, these African Americans inferred, then black Americans might eventually replicate that feat at home. But to a considerable extent, except when sermonizing about the need for Africa's "redemption" and extolling Ethiopia as a "symbol of hope," black attitudes toward matters of foreign affairs, generally, were marked by indifference or were carbon copies of white American attitudes. The period of the Russo-Japanese War, however, was a time when many more African Americans became actively interested in an issue of international dimensions.

As a result of this war African Americans began to look at the Japanese differently. Where previously they had been content to see the Japanese much like other Americans did, African Americans began to view the people of Japan more from a racial perspective and embraced them as a colored people. There even seemed to be more of a tendency to use "brown" rather than yellow as descriptive of the "little people of Japan." African Americans used "yellow" and "brown" usually when trying to designate the color of the Japanese, but there were even references to them as "black" and "blue-black." In 1937 Du Bois still tried to describe the color of the Japanese for the readers of the *Pittsburgh Courier*.[48]

The reason why African Americans were attracted to the Japanese was understandable: the victory of Japan over Russia was the most emphatic refutation of the whole idea of white supremacy. Clearly, members of the "colored branch" of the Young Men's Christian Association in Indianapolis thought so. They held a debate which resolved that "the world would be greatly benefitted by the ultimate victory of the Japanese in the present war." Those who chose to debate the negative proposition were at a serious disadvantage, debating what must have been an untenable position for a black middle class audience.[49]

Even as Roosevelt struggled to settle the war in favor of the white belligerent, African Americans in Indianapolis, probably Republican to the last man, declared their intellectual independence by putting forth three central themes that revealed their distance from doctrinaire Republican opinion: first of all, Japan's emergence signaled a return to prominence of the Asian peoples; second, such an eventuality threated the continued domination of white imperialist powers; and third, the rise of the Orient and demise of the Occident portended well for the future of other oppressed nonwhite peoples.

This view anticipated Japan playing a role in freeing China from the plundering of European powers. According to this way of thinking, once the Chinese and Japanese resolved their differences and became allies, these united Asian powers would assist the peoples of Southeast Asia, India, and Africa in the expulsion of white imperialists. The *New York Age* observed that the "yellow peril" meant that Asia was to be for Asians and that part of the world was to be free of European or American interference or dictation. The African American corollary to this anticipated the future emergence of a "black peril" in Africa. "If the Japanese can inoculate the Chinese with this [martial] spirit," the *Age* surmised, "then let the haughty, masterful sons of Japhet[h] beware." W. E. B. Du Bois, before the war ended, declared that whether Japan won or lost the brown and black races would arise. That, he determined, was "the problem of the yellow peril and the color line."[50]

In summary, in the minds of African Americans who followed the news of the Russo-Japanese War, the victory of the Japanese over the Russians was as vicariously satisfying an event as any achieved in their lifetime. The Japanese most convincingly demonstrated for all the world to see that white hegemony over nonwhites was merely situational, not genetic, a matter of strategy and tactics, not race. From this time and event, African Americans embraced the Japanese as colored people in a way that they had not done previously. The image of the victorious little brown men of Japan, in the consciousness of African Americans, would become an indelible one, an image to be nurtured and savored much like a Joe Louis victory over Max Schmeling or Billy Conn. Some began to dream of the Japanese as allies in their struggle for freedom, more acutely so as they found that increasingly Japanese were becoming fellow victims of white racism in the United States.

PART II

CHOOSING SIDES

THREE

𝄞𝄞𝄞𝄞

FELLOW VICTIMS
OF RACISM

One byproduct of the Russo-Japanese War was an increase in the number of Japanese emigrating to the Pacific Coast of the United States, a region with a strong anti-Asian bias nurtured in conflicts with the Chinese. Westerners, who objected to Asians on economic and racial grounds, had increased anxiety at the thought that an influx of Japanese, some of whom would probably be veterans fresh from the victory over the Russians, would serve as a further drag on the standard of living of white people living in the Pacific Coast states. The *Indianapolis World*, in a series of editorials, ridiculed the attitude of whites, pointing out that what was at stake was "the principle of 'Survival of the Fittest.'" Californians needed to build "a race of white men strong in morals and virtue," the *World* chided. Criticizing the effort to deny Japanese ownership of land, the *World* asserted that the land from which the Japanese were being forced constituted "the bog land and plague plots that could have been offered unto [the Japanese] without suffering too intensely from a remorse of conscience."[1]

Acceding to an anti-Japanese sentiment, the San Francisco Board of Education, in October 1906, passed an order that required that ninety-three Japanese students attend a segregated school designated for Orientals; in 1913 the California legislature led a Western effort to force Japanese from the land. These actions of the San Francisco school board and the California legislature made blacks and Japanese fellow victims of racism. Clearly, this was an opportunity for African Americans to identify with the Japanese in a fashion less remote than the vicarious associations made during the war between Japan and Russia.

When President Theodore Roosevelt, sensitive to the politics of power and prejudice, personally intervened in order to dissuade the San Franciscans from offending the militarily strong Japanese, however, blacks reacted ambivalently. On the one hand, there were some blacks who were strongly opposed to the proposal to segregate Japanese school children in San Francisco. The problem of discrimination that the Japanese encountered in California, obviously, was one with which African Americans were very familiar and opposed in principle. On the other hand, however, a few blacks were perturbed that the American government seemed to act decisively to protect foreign-born people from discriminatory practices and ignored abuses when directed at those "to the manor born."[2]

Many African Americans objected to what they perceived as a capitulation to "colorphobia" and denounced the efforts on the part of Californians to discriminate against the Japanese. The *Colored American*, warning against the release of a "Pandora's box of evils," declared, "We do not subscribe to American race prejudice." The *New York Age* observed that the American sense of fair play had become "as blunt as the broad side of the Rocky Mountains." T. Thomas Fortune declared African Americans out of sympathy with the American injustice to the Japanese. The Japanese, in Fortune's view, were entitled to demand equality of treatment for their children in the public schools of San Francisco. An article in the magazine *Voice* summed up the issue very succinctly, "Japan's demand . . . is surely a righteous one." The Japanese were a "colored race to be respected," and there was no reason why they should be humiliated. "California's folly" resulted from the "clamor of a crazy crowd" of "San Francisco demagogues" and "race cranks."[3]

From his vantage point as a long-time critic of America's racial inequities, Fortune could be more militantly demanding of Japanese rights than the Japanese themselves. He wrote a pair of editorials critical of the "gentleman's agreement by which the Japanese government agreed not to issue passports to laborers and to permit American restrictions on Japanese immigration from Hawaii, Canada, and Mexico as a way to mollify the anti-Japanese agitation on the West Coast. In addition, the Japanese agreed to a categorization that made those who settled here "aliens ineligible for citizenship."

In Fortune's view, there was nothing gentlemanly about an agreement that, in practical terms, denied to Japanese privileges available to whites of Europe and thereby constituted a discrimination solely on account of race and color. Fortune believed that the Japanese had failed to understand that the San Francisco incident was subject to be repeated in any of the other states, but most especially in those of the South. His view of the gentlemen's agreement was encapsulated on the front page of the *New York Age* in March 1907: "Conquerors Vanquished! Proud Japanese Excluded as Laborers from US; Rated with Mongolians; Swap Equality in American Schools for Inequality in Right of Citizenship." Clearly, Fortune was convinced that the Japanese had given away a great deal more than they had gotten; they had surrendered "the substance for the shadow, the principle for the sentiment."[4]

Discrimination, whether against the Japanese in the West or blacks in the South, in the view of some was "no different in kind or degree." Fortune was convinced that neither the people of the Pacific Coast nor the people of the Southern states wanted the Japanese in the United States. The *Nashville Globe* made the point that the anti-Japanese legislation of California was comparable to the anti-Negro legislation of the southern states except that it was also a violation of the treaty-making provisions of the U.S. Constitution.[5]

The view of the Japanese as a people who had little need to "stand for anything that injures them in their pride or their purses" led some blacks to fantasize scenarios in which the Japanese would assist in avenging long-standing wrongs against Negroes. The *Colored American* thought it a good idea to release "the dogs of war" and allow Californians and the southern states which supported their anti-Japanese legislation to fight it out with Japan while the other states stood off and watched. The *Nashville Globe*, in a front-page piece, heralded a "Coming Terrible Conflict" because the Japanese, unlike Negroes of the South, would not submit meekly to segregation. The *New York Age* warned, "Japan . . . will retaliate and America may be made to drink the dregs of sorrow for her present injustice."[6]

At a time when rumors of possible war abounded, some blacks speculated about the role they might play in such an eventuality. In the event of war with Japan, the *Nashville Globe* wanted to know "what position would the Negro take?" The *Globe* asked rhetorically would the black American sympathize with and aid Japan, remain neutral, or "take up his gun and defend 'old glory'?" In its final analysis, the Tennessee newspaper concluded that "in the great struggle that is coming" the United States would need to employ "every able-bodied Negro" in order "to help push the intrepid and death-dealing little Jap from the crest of the Rockies back into the Pacific Oceans." The *Washington Bee* agreed that the services of "colored people" would be required and predicted that blacks would "win laurels." The *New York Age* and *Cleveland Gazette*, on the contrary, predicted the formation of a Negro and Japanese alliance as a result of the white offensive against them. This combination, in the view of the *Age*, would result in a radical revision of the world balance of power and "one of the most horrible spectacles written in blood in the history of mankind."[7]

The image of the Japanese as a militant people disinclined to suffer abuse or insult spurred some African Americans to make some rather extreme remarks. The *Broad Ax* thought it a "solemn duty" for African Americans "to implore the fighting Japanese to assist them to roll back the wave of race prejudice and oppression which is constantly engulfing them in America." The suggestion of W. Calvin Chase, the editor of the *Washington Bee*, that the Negro must fight or be made the laughing stock of other nationalities" was so extreme as not to merit extended discussion. It is important, however, as an indication of the range of responses discussed in an era of black "accommodation." Unfettered by notions of possible war between this country and Japan, there was significant support for Japan within the African American community. The black inclination to support the Japanese was idealistic, pragmatic, and a bit therapeutic. Ideally, American blacks were motivated by concerns for human rights and the belief that anti-Japanese legislation ran counter to the democratic principle of inalienable rights for all people. From a more practical point of view, blacks understood, all too well, that any legislation that had as its ultimate objective the maintenance of the United States as a "white man's country" was legislation that menaced black Americans very directly. The following sums up the view of those who were apprehensive about this kind of legislation: "as California would treat Japanese she would also treat Negroes."[8] Psychologically, African Americans were siding with winners.

Despite their own readiness to empathize with the Japanese of the West Coast, some blacks were critical of the role the Roosevelt administration played in attempting to intercede with officials of California on behalf of the Japanese. In order to resolve the San Francisco dilemma, Roosevelt sent Secretary of Commerce and Labor Victor Metcalf to San Francisco to negotiate a truce; the attorney general instructed a U.S. District Attorney to side with the lawyers representing the Japanese community in injunction proceedings; and Roosevelt himself conferred with the mayor and school board of San Francisco. Finally, he was able to persuade the San Francisco officials to rescind their order barring Japanese from white schools. Professing a "deep sympathy" for the president's efforts to improve the conditions of the Japanese coming to America, the *Indianapolis Freeman,* in an editorial, maintained that African Americans would have had "some real enthusiasm" had Roosevelt equally sought greater jurisdiction with a mind to protecting black lives, black liberty, and black property.[9]

One writer contrasted Roosevelt's efficacy in dealing with the San Francisco situation with his more inept handling of the Brownsville, Texas, incident. Augustus M. Hodges, of Brooklyn, New York, an ex-editor and newspaper writer, wrote an open letter to Roosevelt congratulating him for his attempts "to settle the school question in California in a way that will continue our friendly relations with Japan." At the same time, however, Hodges informed the president that an entire battalion of Negro troops should not be disgraced for "the crimes of a few."[10]

The *Cleveland Gazette* was pleased by what it perceived to be an attack on the doctrine of states' rights, the concept which deterred interference by the federal government on behalf of blacks in the South. "Teddy" was praised as a "wiser head of national affairs" who used a double-barreled, no-nonsense approach to clear up an "international muddle." "The South," the *Gazette* continued, got "its old time hobby of 'state's rights' kicked good and hard by the president, and California, its racial prejudice."[11]

Puzzled by Roosevelt's activism on behalf of the Japanese and his apathy where blacks were concerned, the *Freeman* asked, "Are the wishes of yellow aliens . . . of more consequence to this nation than its loyal Negro citizens?" Noting that black children were "forced into separate schools," made to endure "inferior conditions," and otherwise discriminated against, the *Freeman* answered its own question by pointing out that a torrent of presidential action to redress these conditions was noticeably lacking. "Enlightened selfishness," the *Freeman* reasoned, dictated that the general government owed its own citizens "as deep an obligation" as it owed foreign-born persons. The militant antilynching activist Ida Wells-Barnett used the California brouhaha to highlight her view "that federal power must yet assert itself to protect the nation from the treason of sovereign states." She reasoned, "If the government has power to protect a foreigner from insult, certainly it has power to save a citizen's life."[12]

Some blacks were quick to point out the difference in government response according to whether the victims of prejudice were Japanese or black. The *Nashville Globe* observed that a government unable to investigate "the most flagrant violations of law . . . when the rights of its citizens have been violated . . . moves with an alacrity that is surprising when the Japanese Government calls its attention to the fact that the people of San Francisco . . . had destroyed a restaurant belonging to a native of Japan." No matter how "peaceable, industrious, patient and patriotic," no matter how much nor how important their service to this country, black Americans could not look forward to "friendly intervention to stay [their] deprivation."[13]

In the treatment of its own citizens, mused Archibald Grimke, "America makes no distinction in favor of merit, of achievement when the race is dark, when the skin is dark." No level of intelligence, refinement, or accomplishment could redeem those born tainted. Grimke's lament was that "no amount of eminence in any of the varied walks of American life and civilization by [black] individuals has been able to atone to their white fellow-countrymen, either North or South, for the unforgivable sin of their race and color."[14]

The most glaring case of a double standard was the nation's capitol itself. The *New York Age* observed that the president and Congress had set a bad example for states such as California where there was an inclination to "enforce separation between the children of co-equal citizens." In the District of Columbia, where the federal government had clear jurisdiction, segregation of the races was a fact in the public schools. Grimke believed that much of the blame belonged to Roosevelt. When it came to setting the moral tenor on matters of race, Grimke held, Roosevelt stood "not on a rock foundation of broad humanitarian principles, but on the shifting sands of mere impulse." So from Grimke's viewpoint Roosevelt was wholly in character thinking the achievements of the Japanese ought to make some difference in their favor despite their race and color, while, at the same time, remaining silent regarding jim crow transportation, the riots in Atlanta, and the denial of the vote to blacks. Why did Roosevelt make the "insidious distinction" between the Japanese and black Americans, Grimke asked. Was it because one was strong and the other weak?[15] Indeed, it was.

Many American blacks understood this to be the critical difference that resulted in blacks being of "secondary consideration" and Japanese being respected; the government of Japan could make demands which "nursed a threat backed up by the sinews of war." Japan's unwillingness to "tamely submit to any persecution of its citizens" contrasted sharply with the image of blacks projected editorially by the *Nashville Globe*: "The Negroes, millions strong, peaceable, industrious, patient and patriotic . . . have been stripped of every right of manhood and of humanity without any effectual, friendly intervention to stay the deprivation." The *Portland New Age*, in less than a month, carried two references to Booker T. Washington that contrasted with the image of Japanese militancy: in the first Washington pleaded for the cultivation of "a spirit of racial pride" like that exhibited by, among others, the Japanese; and second, Washington strongly advised blacks to "remain calm during present trouble in the South," a reference to the 1906 riots in Atlanta, Georgia. The *New Age* observed, "The negro race war continues in a small way in many Southern cities."[16]

The *Washington Bee*, in an editorial titled "American Cowardice," accused the government of "a cowardly backdown" and expressed its confidence that "the United States will not enter a contest with a nation like the Japanese or any other nation that has power behind her like Japan." One of the most effective arguments against the segregation or mistreatment of Japanese, in the words of the *Nashville Globe*, was that Japan had some "mighty effective and destructive fighting machines" that the Japanese knew "mighty well how to manipulate." The *Globe* also believed it to be the "height of folly" that Californians seemed intent on fomenting "an expensive and stupendous war with one of the bravest and most warlike as well as one of the greatest naval powers of the world."[17]

The Californians' penchant for exacerbating relations between the United States and Japan manifested itself again in 1913 when the state legislature overwhelmingly passed the Alien Land Law. This law limited to three years the leasing of agricultural lands to Japanese and prohibited further purchases of land by aliens. The *Chicago Defender*'s assertion that the anti-Japanese agitation provided blacks a "kindred element in the situation to their own status in this country" echoed arguments made by blacks when

Californians earlier tried to segregate the Japanese and restrict their
entry into the country. Robert S. Abbott, the editor and publisher of
the *Defender*, a man who could be strident in his opposition to
European immigration, rehashed the theme of retributive justice,
seeing potential benefit in the latest assault upon Japanese sensi-
tivities: "The vengeance of the gods finally may be wreaked upon
our oppressors . . . through the Providential happenings to fellow
sufferers from the Orient who have a flag and navy to demand justice, and not simply ask for it."[18]

A significant difference, in the view of some African Americans, was that the Japanese were not to be taken lightly while
blacks were not to be taken seriously. On this basis, the *Philadelphia Tribune* took issue with a stance assumed by Booker T. Washington during a trip to Montclair, New Jersey. One source had
quoted Washington as saying that blacks spent "too much time in
defending their race and showing resentment of things that had little or no significance." After expressing support for Washington's
overall program, the *Tribune* labeled Washington's alleged remarks
a "serious mistake." According to the Philadelphia newspaper, an
aggressive spirit had garnered for the Japanese the respect of the
peoples of Europe and the United States and "the great trouble"
with blacks had been a lack of sufficient resentment regarding the
indignities that had been heaped upon them. Whites despised
blacks, in the view of the *Tribune*, because blacks lacked the "spirit
to resent an insult" and "smile at the mailed hand that stands ever
ready to smite us." Contrasting blacks and Japanese, one writer, in
a letter to the *Washington Bee*, was broadly condemnatory of the
former: "Uncle Sam had better be on the alert lest he be caught nap-
ping, for the Japs haven't got one drop of Negro blood in their
veins."[19]

The notion of "retributive justice" had a tantalizing and
enduring appeal for some blacks. The *Savannah Tribune* predicted
that the whites of the South would begin "to pay the price of their
brutal mistreatment of the Negro." This revenge, in the *Tribune's*
view, was to be exacted as the colored races united "under the leadership of Japan." At least one black man, a physician from Spring-
field, Illinois, by the name of James E. Henderson, attempted to act
on behalf of his unorthodox views. Over a two-year period, Dr. Henderson distributed what the FBI labeled "riot-inciting literature."
His circular was captioned, "Get off the earth, you Japs, Hindoos
and Niggers," and it included his reply, "No we won't, you stop
shoving." In what he termed "the first shot in the initial skirmish

inaugurating a war of races unless colored people are better treated," Henderson enumerated his grievances. He accused whites of "gobbling up practically the entire surface of the earth, exterminating the natives, and denying those, whom they do not wipe out, the rights of citizenship, Christianity, and religion." The *Afro-American* newspaper, which had received several of the circulars, cautioned that "even the sincerest race patriot should have the sense not to talk about rebellion when there is no chance of its success."[20]

At the opposite pole was the view expressed in the *Freeman*. In an editorial titled "Japanese and Negroes," noting that some of the conferees in Tokyo denounced color prejudice as directed against blacks in America, the editorialist reminded his readers that blacks in this country had "a pretty good thing." Continuing this conservative line of reasoning, the writer proclaimed, "We chafe 'neath the goads we know, yet we should rejoice because of the weights we have flung aside."[21]

Despite differences of view, one would have been hard pressed to refute the argument presented in the *Indianapolis World*: "Race proscriptive measures do not sound good to Negroes." Therefore, the piece continued, "there was only one position for African Americans to take . . . one of opposition to all statutory legislation—precisely because blacks were fellow victims of such laws."[22]

Representative black views of the Japanese and the meaning of Japan's emergence as a world power can be seen better in African American newspapers remote from the Pacific Coast. Strangely, the non-Pacific papers contained more editorial comment about Japan and spoke for a larger percentage of the black population. Pacific Coast papers, if the Los Angeles-based *California Eagle* and the *Portland New Age* were in anyway representative, tended to fluctuate and, at times, seemed more concerned about the comparative status of their advancement vis-à-vis the Japanese than they were interested in the symbolic representation of Japanese as brothers under the skin.

Both papers gave attention to the Japanese at times other than those where U.S.-Japan relations were at flash point. They were also more inclined toward detachment in their reportage than other African American newspapers, and certainly they were free of the Japanophobia found in major Pacific Coast dailies. The *New Age* told its readers that "Japan's pride is hurt by anti-Japanese sentiment," but drew no parallels. It reported that Secretary Victor Metcalf had expressed the opinion that Japanese school children were guaranteed an education in American schools free of discrimination and that the Japanese government understood the situation and beyond punishing the Bay City a bit would make nothing more of the affair. Again, these reports were carried as straight news stories.

On December 15, 1906, the *New Age* carried an item under the title "Race Riot Averted," which it declared "insignificant in itself, but which may be the first of a series of events to strain the relations between Japan and America to the breaking point." The incident, which occurred in San Francisco, had been instigated by Ed Mell, an employee at a stable, who punched a Japanese delivery driver. According to the *New Age*, "In an instant one hundred angry Japanese and a score of young Americans had collected." Mell was reported to have challenged the Japanese. "Come on, all of you," he cried, "I'll lick every d——d Jap in the crowd." The incident resulted in Mell's arrest, but the *New Age* concluded: "The fighting blood of Young Japan had met the fighting blood of Young America." On the same day that this news item appeared, under the "News of the Week" column, there were forty items. The eighth mentioned that Roosevelt was about to send a message to congress regarding the Japanese question; the sixteenth reported that Representative Julius Kahn was "very bitter against Japanese immigration; the twenty-sixth told of Canada "also having trouble with Japanese coolies"; and the thirty-fourth again referred to Roosevelt expressing hope that a treaty of exclusion might be negotiated with Japan.[23]

A week following the alleged riot the *New Age* carried the full text of Roosevelt's message to Congress regarding the matter of the Japanese, an item about the San Francisco school board accusing Roosevelt of "meddling and misrepresentation in the Japanese question," and a report of the return of Frank P. Sargeant, commissioner of immigration, from Honolulu, Hawaii, aboard the Japanese ship *Nippon Maru*. Sargeant returned bearing tales of the Japanese "fast displacing all shop keepers, contractors, carpenters, and tradesmen generally of other nationalities in the islands."[24]

The *California Eagle* was more likely to express opinions than the *New Age*. While an editorial bias for or against the Japanese was not readily discernible in the *New Age*, the *Eagle* was less circumspect. At times there were complaints that Japanese, Mexicans, and Chinese, who were not American citizens, were admitted to saloons, soda fountains, and restaurants which denied service to blacks. The *Eagle* sometimes carried articles that tended to be critical of the Japanese. One such article was about a New York congressman. Herman Metz made the assertion that Japan wanted to do to the United States what it had done to Germany, an obvious reference to the Japanese move into the Shandong Province. The *Eagle* also carried the "Declaration of Principles of the Afro-American Council of California," number 17 of which stated that it was "opposed to the discrimination practiced . . . against the Negro people in favor of aliens, who have never rendered signal service to this nation, especially Asiatics."[25]

The *Eagle* carried positive references to Japan as well. Positive references to the Japanese easily were more abundant. As a matter of fact, Charlotta Bass, the publisher of the Los Angeles newspaper consistently asked her readers to emulate the Japanese. Whether advocating agriculture or business, the *Eagle*'s message was essentially the same: "Now, dear Colored Brother, if you want to emulate something or somebody, here is your chance." A reader also acknowledged that the Japanese walked among the advanced: "I pray God to speed the day when the black man will . . . walk side by side with the white and Japanese in the commercial world of this city." The *Eagle* admired characteristics of the Japanese such as "unity of purpose," their "supreme willingness to help one another," their ability to "build business blocks and become factors in the business world," and their political astuteness.[26]

The *Eagle* blamed the economic status of the blacks on themselves "since strictly speaking in California, NO NEGRO JOBS." African Americans lacked "enterprise and daring," the *Eagle* charged. But at the same time, the *Eagle* also accused blacks of falling "victims to the lure of the cities." While claiming that California offered a black man "unusual opportunity to show his adaptability for changed economic conditions," the Los Angeles newspaper stated that menial labor in California had been preempted by immigrants: Italians and Greeks ran the bootblack stands and did other low-waged jobs; Japanese were the porters. African Americans held their own "as train and Pullman and Dining car porters," but hotels and other areas of public entertainment were "entirely out of reach of Negroes."[27]

An example of the political acumen of the Japanese was carried on the front page of the *California Eagle*, "Japanese Make Strong Protest Against Moving Picture Film Before Welfare Committee of the City Council." Local Japanese residents of Los Angeles were protesting the showing of a film called *The Cheat*, and the public welfare committee was considering whether or not to ban the showing of the film. The *Eagle* promised that the outcome would be watched with interest since the Japanese protest of an obnoxious film was "a different proposition at all hazards from the protest filed by our own citizens when the *Clansman* was first brought here."[28]

Occasionally, the Japanese would do something that endeared them to African Americans and heightened the image of blacks and Japanese as allies in the struggle against white dominion. For example, a headline that certainly caught the attention of *Eagle* readers read, "Japan to Lead Fight for Rights of Colored Races." If readers missed this front page exegesis by a Japanese diplomat explaining why Germany had to be expelled from China, it was repeated a week later. But the notion that the Japanese were champions of colored peoples remained in circulation among African Americans until World War II. When a Japanese daily carried an article on C. J. Walker, the cosmetics entrepreneur, the *Eagle* told its readers that the Japanese were being told that "the Negroes of America are making the most remarkable progress of any race in this country." African Americans only had to learn to have more confidence in their leaders for them to occupy "the higher walks of life."[29]

In response to the arrival of the Japanese, white politicians and demagogues issued the direst warnings about the approaching end of the white race in California, the subversion of American institutions, and the end of Western civilization. However, African Americans refused to entertain such allegations and focused on what they perceived to be the positive benefits of having the Japanese on the West Coast.

James Weldon Johnson, noted writer, poet, field secretary and national organizer of the NAACP, while denying the assertion that the Japanese threatened American institutions, issued his own caveat: "If industry and thrift on the part of the Japanese farmers mean the end of the white race in California," he warned, "well, let it end; for the truth would be that it had already reached the point of decay and rot if it could not stand the fair competition of hard work, industry and energy expended on the soil." Johnson agreed that the biggest problem that whites had with the Japanese was that whites were unable to compete with the industriousness of the Japanese. He pointed out that the Japanese did not lower the wages or reduce the standard of living of Americans. They worked better than whites. According to Johnson, the Japanese worked harder and longer than white workers, made money where whites failed, and set a pace too hard for whites to follow. That, he said, was how the Japanese had come to control the production of certain produce.[30]

White racists, inadvertently, helped to foster among African Americans a greater sense that they shared with the Japanese a common victimization at the hands of white people. Few African Americans of the period would disagree with the Japanese professor who stated, "Inequality among races is indisputable, but injustice comes when the color of the skin is made the criterion equality." Johnson pointed out that after African Americans the chief victims of racist themes in the theater were the Japanese. The experience of Japanese protesting racist movies such as *The Cheat*, the Japanophobic espousal of racial hatred of the Hearst newspapers, all of these increased the African American's sense of comradeship with Japanese.[31] At different times, Japanese tried to encourage this notion of colored unity.

FOUR

𝒮𝒮𝒮𝒮𝒮

CHAMPIONS OF THE DARKER RACES

I n the summer of 1919, which John Hope Franklin called "the greatest period of interracial strife the nation had ever witnessed," a small dedicated band of international-minded African Americans prepared to take their appeal for justice to the Paris Peace Conference. Before an international body contemplating a new world order, African American activists—much like Malcolm X would propose in the 1960s, another period of heightened racial crisis—hoped to dramatize and bring the moral force of world condemnation to bear on American apartheid. In Paris these optimistic crusaders counted on Japanese support for an international solution to America's racial quagmire. The delegation, which included C. J. Walker, millionaire cosmetics entrepreneur; Ida Wells Barnett, indefatigible campaigner against lynching; and Monroe Trotter, visited the representatives of Japan who were staying at the Waldorf Astoria in New York enroute to the peace conference. Also a member of the representation from the African American community was A. Philip Randolph, labor leader, who as co-editor of the socialistic *Messenger* magazine, often railed against Japanese imperial policy in East Asia. Reportedly, they left with assurances that the delegates of Japan were sympathetic regarding the plight of African Americans in the United States. Encouraged, members of the East Calvary M.E. Church in Philadelphia also petitioned the Japanese asking that they work "to remove prejudice and race discrimination in all nations of the earth."[1]

The idea of petitioning the Japanese to support before a league of nations African American protest of racial conditions in the United States lacked universal appeal within the black community. The *Chicago Broad Ax* reported that there was deep division over the issue. According to the *Broad Ax* account, a large portion of the race favored the movement to send petitioners asking for an agreement to grant democracy to citizens of color. Opponents argued that the treatment of African Americans in the United States was a "domestic question." In hopes of coming up with something with which all editors and leaders could agree, the proponents of the petition movement suggested that they ask the member states in the League of Nations "to vouchsafe to their citizens respectively full liberty, rights of democracy and protection of life without restrictions of distinction based on race, color, or previous condition."[2]

Distrustful of Robert Russa Moton, successor to Booker T. Washington at Tuskegee, DuBois, or "any other Colored man whom the government has caused to be in France," the National Equal Rights League selected Walker and Trotter to go as its representatives as petitioners on behalf of African America to the deliberations in Paris that aimed to establish a new world order. After much difficulty and intrigue Trotter was able to get to Paris. Walker did not; she died in May. But the guardian of Boston arrived only after the principal debate had taken place. He did manage to gain an interview with Japanese delegates. According to the *Chicago Whip*, Trotter, "in a masterly and scholarly way," persuaded the Japanese that they and African Americans shared interests and that the Japanese ought to assist in getting the Negro question before the conference. Trotter had tried to gain an audience with President Wilson and was "flatly refused." It was after this refusal that the fiery editor sent a letter to every member of the peace commission detailing several cases where African Americans had been victims of "the most undemocratic class distinction." His petition pointed out that African Americans had done their part in helping to bring about the victory and ought to receive "such equal rights as are to be given the ethnical minorities in Austria, Ireland, or the Jews in Poland." His efforts, according to the *Whip*, were rewarded by a Japanese promise of "their united support."[3]

Among those who supported the move to petition the Japanese, A. Philip Randolph was most ambivalent. In normal times he had little regard for the Japanese. His criticisms of them were largely based on ideological differences. A typical Randolph piece about the Japanese denounced them as "imperialistic," "autocratic," and "reactionary." He called Japan "the Prussian State of the East," but concluded that the Japanese were actually more Prussian than the Prussians. He and Chandler Owen, his collaborator on the *Messenger*, argued that the Japanese were hardly concerned about race or color prejudice. Although he termed the introduction of the race issue a "monkey wrench" dropped at the peace conference, Randolph claimed that the Japanese were not interested in race prejudice because they were untouched by its sting. In order to support his contention, he cited such "evidence" as the Japanese being able to wine and dine at the best restaurants, "divide financial melons" on Wall Street, and ride on trains and buses free of discrimination.[4]

With the end of World War I, the victorious European nations and their allies met in Paris and began the task of restoring order to the international community. Each of these countries had its own agenda of priorities, but collectively they were willing to entertain some proposals from two non-European allies, Japan and the United States.

President Woodrow Wilson went to Paris with Fourteen Points which he hoped would serve as the basis for the creation of a new world order free of some of the irritants which sparked the first of the great wars. Wilson, in his idealism, was suggesting the establishment of a system rooted in a common notion of international law and mortality. The Japanese went to the peace conference advocating a fifteenth point which Wilson, given his southern predilections, could hardly father: the delegates representing the Imperial Japanese Empire proposed that the principle of racial equality be incorporated as a clause of the Covenant of the League of Nations.

Although Wilson went to Paris with dreams of enforcing a new morality in international affairs, the Japanese delegates, as a result of the old morality, arrived with a secret commitment from Great Britain, France, Italy, and Russia which was to leave Japan in possession of former German rights in the Shandong Peninsula and the southwest Pacific. It was in the area of race where the Japanese were prepared to depart from precedent and Wilson was not.

The Japanese proposal, if implemented, would have created an interesting paradox for African Americans. Japan contended that nationals of member states ought to be permitted to travel in the territories of other member states without restrictions as to race or color. Of course, had this proposal been adopted it would have meant that Japanese nationals residing in the United States could demand that no distinctions be made against them on account of race or nationality. In addition, Liberia and Haiti, as members of the League of Nations, would become able to make demands on the United States that native-born African Americans could not. For black Americans to receive the same equal democratic treatment accorded other nonwhite members of the league, they would have to leave their own country and reside abroad.

Regardless of whatever inconvenience it might cause, James Weldon Johnson thought that the racial equality issue ultimately would benefit African Americans. He stood among those convinced that Japan was "perhaps the greatest hope for the colored races of the world." The ascendancy of Japan, Johnson claimed, would benefit all nonwhite peoples. He believed: "One great world power made up of a colored race will have tremendous influence on the treatment accorded to all colored races."[5]

The degree to which Johnson's opinion was shared within black America is uncertain, but Japan's attempt to have the issue of racial equality debated before a world assembly was bound, almost inevitably, to spark a keen interest among African Americans. The Associated Negro Press claimed that African Americans were "manifesting the greatest concern in the momentous fight Japan is making before the Peace Conference on 'Race Discrimination.'" "From every section of the country," according to the ANP, "reports are coming in to the effect that the 12,000,000 colored people of America are watching the developments with the keenest interest." African Americans could hardly be unimpressed by the brave words of Japan's top diplomat at the conference: "We are not too proud to fight, but we are too proud to accept a place of admitted inferiority in dealing with one or more associate nations. We want nothing but simple justice." African Americans sought the same.[6]

There were more than a few African Americans who thought the chance to put their grievances before the world body using Japan as their intermediary was a real opportunity for African Americans and Japanese to ally themselves in the cause of ending racial discrimination. A year before the peace conference the *New York Age* and the *Cleveland Advocate* had predicted that Japan would seek nothing less than "no further racial discrimination throughout the world." Du Bois pursued this same theme. In Paris to attend the meeting of the Pan-African Congress, Du Bois had faith that the two great confabs would be significant for the advancement of the rights of black people. Resolutions passed at the Pan-African Congress, he announced, contained principles of equality which Jews and Japanese demanded. He believed that to ward off the inevitable specter of the Great War of the Races it was absolutely necessary to have the Great World Congress where black, white, and yellow people sat down, spoke, and acted. This "supernational entity," he believed, would check race antagonism by bringing to bear influences of a multiethnic civilization and culture. Such a body would also represent the organized public opinion of the World.[7]

Some African Americans distrusted Japan's commitment to a broad principle of racial justice. Most, however, understood that there was "but one great power among the darker races signatory to the covenant of the League of Nations." "Any other [nonwhite] country could only resort to the petition with no power of enforcing any demand," the *Chicago Defender* dutifully pointed out. But the *Afro-American* accused Japan of fighting for the rights of the Japanese alone, not the darker races. What made African Americans apprehensive about Japan was China. Because of Japanese aggression in China, African American suspicions turned to convictions, at least in the minds of some. If the Japanese were ruthless in dealing with kissing cousins, blacks reasoned, they would have less regard for those further removed. When the League of Nations consented to Japan's acquisition of the Shandong Peninsula, a number of African Americans were critical of what they perceived as Japan's interference in the internal affairs of China and fretted that the Asian power was trying to "bulldoze her neighbor." The *Philadelphia Tribune* denounced this turn of events as unjustifiable and declared China "forsaken."[8]

While some African Americans were critical of Japanese imperialism in China, others saw it as a necessary development in Japan's rise and acceptance as a great power. Acknowledging that China had grounds for protesting the alienation of Shandong to Japan, James Weldon Johnson, after stating his basic opposition to the "whole business of domination and exploitation," declared that "if other nations are going to be allowed to hold and dominate parts of China, we are in favor of seeing Japan do the same thing." Observing that nothing appealed to modern white civilization except power, Johnson saw Shandong as part of an entity that lay within Japan's sphere of influence: "The victory which Japan has gained does violate the principle of 'self-determination' so far as China is concerned, but we feel that on the whole it is better for China to be dominated by Japan than to be dominated by some European govenment."[9]

The image of Japan standing up to the combined powers of Europe and the United States inspired heroic headlines and editorial comment in the black press. The black press depicted Japanese imperialism as an outgrowth of higher, more moral motivation than that of white imperialism: "Japan to Lead Fight for Rights of Colored Races," "Japan Speaks for Darker Races in Asia," "Japan Greatest Hope for Colored Races," "Japanese Principle Asia for Asiatics," "Asiatic League Forming to Combat White Supremacy." Johnson already envisioned and welcomed an Asiatic Monroe Doctrine."[10]

Some African Americans, in their reverie, relished the idea of a coming racial Armageddon whereby the colored peoples of the world, probably under the leadership of Japan, would rise up and overthrow white hegemony. John Edward Bruce, a columnist who used the nom de plume "Bruce Grit" found this kind of imagery pleasurable. In the view of Peter Gilbert, the editor of Bruce's selected writings, Bruce Grit "not only spoke to, but probably for the average black citizen." Whether or not his musings reflected those of the average black citizen, Bruce, at least, left a record of his own dream for Japan. In an undated, never completed short story, Bruce fantasized a scenario in which East and West locked in a "death grapple for the mastery of the Pacific and the Orient won." "The Philippines and Hawaii," he prophesied, "were lost to America and the flag of Japan waved proudly from the fortifications lately occupied by American troops." Was it possible in the early 1900s for the average African American citizen to dream, as Bruce did, of the end of white rule in Asia? Not only was it possible; it was highly probable.[11]

The tendency for seeing Japan in heroic proportions and the cavalier disregard that some African Americans displayed toward Japan's trampling upon China's sovereignty both resulted from blacks projecting aspects of their own circumstances upon the East Asian situation. A Japanese acquaintance told James Weldon Johnson that there was no difference between an "Uncle Tom" and a "nagging China." Admitting that Japan had been at times "overbearing" and "unjust," Johnson, nevertheless, agreed that China had "never sought in any way to cooperate with Japan" in an effort to reach "a mutual understanding." He accepted the view of his Japanese source who maintained that the role of the Chinese was comparable to that of Negroes who, when plans were being made to advance the race without help or hindrance from whites, "run and tell the white folks."[12]

Few African Americans, however, would dissent from Mary Church Terrell's assessment of events in Asia. Contemplating the coming clash of war machines and martial spirit, she pronounced it "a great pity." She thought it "heartbreaking to see those colored races" poised "at sword's point." "What a wonderful power they would be if they could be persuaded to unite their forces instead of cutting each other to pieces" Terrell mused.[13]

The reactions of African Americans to the Washington Disarmament Conference, which took place almost two years after the Paris Peace Conference, demonstrated the extent to which African Americans were prepared to accept the view that Japan labored on behalf of all colored peoples. Those African American pundits who commented on it invariably saw race as a paramount issue. They tended to see it as a western stratagem to limit Japanese naval expansion in the Pacific. Ultimately, they believed its aim was to hobble Japanese naval power. In the view of the *Philadelphia Tribune*, the Anglo-Saxon powers only invited "a colored nation" because of Japan's rapidly growing power. The *Tribune* also expected the "one colored nation represented among the 'big five' nations" to "bring up the question of plain human rights again." The big question of the conference, from the point of view of the *Savannah Tribune*, was "Is this a white man's world?" From the viewpoint of people "born to blush unseen," Japan was the foremost contender in the battle of brains, conscious of its responsibility and mindful of the "background of color."[14]

African American observers became more convinced that racial motives lay behind European and American initiatives when China "joined hands on the issue of the hour" with Japan, a "long time bitter contender with China on many things." Both China and Japan, acting in concert, matched "at every stage of the game, the wisdom and diplomacy of the United States, Great Britain, France and all others," marveled a reporter for the *Savannah Tribune*.[15]

Both William Pickens, field secretary with the NAACP, and Johnson agreed that calling the naval powers together in Washington was part of the West's strategy for hamstringing Japan's naval development more than a desire for disarmament. Pickens called Japan "the first real threat against white domination of the world since the keys of the Alhambra were last handed over." Johnson seriously doubted that disarmament could result from a scheme designed "to isolate [Japan] and put her more at the mercy of the two great Anglo-Saxon nations."[16]

In a series of columns for the *New York Age,* Johnson followed closely the proceedings of the disarmament conference and recommended that other African Americans do the same because it would "revolve around the status of the colored races of the Orient directly and the colored peoples of the world indirectly." In Johnson's opinion, Japan's position was precarious. Citing the American government's position at Paris and its opposition to the renewal of the treaty inaugurating the Anglo-Japanese alliance in 1902, Johnson maintained that the U.S. government was opposed to the Japanese because of race. Johnson was equally convinced that the British were playing their "same shifty diplomatic game" and that they would readily let Japan "go adrift" if such an abandonment would result in a closer Anglo-American nexus.[17]

The Japanese, Johnson understood, had considerable skills and resources when it came to coping with the "tricks of diplomacy." He saw them as having three advantages: first, the Anglo-Japanese treaty remained in force; second, Japan benefited from certain secret agreements; and the United States as a result of the Lansing-Ishii Agreement acknowledged that Japan had "special interests" in Asia. Before consenting to participate in the conference, he asserted, the Japanese would insist that parameters of discussion be clearly articulated in advance and they would stand firmly on the Lansing-Ishii Agreement of 1917. When all else failed, Johnson claimed, the Japanese could play their "trump card," the demand for racial equality. This, Johnson explained, was a pressure to which the English and Americans were determined not to yield: "Therefore, whenever Japan plays it she forces these two nations to compromise on demands which they are making upon her."[18]

In Johnson's view, Japan's considerable diplomatic advantage was complemented by "an underlying moral advantage." He maintained that the Western powers only sought commercial and trade benefits in the Orient, but Japan, with a rapidly increasing population and a sparsity of living space, vitally needed an outlet for its surplus population. Johnson summed up his view simply, "The right of the western powers in the Orient are artificial and questionable while those of Japan are natural and moral."[19] But if the Western powers seriously negotiated "real disarmament," Johnson believed, it would be advantageous for Japan. Real disarmament would mean that Japan could reduce its military budget and would gain greater security as the Anglo-American naval power was reduced and Pacific fortresses dismantled, he explained.[20]

The Washington Disarmament Conference had proved to be yet another instance in which African American intellectuals had sharpened their racial consciousness by contrasting the black condition with that of the Japanese in the international arena. By seeing the Japanese and themselves as both "colored" it was a logical extension to anticipate, as the *Savannah Tribune* put it, "the great shadow of the darker races of the world contending with whites for justice and equality of opportunity."[21] That is, through the Japanese, African Americans had invented a metaphor that gave worldwide dimensions not only to their plight but to its solution. Thus, given the chance to meet and interact with Japanese, African Americans were predisposed to greet them with cordiality.

Demographic circumstances pretty much guaranteed that the average African American would have little opportunity to meet Japanese face-to-face. If African Americans were to meet Japanese, that meeting would most likely occur in the Pacific region. Robert E. Park, noted sociologist at the University of Chicago, provided evidence of the cordial interpersonal relations that occurred in the 1920s between African Americans and Japanese on the Pacific Coast.

The "Pacific Coast Race Relations Survey" was a sociological research project directed by Park and sponsored by the New York–based Institute of Social and Religious Research, which had supported some of the most important sociological research of the period. Researchers under Park's overall direction conducted interviews in a transitional neighborhood where whites, African Americans, and Japanese lived together "experiencing conflicts and accommodations. In this target area, the three groups "intermingled even to the extent of whites and Negroes, whites and Japanese, Negroes and Japanese living in the same flats." Whites had occupied this neighborhood until 1910 before African Americans began to move into the area. A few Japanese began to trickle in about 1914, but "the real Japanese increase" started in 1921. Among whites, as the neighborhood became increasingly triracial, there occurred "conflicts of opinion . . . with references to both Japanese and Negroes." Some whites liked African Americans better than Japanese, and other whites preferred the Japanese before African Americans. When asked about their preference for one or the other, whites tended to reply that the group of their choice minded its own business, kept nice homes, and was neat. The overriding fear among those whites who wanted neither group as neighbors was that property values would depreciate as a result of the presence of African Americans or Japanese. A third group of whites did not object to living next door either to African Americans or to Japanese.[21]

Japanese who were interviewed indicated that white people tended to avoid them but African Americans were cordial toward them. One respondent admitted that he had moved to be "with the Negroes because they have less prejudice against us than whites. They befriend us, and act glad we are here." The responses of black interviewees typically supported the assessment of the Japanese. The study indicated that African Americans and Japanese, in practical day-to-day associations, got along quite well together. In commenting on this Pacific Coast survey, the *Philadelphia Tribune* attributed the cordiality between African Americans and Japanese in the study to the ability of the Japanese to "mind their own business" and to the fact that they were also an "oppressed people."[22]

In 1923 African Americans outside the Pacific region demonstrated their strong feelings for the Japanese when Japan was devastated by a great earthquake and tidal wave. In Chicago, the white political elite began to organize a relief campaign without seeking input from the black community. Upon reading about this, one reader of the *Chicago Defender* urged it to appeal to "the Race people of this country" so African Americans, "as a Race," might help the sufferers of Japan. The *Defender* promptly launched such a campaign. The first contribution of one hundred dollars was donated by Jesse Binga, president of the Binga State Bank. Binga, who began his state bank in 1921, amassed a fortune speculating in real estate before going into banking. About ten months before the tragic earthquake, some prominent Japanese, who were studying social conditions in the United States, "particularly as they effect [*sic*] the Negro," reminded Binga of Japan's efforts to have racial equality made a principle of international behavior. The *Defender* asked its readers to "make a creditable showing." "None of us are so poor that we cannot give something to such a worthy cause," the *Defender* admonished the hesitant.[23]

At first glance, it might seem that the black response was a humanitarian gesture little different from the outpouring of sympathy which flowed from any community in a time of great crisis. But A. L. Jackson, a columnist for the *Defender*, in alluding to the dual impact of the calamity that struck Japan, insisted that it had particular meaning for African Americans as well as the Japanese. On the one hand, he wrote, "the world stock of brains had been depleted by the lost lives of skilled artisans and progressive citizens who might have contributed to the advancement and welfare of nations." On the other hand, he believed that the loss was especially poignant for African Americans because, having succeeded in science, commerce, engineering, war, and other areas long thought the special preserves of white people, the Japanese were the "living refutation of the white man's theory of white supremacy." The *Savannah Tribune*, taking a position comparable to that of Jackson, reported that black leaders across the country endorsed aid to Japan precisely because it was a nation made up of a "colored race."[24]

Marcus Garvey, the self-styled provisional leader of Africa, certainly the foremost mass leader of black America, on behalf of the Universal Negro Improvement Association and the Negro people of the world, sent a telegram expressing deep-felt sympathy to the emperor of Japan, whom he addressed as "a friend in the cause of racial justice." After receiving acknowledgment of the cable, Garvey and the UNIA membership donated five hundred dollars to the Japanese relief fund, predicting the reemergence of "a new Japan, greater, stronger, and more substantial than before."[25]

Garvey, as the individual who captured the imagination and following of .5 million African Americans of the lower end of the social and economic scale, helped fashion the image of the Japanese found among lower class African Americans. In a sense, Japan's resurrection was vital to Garvey's own continuing scenario of the redemption of Africa. "Asia for the Asiatics," in Garvey's preaching, was to be prelude to that time when Africa would be for Africans. As he envisioned the expulsion of imperialist powers and the restoration of Africa's former greatness was to be preceded by the revival of Asia's eminence. Under the direction of Japan this revivification of Asia pointed toward an eventful lining up of Asia, after which the yellow races would "call in all Africa," Garvey taught. Garvey told his followers that it was because he foresaw this eventuality that he "brought into line the Universal Negro Improvement Association."[26] Both contingencies, he recognized, would come only after strength, group, and intergroup solidarity had garnered the respect of Europeans and Americans.

Garvey and others among the leadership of the UNIA held forth the Japanese as models worthy of emulation. Garvey compared the accomplishments of Japan, China, and India:

Marquis Hirobumi Ito sent Japanese students to American, English, French and German universities to learn all that Western civilization could teach. The result is that Japan is a force to be reckoned with. China and India paid little attention . . . remained rooted in the past. . . . The result is as follows: India is now dominated by England and China by Japan. . . . The Negro must prove of what mettle he is made. He must demonstrate his originality and his initiative by building a standard civilization comparable with that of other races."[27]

He keeps the best he finds and needs in any other race, but fundamentally he remains a Japanese. Garvey's typical message was that the Japanese had once been humbled, but through pride, unity, and determination built themselves up so that no one could again humiliate them without fear of retribution.

Compared to the Japanese, Garvey and his minions charged, others among the darker races lacked the right stuff. William L. Sherril, who bore the Garveyite title "titular leader of American Negroes" critiqued the difference between African Americans and Japanese as follows: "The Negro is something you can lynch . . . something who is ashamed of himself and thinks . . . he has got to use all the bleaches and hair-straightening that Walker and Poro can put out. He does not like the color of his skin." The Japanese remains a Japanese and is proud to retain the color of his skin; he has evolved his own culture, his own art, distinctly for the Japanese people. T. Thomas Fortune, converted to Garveyism, drew upon his experience in Asia, "The white man nowhere is disposed to bully the Japanese, because he will not stand for it, but he does not hesitiate to bully the Chinaman, the East Indian or the African." In another piece Fortune wrote, "An American could cheat and abuse a Chinaman and he would accept it, and his companions be they few or many, would accept it, with the stolid humility of those whom the spirit has broken on the race rod." Hordes of Africans and Asians, he charged, had been "broken in their pride of manhood and race." Fortune said, "But the Japanese are not broken in their pride of race and manhood. They have no right cheek to turn when the left has been smitten." This Japanese spirit, he felt, "should animate everyman, every race, and every nation, and only those who possess it are respected in their lives and property by others."[28]

When the California-inspired agitation against the Japanese resulted in a national policy of exclusion in 1924, Garvey was among those African Americans who anticipated a war between Japan and the United States. His newspaper characterized the Japanese as a people "slow to anger slow to forgive and forget," who would "nurse a grievance against the time when they are ready to exact vengeance."[29]

When talk of possible war between Japan and the United States cropped up among African Americans, someone invariably asked what should be their role. Should African Americans forget that Japan would be fighting against conditions about which they complained and defend "old glory"? Should they sympathize with the Japanese and render aid? Should they remain neutral? The *Chicago Defender* articulated the black dilemma and offered a formula for dealing with it. Noting that some African Americans anxiously hoped for war between Japan and the United States, with the idea of Japan becoming victorious over the United States, the *Defender* dismissed such thinking as "idle dreams" and cautioned African Americans, "Your sympathy to Japan, but your heart, your hand to Uncle Sam." The *Defender* shared its perception of reality with its readers: "To follow our white people . . . you will have to wade out into deep water. Sink or swim, go along with them." In the final analysis, the *Defender* concluded, African Americans were expected to answer the roll call "when Uncle Sam says so."[30]

Other than the issue of possible war with the United States, African Americans aligned themselves on the side of the Japanese where Japan was involved. A contributing factor was the nature and quality of contact between the two groups. It was often typified by a "friendly spirit of cooperation and sympathetic understanding." In Oakland, California, Japanese advertised in the local black newspaper. The *Oakland Sunshine* carried advertisements for an Osaka silk agent, the Nadaokaco soft drink stand, a Japanese dentist, the Mikado laundry, and a Japanese shoemaker.[31] In turn, a Japanese newspaper carried profiles on distinguished African Americans such as C. J. Walker. Furthermore, the Japanese media often ran items protesting American racial conditions and the lynching of African Americans. For example, the *Philadelphia Tribune* carried an editorial that ran in the *Asian Review*, which was published in Tokyo, condemning a lynching in Arkansas in the summer of 1921. It was based on information supplied to the foreign press by the New York office of the NAACP.[32]

Individually and in groups, Japanese tried to boost the morale of African Americans. A Japanese delegation of filmmakers visited the Lincoln Motion Picture Company where they watched the newly completed *By Right of Birth*, a film they applauded for its "moral appeal and human interest."[33] In Los Angeles, the head of the Japanese Chamber of Commerce spoke before the Negro Businessman's League. In New York, Claude McKay, noted poet of the Harlem Renaissance, became acquainted with Sen Katayama while both worked on the *Harlem Liberator*, a Communist newspaper. McKay wrote of the exploits of Katayama and told how this Japanese activist went to the Soviet Union and worked "unceasingly and unselfishly to promote the cause of the exploited American Negro among the Soviet councils of Russia."[34]

Within the United States, African Americans saw the Japanese as more than fellow victims of racism: they saw them as people ready to treat black people with dignity, respect, and equality. The Japanese hospital in Los Angeles employed two black surgeons. "At a time when seemingly all hospital doors are being closed to members of the race, it is gratifying to know that Japanese leave their doors wide open to all people, where one can have the care of his own physician," the *California Eagle* noted. The image that Japanese were fair to African Americans was further enhanced by occasional rumors that Japanese were intermarrying with African Americans on the Pacific Coast.[35] Given the abhorrence with which whites generally regarded miscegenation, African Americans tended to interpret the reported Japanese willingness to intermarry as a testament of their commitment to social equality.

A few African Americans visited Japan. Reverend Henry Allen Boyd of Nashville, Tennessee, who attended the World's Sunday School Convention in Tokyo, gave a talk titled "My Impression of the Japanese People" at the Spring Grove Baptist Church in Toledo, Ohio. Dr. and Mrs. Charles Thompson returned to Chicago from a ten-month jaunt around the world with a picture of one of the highlights of the trip: it showed them seated around a banquet table "Tokyo fashion" as guests of honor in the modern capitol. The NAACP's Johnson visited Kyoto, the imperial capitol, as delegate to the Third Biennial Conference of the Institute of Pacific Relations. Returning full of praise for the hospitality bestowed by the Japanese, members of the elite were joined by servicemen, domestics, musicians, and assorted others.[36]

Further evidence of the African American identification with the Japanese can be seen in the result of a public opinion poll taken in 1920. The Associated Negro Press conducted the survey in an effort to ascertain the issues African Americans thought most important. The respondents ranked "the Japanese problem in the

West" their fifth issue of concern, behind lynchings, disfranchisement, jim crow transportation, and European immigration.[37]

Among African Americans there was some criticism of Japanese imperialist policies toward Korea and China, but the one other
area where Japanese generated the highest disapproval rating was
that mentioned earlier, where they threatened to show up as economic competitors. African Americans understood very well that
racial prejudice toward the Japanese was compounded by and partially derived from fears of economic competition. During times of
economic sluggishness, African Americans were as likely as whites
to resent interlopers who would make the snatching of crumbs a
fiercer competition. The *Chicago Defender* feared African Americans would be unable to hold their own in the American labor market against Japanese competition and admitted, "The white man
does not want him, for economic reasons; neither do we." The
Savannah Tribune put forth a novel argument to support its contention that Japanese workers had an unfair advantage over African
Americans. They had an uncanny ability to live more cheaply than
native Americans. Why? Because the "wily Nippon," the *Tribune*
answered, was not a witness to "the wanton waste and destruction
of American improvidence"; therefore, it was easier for the Japanese to learn thrift than it was for African Americans who were
"born within the view of the white man's lavishness."[38]

As critical as it might be of foreign competition, the African
American press denied the allegation that Japanese menaced the
American standard of living. The "far greater menace" to American
institutions and values beckoned at "her eastern gate, not her western," the *Defender* proclaimed. In the impassioned rhetoric of the
nativist, the *Defender* declared, "If we are to survive we must dam
the European flood." It was the position of the Chicago newspaper
that America's "Huns and Vandals are not black, not yellow, but
white, and they are coming through Ellis Island at the rate of three
thousand per day." The number of Japanese landing on the Pacific
Coast, by the *Defender's* calculations, paled into insignificance
alongside the figures quoted for Europeans. "Just why are Japanese—a thrifty, industrious, progressive people—more objectionable
than the Nordics, some of whom are far less progressive?" the
Atlanta Independent wanted to know. The *Independent* noted
rather caustically that the "more largely intelligent and very adaptable" Japanese constituted less of a danger than did a foreign element made up of "largely radicals who eat peanuts and make
bombs."[39]

African Americans were more inclined to defend than knock the achievements of the Japanese. The Japanese stood as living statement to the ideals of race pride, economic cooperation, group solidarity, and self-reliance.\They were the practioners and embodiment of the virtues of thrift, industry, and economy. The Japanese work experience was a vindication of Booker T. Washington's admonition that "the individual who can do something that the world wants done will, in the end, make his way regardless of race." Washington himself once had designated the Japanese as a "convincing example of the respect which the world gives to a race that can put brains and commercial activity into the development of the resources of the country."[40]

As whites intensified their efforts to expel the Japanese from their agricultural lands in California, some African Americans looked covetously at the "exceptional agricultural opportunities" the Pacific Coast potentially offered. The national convention of the Industrial and Commercial Council of Peoples of African Descent, which met in Los Angeles, discussed the possibility of importing black farm workers, especially from the South. One delegate claimed to be in direct touch with at least five thousand colored men who were prepared to move to California to take up truck farming. These workers were supposed to be led by graduates of the agricultural department of Tuskegee Institute.[41]

Four years later the *Afro-American* newspaper was still advising black banks, insurance companies, and realtors to get busy and investigate the possibility of settling black farming migrants in voids left by the Japanese. For thousands of African Americans who had left the South and gone north only to find disappointment, the *Savannah Tribune* now advised that they redirect their hopes and aspirations for a better life westward toward California.[42]

At the same time that it suggested that there might be a future for African Americans where Japanese had formerly made a living, the *Afro* cast doubt that it would ever be so. It pointed out that the "big sin" of the Japanese was their "thrift and progress." The "bloody flag of race prejudice," the *Afro* exclaimed, was raised and they were legislated out of the state because they were disinclined to serve as "beasts of burden and slaves" in the service of white overlords. The experience of the Japanese did not bode well for African Americans. The message whites of California sent out was work hard and then get expelled.[43]

The more the Japanese demonstrated ability, the more they overcame adversity and moved nearer the realization of the American dream, the more whites seemed to resent and persecute them, and the more African Americans understood that they themselves also were likely to bear some of the brunt of assaults against the Japanese. For as William Pickens pointed out, both African Americans and Japanese were "jinx" in California. "And queer varmints like race prejudice," he stated, "will naturally spawn all other sorts of queer things: queer laws, queer customs, queer complexes, and queer antics."[44]

A Philadelphia minister, back from a not too enjoyable visit to California, touched on a major weakness in any scheme to displace the Japanese: African Americans on the Pacific Coast freely patronized Japanese establishments. In his words, the "Jew" and the "Jap" had settled, "like the sucker shark on the whale," near African Americans and sold them the "necessities of life." Being a resident of Philadelphia, he, evidently, was unable to appreciate the cordial relationship between black Californians and Japanese. He certainly displayed no brotherly love toward Jews or Japanese.[45]

Many African Americans came to dislike Takao Ozawa. Ozawa, who sought to prove he was eligible for citizenship because he was white, had his case reach the Supreme Court of the United States. His suit was based on his contention that the Japanese as descendants of the aboriginal Ainu were a Caucasian people. Ozawa labored through the American judicial process to learn what Kelly Miller long understood intuitively, that is, "no amount of learned ethnological disquisition can seriously disturb" the American racial structure. Yet, underlying the Ozawa argument, Miller detected an abstract claim of human brotherhood that appealed to him. With regard to that notion, he believed that "the Negro cannot but sympathize with the Japanese position." The world ought not be made into "air-tight compartments along lines of racial cleavage," Miller asserted.[46]

If the Supreme Court had accepted Ozawa's position, it would have exacerbated the domestic issue of longer standing since there were countless numbers of African Americans who could claim Caucasian forebears without reaching back into a primeval past. The case was interesting in a number of respects. Ozawa had two lawyers, "one white and the other non-white, trying to prove that a yellow race is a white race," and most important, the decision, in essence, reserved America for the white race and Africans.[47]

The *Chicago Defender*, two years subsequent to the Ozawa decision, still managed to sound an irate tone. Japan had risen as a yellow people but "as soon as it got up it wanted to be 'white,'" the

Defender complained. Until Japan made her "great blunder," the sympathy African Americans had for her was "universal," the *Defender* asserted. According to the militant Chicago newspaper, the support African Americans gave Japan in its stand against the "swash-buckler and braggart" dissipated with the image of Ozawa "begging to be classed not as a yellow people, but as a branch of the Aryan tree." By this act, the *Defender* remonstrated, Japan had served notice "that her yearnings were beyond her blood."[48]

In the opinion of Kelly Miller, the Ozawa decision was the international equivalent of the Dred Scott decision. He denied any correlation between the respective claims of African Americans and Japanese regarding citizenship. The political status of the two groups, he thought, were so far removed from one another that "a comparison becomes odious." The claim of one was based on "an inheritance of three centuries of ancestral toil," while the other was that of the eleventh hour comer." He believed that Japan, however, was facilitating a movement toward some kind of "moral unity." Such a movement could never occur "so long as any race smarts under the stigma of unfair discrimination," he conceded. In time, he felt, the Ozawa decision would have to be overturned or stand "as a stumbling block in the way of international peace and good-will." Unless the decision was overturned, it would serve to engender a common resentment among the darker races who were "victims of Anglo-Saxon proscriptions," save the African.[49]

In summary, between 1919 and 1929, African Americans watched as the Japanese performed on the world stage of international politics: they applauded when Japan appeared at the Paris Peace Conference with a proposal to make racial equality a principle of the League of Nations Covenant; they jeered when Takao Ozawa appeared before the Supreme Court in an aborted effort to prove Japanese white. On balance, however, the period was one in which certain African Americans and Japanese actively fostered the idea that they should be allies in the struggle against white hegemony. African Americans sent delegations to meet with Japanese; they were uncritical of Japanese aggression in China and Korea; Garvey projected a vision of a Japan-led redemption of Asia as precursor to Africa's resurrection; some Japanese actively promoted the idea of an African American and Japanese alliance.

⚝⚝⚝⚝

FIVE

PRO-JAPAN
SENTIMENT UPSWING

The 1930s was a critical time when the relations between the governments of the United States and Japan took an irreversible turn for the worse as Japanese troops invaded Manchuria and pursued policies in China defiant of American remonstrances. During the same period, however, the image African Americans held of the Japanese actually became more sharply focused and more favorable. Until this time, the intellectual electricity that took place between black America and Japan occurred in a political and diplomatic vacuum in that neither could directly affect the other. This, to a considerable extent, would continue to be the case until Pearl Harbor. What helped to hone the image of the Japanese among African Americans were interpretations of Japan's role in China, reports of Japan's efforts to aid Ethiopia in its war with Italy, certain goodwill gestures of the Japanese, the despair felt by southern agricultural workers, and a visit to Japan by W. E. B. Du Bois.

In 1931 the Japanese Kwangtung Army invaded Manchuria and earned the unequivocal condemnation of the League of Nations. China, seemingly, had been the victim of an unprovoked attack. Was the aggressive policy of the Japanese merely the aping of white imperialism, or did that policy, to the contrary, represent an altruistic effort to uplift the Chinese, even in spite of themselves? African American opinion split on this issue along an idealists versus realists bifurcation. The former criticized Japanese policies of force in China as no different from what other exploiters of the militarily weak did. The latter saw aggressive actions as regrettable but necessary. As leader of the nonwhite nations, like other strong governments, realists believed, Japan must display the perks of power.

A great number of African American intellectuals held the view that the Japanese were acting on behalf of all Asia in throwing off the shackles of Western imperialism. From this perspective, they believed that the Chinese were either naive or too dumb to understand Japan's altruistic attempt to assist them. An editorial in the *Philadelphia Tribune* characterized the Sino-Japanese conflict as "much like a father trying to whip a child into a correct appraisal of his opportunities." Like a strict parent, the Japanese were tough but not malicious. Wary of Euro-American intentions, the Japanese, in the view of the *Tribune*, were defending their security zone and working toward "the fall of white rule in Asia." This was all that the Japanese intended. To accomplish this end, Japan needed to secure access to the coal and iron resources of "her cousin" before other powers acted to take these resources "under their protection."[1]

"China might well cooperate" with the Japanese, the *Philadelphia Tribune* asserted, "for the burdens of all dark skins are common ones." The *Tribune* believed that such cooperation would preserve "the East for those [to] whom it rightfully belongs." The *Baltimore Afro-American* newspaper, a little more dramatically, expressed the same sentiment, "The Chinese have become a kind of 'Uncle Tom' of Asia." Chinese leaders, the *Afro-American* declared, "have kow-towed to the white exploiters, licked their boots and allowed themselves to become the footstools of Western conquerors." "As we see it," the *Afro* reasoned, complete with cartoon, "Japan is kicking China in the pants to make it stand up straight and be a man."[2]

Among those who thought the Chinese naïve, W. E. B. Du Bois faulted them for being "utterly deceived as to white opinion of the yellow race." What motivated the Japanese to act was Japan's fear that China misunderstood the politics of European aggression, he surmised. In Du Bois's view, the Chinese failed even to recognize the insult implied in the Chinese Exclusion Act. He regarded it "a matter of fact" that Chinese were "despised and insulted in Amer-

ica almost as much as Negroes" and any coddling of China by white
nations was strictly for the purpose of later advantage.[3]

The *Chicago Defender* agreed that the reason Japan marched
against China was because of China's inability to ward off "the
scoundrels of western diplomacy." The *Defender* assumed that it
was Japan's "manifest destiny" to shake China from its slumber.
While chastising China, the *Defender* argued that Japan was whip-
ping race prejudice. The Japanese were defeating the ignominy of
color, cutting down the weed of ignorance, and setting the principle of human equality upon a firm and proper foundation through
the "infusion of the blood of genius into that of weary reknown
[*sic*]."[4]

Some African Americans questioned whether the aggression
of the Japanese in China was meant to bring together the colored
peoples of the world in some kind of anti-imperialist coalition, but
Japan's reported efforts on behalf of Ethiopia seemed to be positive
proof that this was indeed the case. When Italy threatened the East
African country, African Americans saw Japan acting more aggres-
sively protective of Ethiopia than the League of Nations.

The *Pittsburgh Courier* sent J. A. Rogers to cover the war
between Italy and Ethiopia, and Rogers reported that the association with Japan was beneficial for the Africans. He told readers of
the *Courier* that Ethiopians were in Japan training to be pilots and
that there was speculation that they were to be provided with
planes. Rogers believed that the trade relationship that developed
between Japan and Ethiopia contributed to the health and comfort
of the East Africans through the introduction of affordable Japanese
goods. According to the *Philadelphia Tribune*, even before resign-
ing from the League of Nations, Japan had sought "a formidable
political and commercial alliance with Abyssinia on the basis of
racial security."[5]

There were some African Americans, however, who believed
that there was little difference between Italy's role in Ethiopia and
Japan's in Manchuria. Japan, Kelly Miller argued, had done in China
"precisely" what Mussolini intended in Ethiopia. In both cases, he
believed, it was "primarily a question of greed and imperial aggression."[6]

More typically, however, the African American press seemed
to support the idea that Japanese were committed to Ethiopia's
well-being. The *Indianapolis Recorder* denied that Italy and Japan
were pursuing similar policies. The *Recorder* took the position that
China was saddled with warlords who were "so grasping in their

desire for power and bitterly jealous of each other" that they caused China to be too divided and weak to ward off the predatory Europeans. The pettiness and bickering of the Chinese warlords, according to the *Recorder*, made "leadership a joke and principle a word glutted of all potency." The *Chicago Defender* reported that General Kazushige Ugaki, a member of the Japanese Supreme War Council, had declared that "Japan could not be neutral in the event of an Italo-Ethiopian conflict." The *Defender* speculated that in the event of war thousands of Japanese would "go tramping through African hinterlands to the aid of their darker brothers on the lofty plateaus of Ethiopia."[7]

The *Indianapolis Recorder* reported that Japanese, Chinese, and Egyptians were offering to serve in the Ethiopian army in order to fight against the Italians. This was in spite of the Japanese government's efforts to discourage such "volunteerism." The article included the call of arms issued by the Great Japan's Young Men's Association:

> Arise, colored brothers, Slay the Mediterranean white wolf pounding on the black lamb in East Africa.
> Colored brothers throughout the world, stand up and save your poor brother Ethiopians who are in the clutches of the white wolf.
> Slay the white-skinned beast who is threatening the innocent black lamb.

Although the Japanese government for reasons of *realpolitik* tried not to upset its diplomatic relationship with Mussolini, the ordinary people of Japan clamored to support the regime of Haile Selassie. Americans who regarded it as a sinister organization "conjectured that the Black Dragon Society [was] attempting to influence the Japanese government to intercede on behalf of Ethiopia." And they were right.[8]

Members of the so-called Black Dragon Society or Kokuryukai had earned a reputation for assisting armed resistance to white rule. Kokuryukai members engaged in paramilitary operations in support of Emilio Aguinaldo and against the Americans in the Philippines and cooperated with Dr. Sun Yat-sen against the Manchus in China. Taking their name from the river that served as a border between Manchuria and Siberia, the members of the Amur River Society dedicated themselves to furthering Japan's imperial mission and checking the expansion of Western powers into Asia.

When Chinese wrote the name of the river, they used characters that together in Japanese are read *koku* (black) and *ryu* (dragon).

Founded in 1901 the Kokuryukai was the most important of many patriotic groups formed in Japan. It was founded by Mitsuru Toyama, the "outstanding nationalist of modern Japan," and dominated by men who were the spiritual heirs of samurai who pledged to revere the emperor and expel the barbarians, in this case from Asia. Mainly, they came from the city of Fukuoka on the island of Kyushu, the closest to the Asian mainland of any point in Japan, "the spiritual home of the most rabid brand of Japanese nationalism and imperialism." The original aim of the organization was containment of Russia. Toward this end, the members advocated the Amur River as Japan's boundary, an eventuality that would give Japan a comfortable zone into which it might expand. Although they were first and foremost nationalists, the Kokurykais envisioned Japan leading in the revival of nationalism among other Asian peoples. Members of the group wielded considerable influence within government circles since they shared views with high-ranking officials and often carried out information gathering expeditions. Members of the Kokuryukai viewed themselves as heirs of samurai zealots who helped to end the rule of the Tokugawa shoguns and restore the emperor to his rightful place as head of the nation. Thus, they could be rather critical of what they considered to be mistaken policies of the Japanese government and were not reluctant to act independently of and in opposition to it. The association opposed its government's official policy of recognition of Italy's conquest.[9]

American blacks, in groups and individually, tried to lend support to Ethiopia. They held mass meetings to express sympathy for the plight of Ethiopia, and Japanese were among the speakers. One such meeting was held at the Roseland ballroom in Chicago; the audience was estimated to be 3,500 people. At these gatherings, American blacks bewailed their own government's refusal to take heed of the plight of Ethiopia. A school teacher, who responded to an inquiring reporter regarding the issue, felt that the greatest contribution a people burdened with their own unresolved problems could make to an overseas crisis was "silent sympathy and prayers." Yet there were countless others who were interested in extending to Ethiopia more than the benefit of their prayers. When Italy invaded Ethiopia, according to the noted historian John Hope Franklin, "almost overnight even the most provincial among Negro Americans became international-minded." American blacks organized and raised money to aid Ethiopia to stave off the destruction that would have symbolized "the final victory of whites over blacks."[10]

Of the many groups that proliferated with the intent of helping the beleaguered African country, two, the Ethiopian Pacific Movement, Inc., and the Peace Movement of Ethiopia, would gain notoriety in the 1940s as pro-Japanese groups when their leaders were indicted, convicted, and imprisoned for their partisanship. Among the stated objectives of the Ethiopian Pacific Movement when it incorporated under the laws of New York in 1935 was the desire "to promote better understanding and more friendly relations between races, nations and classes of people.[11]

The very name of the Black Dragon Society disturbed, perhaps even shocked white American psyches. Hordes of Asians overwhelming white civlization had long been a nightmare of Europeans, and in the racial climate of the new world, white Americans, especially those of southern origin, easily imagined Europe's yellow peril metastasizing into a more horrific yellow and black menace.

African Americans, however, liked the image of strength connoted in the symbol of a black dragon. African Americans in the 1930s, much as a later generation that adopted a black panther to take on a white cock, liked the symbolic imagery of a Japanese black dragon doing battle with the American eagle or British lion. In the United States both the Ethiopian Pacific Movement and the Peace Movement of Ethiopia would claim that they were affiliated with the Black Dragon Society.[12]

Although members of the intellectual elites in Ethiopia and Japan began a mutual admiration pact in the latter part of the nineteenth century, a formal diplomatic and trade relationship started in the 1920s. The symbolic importance of the Tokyo–Addis Ababa nexus was to be underwritten by the marriage of a nephew of Haile Selassie to a daughter of a member of the Japanese peerage. When the proposed union was aborted, the Chicago Defender carried the photographs of Masako Kurode and Prince Arya Ababa over the caption "objection of Mussolini to union of Japan and Ethiopia . . . shattered the international planned romance."[13]

The story of a daughter of Japanese nobility preparing to marry an Ethiopian prince was celebrated in all of the ladies' magazines. According to one Japanese historian, the aborted wedding and Mussolini's role in it stimulated greater awareness of Ethiopia for ordinary Japanese. The proposed wedding had more than symbolic significance for African Americans. They often interpreted marriage across racial lines as a statement of social egalitarianism. Whenever blacks had opportunities to meet with Japanese, they invariably asked how the people of Japan regarded Negroes and if there were laws in Japan proscribing marriage between blacks and Japanese. On the basis of such encounters, blacks often concluded that the Japanese were people who "know no color prejudice."[14]

While the image of Japan as a friend of Ethiopia was still fresh in the minds of African Americans, the officers and crew of two Japanese training ships arrived in Baltimore harbor, seemingly to demonstrate solidarity with black America. Actually, the *Iwate* and *Yakumo* visited Baltimore, Maryland, as a part of a goodwill tour of several countries in 1936, but the Japanese sailors carried a message that was bound to have particular appeal in the black community. They sketched a Japan for their audiences that offered idyllic respite from the constant stings of racial prejudice. Officers and crew assured Levi Jolley, a reporter for the *Afro-American* newspaper, and other black visitors that Japan had "a liberal attitude toward all persons of darker races, and especially toward those of African extraction." Shipboard visitors were reminded that Japan had "always aided persons and countries ruled over by persons of the darker race." The Japanese crewmen told their guests that members of the darker races were invited to come and live in Japan. This had to be tailored for the black audience since Japanese historically have prided themselves on the homogeneity of the people and rarely extended the welcome mat to immigrants. Koreans, after living in Japan for many generations, historically have not been regarded as citizens of Japan. They have been segregated in jobs, education, and even dress. The route to Japanese citizenship has remained a test of will and determination.[15]

Contrasting the circumstances of natives of India, Africa, and Ethiopia who had resettled in Japan with the lot of blacks in America, the sailors touched on several sore points. They told their listeners that people from nonwhite nations were permitted to operate businesses in Japan, that public schools and universities were open to colored immigrants and their children, and that there were no restrictions against interracial marriages.[16]

During the discussion of American marriage taboos, one Japanese officer expressed "unusual surprise" upon hearing that racial factors dictated matrimonial patterns of the United States. This officer, to the delight of his audience, expressed the view that a man ought to be able to marry whomever he pleased and implied that any notion to the contrary was alien to Japanese. The Japanese sailors and Baltimoreans casually discussed music and sports. They spoke of the recent successes of Jesse Owens and of the plans Japan had for hosting the 1940 Olympics. The commander of the *Iwate* told of his preference for the classics over jazz. He also mentioned that he had seen Ralph Metcalf and Eddie Tolan, the black heroes of the 1932 Olympic games when they toured Japan. The Japanese hosts dispensed pleasantries and souvenirs in a manner that convinced the African American visitors that these sailors had extended themselves beyond the normal dictates of protocol; it was a clear gesture of solidarity.[17]

Among the Japanese who came to the United States were some who were activists on behalf of the idea that there ought to be a closer rapport between African Americans and the people of Japan. Naka Nakane was one of these. Better known by one of his several aliases, Nakane was a successful organizer. Claiming to be a former major in the Imperial Japanese Army and a member of the Kokuryukai, Nakane took charge of a fledgling group called "Development of Our Own." Only 5'5" in height, bearded, Nakane was a bundle of energy who, with briefcase in hand, carried himself in a military manner aptly earning the appellation "the Little Major." The director of the FBI, J. Edgar Hoover, said that within six months of his first meeting, Nakane had sixty thousand members in Michigan. Entering the United States by way of Saskatchewan, Canada, around 1918, Naka Nakane ultimately arrived in Detroit and devoted himself to organizing African Americans there supposedly on behalf of Japan in preparation for the war that was surely coming. His credentials as a member of the Kokuryukai or as a former officer of the Imperial Army of Japan unchallenged, Nakane became a celebrity fixture identified with Development of Our Own (DOO), an African American organization that was incorporated in Lansing, Michigan, on October 5, 1933 as a patriotic, independent brotherhood proposing the advancement of its members along cultural, social and commercial lines. Under Nakane's leadership DOO attracted the attention of police and intelligence agencies as a vehicle of Japanese propaganda more notable for its advocacy of the overthrow of white supremacy. According to the FBI, Nakane organized DOO and used it to disperse Japanese propaganda. Namely, special agents charged that he aroused "prejudice among [N]egroes against alleged white supremacy" and pledged that Japanese would preserve and protect their interests.[18]

During interrogations by federal authorities, Nakane was never a slave to the truth, but he did reveal much. In a sworn statement before the Immigration and Naturalization Service, Nakane testified that he was born in Tokyo, Japan, on May 24, 1880. In his youth he studied Japanese history and ethics at Kansai Gakuin. For his occupation, Nakane described himself as a preacher of "special doctoring." When he was thirty-one, he married Yasuko Nakane, who died shortly after the marriage. He stated that he went to Victoria, British Columbia, Canada, around 1901 or 1903 and to the United States in 1918. In Canada he married Annie Craddock, an English woman. They had four children, one adopted. In 1921 the family went to Tacoma, Washington, where Nakane had a brother who was principal at a Japanese school. Nakane worked as an insurance agent for New York Life Insurance Company in Tacoma from January 1923 to December 1927, when he disappeared, apparently after misappropriating a number of checks, leaving behind his family and gambling debts.[19]

In 1930 Nakane, using his alias Major Takahashi, went to Detroit. While still in Tacoma, Nakane had met an African American clergyman who invited him to preach among his folks in Detroit. On February 24, 1934, while awaiting deportation for giving false information to immigration service personnel, he married Pearl B. Sherrod, a woman he met a year earlier at a church meeting. Evidently, he had hoped to run the organization through his wife, but a dispute between them led him to oust her from the position of acting chief executive and national organizer. With things beginning to go badly, a drop in membership, exchanges of charges of infidelity, and a decline in his allotment, Nakane decided to reenter the United States surreptitiously. He reorganized those who remained loyal to him as the Onward Movement of America. He was apprehended again when his wife turned him in.[20]

Although presenting himself as a former military officer, under interrogation, Nakane carefully denied that he was employed by the Japanese government. FBI reports stated that he admitted to being a member of the Kokuryukai, but that was not quite accurate. Nakane stated that when in Japan, because of his organizational work among the colored people, he had an interview with Ryohei Uchida, president of the Kokuryukai, and that as a result of the interview he considered himself "more or less a self-styled representative of the Kokuryukai." According to an FBI report, during this interview an agreement was reached whereby both Nakane and Uchida were interested in effecting the same end, namely, the unification of all dark races and that although he was not designated as an official of the organization, the general agreement was that he was to be the representative of the Kokuryukai in the United States.[21] The symbolism, the thought of association with the dreaded Black Dragon Society had wide appeal among lowly ghetto dwellers. Nakane understood this well. Before his followers, he claimed that he was sent from Japan to organize in order to create a strong nation within a nation. One speech that he wrote was titled "Japan's Divine Mission."[21]

The agents of the FBI and other federal agencies paid meticulous attention to Nakane's activities, but the resulting profile turned out to be more of a rogue than a spy. One of the reasons the authorities suspected him of being a spy was because he always seemed to have plenty of money, dressed immaculately, but had no visible means of support. His means of support was invisible only to those unfamiliar with church organization and practice in the African American community. Nakane was no different from others who preached in the black community and found it a good living. Somehow he found out what others who became celebrity preachers discovered. Preaching about putting an end to the reign of the white devils and freeing those who perennially survived on the periphery of society, Nakane lived a life-style of comfort. While admitting that he was dependent on DOO for forty to fifty dollars a month for his livelihood, Nakane, in an angry letter to his wife, detailed the largess his poor parishioners provided her. They provided food and clothing, paid her rent, bought whatever she wanted, including a $300 fur coat and a $1,300 Packard automobile. Members of DOO, as were other seekers after the promise of salvation, were willing to pay. Nickles and dimes were a small price to pay for a peek at paradise, otherworldly or of this earth. As historian Ernest Allen points out, "More than anything else, the flowering of pro-Japan tendencies among American blacks in the era of the Great Depression represented a confluence and crystallization of two long-standing trends in African American thought: nationalism and millennialism." For African Americans fed up with the unfilled promises of a better future, for those who looked up from a bottomless pit of poverty, reaching out to the Japanese offered a flicker of hope. "Japan," according to Allen, "arose as the impersonal messiah—and General Tojo as a more intimate one—of tens of thousands of black Americans."[22] The enormous prestige that Japan enjoyed among African Americans gave Nakane, who probably did not labor to disabuse his listeners of the idea that he was a direct representative of Japan, almost unbelievable influence. Rather than dispel the notion that he represented Japan, Nakane, on the contrary, told his followers that he represented the one association in Japan, one the FBI characterized as a "jingoistic, half secret society of super patriots," that had an unimpeachable reputation for trying to end white domination and unite the so-called darker races. Posing as an ex-military officer of the Japanese army, Nakane generated messianic expectations among tens of thousands of African Americans throughout the Midwest, the upper and lower Mississippi Delta, east-central Oklahoma, and the New York–New Jersey region.[23]

Nakane's reputation was such that those who proselytized in his name reaped success. Federal agents questioned him closely regarding the establishment of units outside of Detroit, and Nakane absolutely denied that he had operated in any city other than Detroit. At the same time, he told his interrogators that there were certain Japanese and Chinese who were capitalizing on his name and on the name of his organization. Actually, after meeting in a UNIA-sponsored meeting in Chicago in 1931, Nakane had recruited Policarpio Manansala, a Filipino who also went by the name Mimo de Guzman, and his Chinese partner Moy Liang. Manansala spoke at UNIA-sponsored meetings across the country and took credit for recruiting twenty thousand members in Chicago over a two-year period. Nakane introduced Manansala to various audiences as Dr. Ashima Takis, a Japanese . The three would begin the Pacific Movement of the Eastern World, primarily in St. Louis. When recruited, Manansala's duties were to organize African Americans into groups that would follow Nakane's principles. He subsequently had a disagreement with Nakane and started out on his own to organize a similar movement in various cities of the United States. Perhaps because of Manansala's ego, he and Liang were itinerants who helped to organize pro-Japanese groups, subsequently had fallings out with local would-be leaders, and moved on. In New York, during a leadership struggle with Robert Jordan, Jordan exposed Manansala as a Filipino posing as Japanese. In 1942, Manansala was sentenced to three years in prison for cashing a forged money order.[24]

Nakane's original affiliation with Manansala and Liang was fully in keeping with his effort to fortify the impression of his official and broad support at home and abroad. He sometimes had an Indian national share his platform, Momahed A. Kahn, and testify that India had agreed to join the League of Dark Races and was ready to fight for freedom, having tried without success to do so through humbleness. From time to time, various Japanese would be invited. Materials distributed by the Japanese consulate were displayed prominently.

In his Onward Movement of America phase, Nakane introduced four projects of social uplift: a kitchen that fed on average ten or fifteen indigents a day; schools to teach older people to read and write and arrange lectures by prominent people to give African Americans insight into community life; a medical unit to provide treatment for people who could not afford it; and general stores so that the less fortunate could buy provisions at a savings. For the latter purpose, Nakane created the Producers and Consumers Market, Inc. The authorized capital stock was five thousand shares of common stock, $1 par value, and the paid-in capital $1,500.00.[25]

According to Allen, "Although Takahashi was far removed from the political scene in 1943, the seeds of Afro-Nippon solidarity which he had sown in the 1930s had taken root in manifold ways." Of the many organizations that had a pro-Japan bias, none blossomed like the Nation of Islam, under the leadership of Elijah Muhammad (Elijah Poole). He taught that the African American, the "original" black man was "Asiatic." In the eschatology of the Nation of Islam, Muhammad acknowledged Japan's role as leader in returning whites to a predestined role of subordination.[26]

A university professor from Japan, speaking before an NAACP gathering, related how embarrassed he felt when a New York restauranteur attempted to refuse service to a black companion. The Japanese professor declared that he was prepared to fight on behalf of his friend if the restaurant manager had persisted. The professor than admonished his listeners, saying that blacks "must fight this evil" whenever and wherever "the objectionable doctrine" reared its head.[27]

Perhaps no Japanese worked more diligently to foster a bridge of understanding between the people of Japan and American blacks than the ubiquitous Yasuichi Hikida. Hikida, who was associated with the Japanese consulate in New York, numbered among his friends and acquaintances many of the notables of African American society. The Negrophilic Hikida generated suspicion among white Americans, but African Americans regarded him as a serious and sympathetic student of the "Negro problem." Walter White, in a letter to James Weldon Johnson, introduced Hikida as "my very good friend," "one of my most esteemed friends," "a man who wrote articles to educate the Japanese about the real facts regarding the Negro in the United States."[28] Hikida had been a member of the NAACP for twenty years.

Hikida wanted to promote between African Americans and Japanese an "intelligent understanding of each other." Toward this end, he dreamed of the establishment of an "Information Research Center of Negro Race and Culture" in Tokyo. By this means he hoped "to promote a sentiment and understanding among Japanese for blacks" and "to stimulate among black students an interest in international affairs and the Orient." He thought that African Americans might divert some of the monies used to send missionaries to Africa and India in order to locate one or two "bright Negro students or journalists" in Tokyo on a permanent basis.[29]

Hikida also worked on a manuscript that he hoped would chronicle the views blacks had of Japan from the time of the Russo-Japanese War. When he originally circulated his manuscript to elicit comments, it was titled "The Canary Looks at the Crow." After James Weldon Johnson and Rayford Logan persuaded him that African Americans attached very negative connotations to the imagery of a crow, Hikida reluctantly changed the title to "A Japanese Sees the Negro American." Personally, he favored the symbolism of the first title and thought his reviewers a bit hypersensitive. In his own words to Du Bois, he explained, "Many objections and advises were given to me from the side of the 'crow' line; and I had to kill the bird—together [with] the Canary."[30]

As a member of the Japanese consulate in New York, Hikida was arrested shortly after Pearl Harbor and deported. At the time of his arrest, Hikida had in his possession "several hundred pounds of literature pertaining to the American [N]egro." These materials, according to a War Department memo, "apparently must have been prepared for the benefit of Japanese."[31]

The positive impressions Japanese might have made while in the United States paled by comparison to the hospitality they extended to African Americans who visited Japan. Three school teachers from St. Louis, Missouri, who sampled Japanese conviviality and were won over during a summer vacation spent in Asia, shared their impressions with readers of the *Indianapolis Recorder*. On the way to Hawaii, L. M. Turner met several Japanese girls whom she characterized as "more prejudiced than the American white man." After her arrival in Japan, the St. Louis teacher revised her earlier evaluation of the Japanese as a people and concluded that those born in the United States were merely "trying to act like white Americans." In Turner's opinion, the Japanese in their own land were "adorable." She became convinced that Japanese uncontaminated by whites knew no color prejudice.[32]

Alice McGee, who had traveled in Canada, Mexico, the West Indies, South America, the Philippines, Hawaii, and China declared that in none of the other places where she visited had she met "a more kind-hearted people" than the Japanese. McGee was persuaded that if the Japanese were biased, "it was rather in our favor." She confessed that she had gone to Japan expecting to encounter some prejudice. The Japanese, she claimed, treated whites with politeness as a matter of "duty" but behaved toward blacks as they might toward "brothers and sisters." McGee reported that the Japanese tended to single out the black women for "posts of honor." "We seemed to be the ones," she felt, "they were most proud to have with them."[33]

The highlight of their stay in Japan, as far as McGee was concerned, was the Pan-Pacific New Educational Conference in Tokyo. This conference was attended by more than three hundred delegates from those countries bordering on the Pacific Ocean, and McGee, who attended with Isabel Dickson, a critic teacher from the Simmons Demonstration School in St. Louis, was one of five delegates asked to give a "farewell talk." As she remembered, they were the only Negroes present. Feeling a sense of mission, she said, she spoke about the Negro American, the United States, and "the ideals of brotherhood and harmony toward which all races and nations should strive." According to McGee, her "plain, unvarnished plea brought tears to the eyes of Japanese men and women who listened." Her reaction to the people of Japan, in response, was equally emotional: "I had the feeling that I stood before a new people, whose existence I had hitherto not suspected, a pious, [t]ender, sympathetic nation in the hearts of whose citizens are watered the principles of brotherly love which most other people give but lip service to."[34]

Those African Americans who were concerned about Japan's invasion of Manchuria had serious reservations about the depth of the Japanese sense of brotherly love; Manchuria was an issue that divided black opinion regarding Japan. The black internationalist was as likely as his white counterpart to look at world events through culturally biased filters, but when blacks zeroed in on an issue they were more likely to interpret it in terms of a racial perspective conditioned by the black/white milieu of the United States. In other words, blacks were more likely to emphasize racism as a root cause in matters of dispute involving whites and nonwhites.

The split in black opinion occurred according to the extent to which partisans could accept naked aggression as a means to an end. Du Bois and people of comparable persuasion thought themselves pragmatic in their willingness to tolerate from Japanese actions that would have been intolerable and deserving of censure had they been committed by whites. Other blacks resented and were appalled by the raw Japanese aggression, which seemed aimed at the destruction of China's independence, the killing of unarmed civilians, and heightened savagery introduced with newer, more advanced military technology. Yet, when all was said and done, the racial aspect weighed more heavily in the evaluations of many blacks than the niceties of international law or even the horror of mass killings.

An editorial in the *Pittsburgh Courier* claimed to see little reason for African Americans to get excited over the outcome of the Sino-Japanese War since events in East Asia would hardly have an appreciable effect on the status of blacks in the United States. Besides, the *Courier* declared, neither China nor Japan had any particular concern for the fate of colored Americans. Yet J. A. Rogers, George Schuyler, William Pickens, A. Philip Randolph, and Du Bois, all of whom wrote columns for the *Courier*, did see the war in China as having significant bearing on the struggle of nonwhite peoples for status recognition in a white-dominated world.[35]

Most American blacks who read of the ongoing killings in East Asia were probably appalled. Particularly gruesome was the image of the technologically efficient Japanese bombing innocent civilians. But when Secretary of State Cordell Hull lodged a protest of the Japanese actions in China in 1937, Charles W. Cranford, a resident of Cassville, West Virginia, who also claimed to deplore the killing of noncombatants, became irate as a result of what he perceived to be the government's hypocrisy. Cranford denounced his country's official complaint as a "travesty on decency and justice" since it came from a nation that had not protested Italy's "rape of Ethiopia" only two years previous. Furthermore, Cranford argued that Hull's protest was "gruesomely paradoxical" when the United States was a "nation whose hands are gory with the blood of 4,000 lynch victims."[36]

W. E. B. Du Bois agreed that the Japanese were not uniquely callous. He characterized the bombings as an "awful business," the "killing of the unarmed and innocent in order to reach the guilty." Du Bois further cautioned, "Americans would have you believe that the method began with Japan. Oh, no!" The *New York Age* argued that the "horrors of war" sometimes result in "many benefits unexpected at the time" and predicted that "China will yet come to bless the day that she was beaten by Japan."[37]

A Japanese graduate student at the University of Pennsylvania tried to explain to the readers of the *Philadelphia Tribune* how Japan's policy was to weld together a weak and divided China as a step toward the creation of a strong Oriental power bloc. Seiichi Furuya, who had been a staff member of the South Manchuria Railway Company for five years explained that the obstacle to that policy was China's lack of "cohesion and unity." The picture Furuya drew was a grim one: territories were divided and ruled over by warlords who, within their "spheres of indulgence," greedily exploited the people of China; the central government seemed powerless in the face of repeated affronts to its nominal authority; consequently, China was unable to fulfill its obligations as an independent and sovereign state; and civilian authorities at the various levels of government had become no more than "parasites of the warlords" as politicians vied with each other in pursuit of personal gain.[38]

Fururya argued the Japanese case zealously. He maintained that any interest the United States or Great Britain had in China was slight when compared to that of Japan. The apprehension with which the Japanese regarded events in Manchuria, he asserted, was like that of a homeowner when his neighbor's house was on fire. Was it an act of invasion, Fururya asked rhetorically, to step in and extinguish the fire when the householder was unable to do so?[39] His analogy of the endangered neighbor who had to be protected from his own incompetence or malfeasance, not merely for his own sake but also for that of the larger community, made Japan's assumption of a guardianship role in China seem very logical. Thus, Japan's assumption of proprietorship rights as a result of vital interests in Manchuria seemed more convincing than American claims with regard to the Western Hemisphere, the Hawaiian Islands, or the Philippines.

Black America had its own interpreter of events regarding East Asia. Few black intellectuals were as consistently observant and informed about issues concerning East Asia as W. E. B. Du Bois. In 1936 Du Bois went on a two-month trip around the world. This was the occasion of his first visit to East Asia. He spent one week in Manchuria (then called "Manchukuo" by the Japanese), ten days in China proper, and two weeks in Japan. During his visit, Du Bois wrote a series of columns for the *Pittsburgh Courier* in which he discussed Japan and its meaning for world affairs and the black experience in America.

In the series, which appeared from February to September

1937, Du Bois shared "an experience never to be forgotten." Declaring himself a private citizen "none too welcome in his native land," Du Bois chose to interpret the stupendous welcome he received in Japan as a tribute to all of black America. He saw this as the Japanese way of saying through him to 12 million African Americans that they recognized a "common brotherhood, a common suffering and a common destiny."[40]

Infatuated with the ideal that Japan represented in his mind's eye, Du Bois was uncritical of imperialistic actions in Manchuria, although the very same acts undertaken by a white nation would have evoked a sound denunciation. Much like Furuya, the Japanese graduate student, Du Bois discussed the status of Manchuria within the context of Japan's vital interests. His week in Manchukuo was undoubtedly an exhilarating experience for an African American man of his time. "The colonial effort of a colored nation is something to watch and know," he enthused. The social scientist saw no ambiguity in his reaction. He discerned a difference between what the Japanese had accomplished, which was "nothing less than marvelous," and what he perceived to be the lot of subject peoples under white imperialist domination.[41]

Du Bois professed his continued commitment to the idea that no nation should rule a colony whose people they cannot conceive of as equals. But whether or not Manchukuo was an independent nation he dismissed as irrelevant. In his opinion, the important issue was what the Japanese were doing to provide for the health and welfare of the people of Manchukuo. Were they happier or more miserable as a result of the Japanese presence? Du Bois deemed them to be happier for two reasons: first, there was an absence of racial or color "caste" and lynchings were unthinkable; second, there was ample evidence that Japanese activities in Manchukuo benefited the "natives." He believed that the Japanese colony was a region with a system of law and order that was impartial in administration. The Japanese, he understood, also had instituted good health and education services, city planning, and other activities with socially beneficial ends. Finally, to the best of his knowledge, public peace and order prevailed and the people of Manchukuo "appeared happy." The fact that the children of Japanese and Manchurians attended separate schools, Du Bois pointed out, was not due to any difference in race. Japanese children spoke Japanese, and the native children had their own language, he observed.[42]

From Manchuria Du Bois went to China where he was overwhelmed by China the historical entity. Not even Africa had had such a profound impact on his emotions as when he stood on the Great Wall, he confided. But, when all was said and done, Du Bois thought that China had become stymied by "impenetrable walls of custom, religion and industry," which resulted in attempts at reform being frustrated by a "rock wall of opposition and misunderstanding."[43]

By contrast, the singular most important fact about Japan, as far as Du Bois was concerned, was that, above all else, it was a country of colored people run by colored people for the benefit of colored people. When he touched foot to Japanese soil, for the first time in his life he felt that he stood in a land where white people controlled neither directly nor indirectly. Furthermore, he was convinced that both Americans and Englishmen acknowledged this through their behavior. Du Bois could detect none of the "English overbearance" nor "American impudence" that he had grown to expect in China, India, Africa, the West Indies, and the United States. An added consolation was that even the physical features of the Japanese were such that they easily might be mistaken for American mulattoes.[44]

Du Bois related two incidents that, for him, seem to reflect the contrasting spirits of the Chinese and the Japanese peoples. In Shanghai he watched a little white boy, whom he guessed to be about four, order three adult Chinese out of his path, and the Chinese adults meekly obeyed.[45] In Du Bois' opinion, this replication of southern protocol symbolized an orthodoxy that attested to white domination and nonwhite humiliation.

The second incident occurred in Japan and involved Du Bois directly. As he was paying his bill at the Imperial Hotel in Tokyo, a "typical loud-mouthed American white woman" barged in and demanded service as she might have been accustomed to doing in the United States. The Tokyo desk clerk "neither winked nor turned his head," but continued to wait on his burnished guest until the business at hand had been transacted. Once he settled Du Bois' account, the clerk took time to bow politely and then "turned to America." This Japanese attitude of self-assurance in dealing with white people, Du Bois hoped, was to be the harbinger of the coming new world.[46]

While in Japan Du Bois became caught up in the heady atmosphere of sukiyaki parties, dancing geisha, and a preeminence he rarely experienced at home. He was the honored guest at banquets given by the *Osaka Mainichi* and the *Tokyo Nichi Nichi*, two of the major newspapers, the Pan-Pacific Club, and the Tokyo PEN Club. He lectured on black literature and the Negro's role in American society at some of Japan's most prestigious colleges and universities. He reminded his hosts that collusion between southern foes of an antilynching bill and western proponents of anti-Japanese legislation had resulted in Japanese exclusion in 1924 and told them that this was indicative of the bond of rejection that blacks and Japanese shared in the United States.[47]

Du Bois was effusive in his praise of the Japanese. Living in houses where the "dust of dirty feet" never penetrated, they were a superlative people. "Nowhere else in the modern world," he exclaimed, "was there a people so intelligent, so disciplined, so clean and punctual, so instinctively conscious of human good and ill."[48]

Commenting on the religion of Japan, Du Bois admired the way in which the Japanese had used an indigenous belief system in their upward drive. The Japanese, he explained, had transformed an "old heathenism" into a "modern ethic of Patriotism, Honor, and Sacrifice." Du Bois labeled Shinto a "system of action, a philosophy of right and wrong into a dogma of revealed religion." He understood the emperor to be the personification of that system that made all of Japan a "Holy Land to the Japanese." "Within the parameters of the reforged creed," Du Bois believed, "the spirit of freedom and expression was hampered but not stamped out, and change was slow and difficult but not impossible."[49]

Acknowledging "a mad muddle of motive," Du Bois attributed the Sino-Japanese War largely to the contrasting attitudes of the Chinese and Japanese and the acquisitive designs of the Europeans and Americans. Du Bois portrayed Japan fighting China in order to save its continental neighbor from Europe's domination. Japan, he contended, was "showing the way to freedom," while China "preferred to be a coolie for England." According to his logic, the "curse and blame" for the fratricidal strife rested squarely with "all those white nations, which for a hundred years and more, have by blood and rapine forced their rule upon colored nations." They had coerced Japan into a "horrible and bloody carnage with her own cousin."[50]

While able to appreciate and condone Japan's motivations for moving into a presumed power vacuum, Du Bois still found it "disconcerting" that a "burning hatred" existed between China and Japan. "With China and Japan in understanding and cooperation," he hypothesized, "the domination of Europe—the enslavement, insult and exploitation of the darker majority of mankind is at an everlasting end."[51] Du Bois shared his impressions with those Chinese and Japanese with whom he came in contact during his sojourn in East Asia.

In the final analysis, Du Bois' uncritical attitude toward the Japanese was an outgrowth of his belief that Japan represented "the only world leadership that did not mean color caste." He was willing to accept Japanese aggression in China as the best way to preempt a potentially more obnoxious European suzerainty in the region. Shanghai dramatized for him the seeming gulf between where Japan was and where he thought China ought to be. He depicted Shanghai as "an epitome of the racial strife, economic struggle, the human paradox of modern life" due to the fact that the "greatest city of the largest nation on earth" was in large measure "owned, governed and policed by foreign white nations."[52]

Du Bois' outspoken pro-Japanese remarks prompted some critics to charge that he was being paid by the Japanese government for propaganda work in this country. The pro-Chinese *China Weekly Review* even made the charge in an editorial. One reader of the magazine, professing to believe that Du Bois had not become "an agent of Japanese fascism," asked him to make a public statement in order to lay to rest the "ugly rumors." Not one to duck controversy, Du Bois forthrightly responded, "I believe in Japan." While denying emphatically that he had ever taken money from the Japanese government, he readily admitted that he thought Japan was the best hope for making Asian hegemony over Asia a reality.[53]

Despite his denial that he received any money from the Japanese government, Du Bois, at Hikida's suggestion, had traveled with a press pass, which allowed him to travel on trains at reduced rates. The Ministry of Foreign Affairs granted him a free pass for the trip from Kobe to Tokyo. Before leaving for Japan, Du Bois had written Hikida informing him that if possible he would go to Japan at his own expense. He also admitted, however, that it would be helpful, once he arrived in Japan, if he could add something to his income.[54]

In all probability, this small gratuity was the basis for subsequent accusations that the Japanese government was subsidizing the NAACP. Walter White would expend considerable time and energy tracking down such a rumor. Whatever the sum Du Bois might have received, it did not constitute a bribe, nor did it influence the tenor of his remarks.

☒☒☒☒

SIX

REACTIONS TO
WAR IN THE PACIFIC

I n his analysis of the American racial scene, Swedish economist Gunnar Myrdal indicated that prior to the outbreak of war between the United States and Japan poor Negro sharecroppers in the South dreamed of "a Japanese army marching through the South and killing off a number of 'crackers.'"[1] Roi Ottley, a black journalist, indicated that the fruits of a sophisticated Japanese propaganda campaign had blossomed in urban areas among "a few radical nationalists, fiercely anti-white, who would lend an ear to talk of an all-colored utopia."[2]

Both Myrdal and Ottley underestimated the black attraction for the Japanese. Actually, Myrdal was aware of the OWI survey of New Yorkers, which disclosed that two-fifths of the sample believed it was "more important to make democracy work at home than to beat Germany and Japan." "Nearly one half of the same sample voiced the belief that they would be at least no worse off under Japanese rule," investigators discovered. Charles Siepmann of the OWI concluded that this was "an indication of the kinship [Negroes] feel for the Japanese as a dark-skinned race." This is important because the respondents represented middle-class types who readily expressed themselves before interviewers. Lower-class African Americans were reticent regardless of whether the investigators were white or black.[3]

Clearly, Horace Cayton did not fit the Myrdal-Ottley characterization of a pro-Japanese Negro. Horace Cayton graphically recalled how he felt at the time that he learned of the bombing of Hiroshima. He was angry at white people generally and refused to celebrate Japan's defeat when invited to do so with his liberal white friends and his white girl friend. He admitted being "torn a dozen ways." While not wanting the Japanese to win because he was an American, Cayton confessed that he drew satisfaction from the sight of "the mighty white man" humiliated "by the little yellow bastards [whites] had nothing but contempt for." The bombing of Hiroshima stirred in Cayton sympathies for Japan and himself. The Japanese, he acknowledged, were imperialists, but they were imperialists with "more right to the Orient than white imperialists." "The Japanese at least tried to break the color line," he stated. Cayton believed that most African Americans felt much as he did.[4]

If African Americans were not pro-Japanese, neither were they anti-Japanese. Actually, in the minds of a significant number of African Americans black grievances against domestic American racism converged with a notion that the Japanese were giving whites a dose of their own medicine. This attitude was pervasive enough among African Americans that the attack on Pearl Harbor, Hawaii, presented black leaders and government officials with a serious dilemma.

The government wanted a consensus statement of support for the war effort from representative leadership groups of the black community. Judge William Hastie, civilian aide to the secretary of war, represented the government as an observer at the Conference of National Organizations which convened on January 10, 1942, at the Harlem branch of the YMCA to contemplate the posture to be assumed by African Americans during World War II. Represented in this coalition were groups such as the National Urban League, the National Bar Association, the Federal Council of Churches, the National Alliance of Postal Employees, the American Teachers Association, and about ten other groups.

After much heated debate, delegates representing these various groups were unable to give the government what it wanted. By a lopsided margin, the conference passed a resolution that read, "The Negro is not unreservedly and wholeheartedly all-out in support of the present war effort." Lester B. Granger, the head of the Urban League, fearful that the enemies of the Negro would misuse such a resolution, argued that the conference participants represented "certain fields of activity" and were not qualified "to

express an opinion on the thinking of 13 million Negroes." Arthur
Spingarn, a longtime friend of the Negro and a driving force behind
the NAACP, however, thought it just as important that the government was being made aware of the depths of resentment, frustration, and cynicism among African Americans.[5]

The resolution clearly underscored deep divisions within the
ranks of black America. Moderate leadership groups were aware
enough to know that they did not have a firm grip on the allegiance
of the masses who were, as George Schuyler suggested, both "skeptical and cynical" and not anxious to soak up the promises reminiscent of those made during World War I.[6] To have given the government what it had wanted, black leaders would have had to drive
a wedge between themselves and the masses they aspired to lead. It
was significant that a coalition of black leadership groups could not
assure the unqualified support of most African Americans in America's hour of trial.

The fact that Japan was the enemy was a very important factor contributing to the reluctance of the nominal leadership groups
to come out in support of a war against Japan. The connection
between the conference and concern regarding the influence of
Japanese among the masses of African Americans was clearly articulated in the statement of purpose of the Conference of National
Organizations. Lester Granger reminded the participants at the
conference that "attempts by enemy agents to turn the justifiable
dismay of Negro citizens to the profit of the Axis powers" had led
to increased cynicism and frustration among large groups of Negro
citizens.[7]

George Schuyler, the acerbic columnist of the *Pittsburgh
Courier*, ridiculed the conference, finding it "laughable" on two
counts: he was amused first by the "roster of participants supposedly representing the masses" and second, by the "consternation at
the answer to the question whether African Americans supported
the war 100%." Schuyler pointed out the dilemma of the black
John Doe, "No matter what a large proportion of Negroes may
think in private about Japanese aggression . . . they are publicly
behind the government 100%. No alternative to going to jail."[8]

In the immediate wake of the attack on Pearl Harbor, black
opinion regarding the Japanese varied: there were those who
believed that America had been attacked and that African Americans should be prepared to fight without reservations, putting aside
outstanding grievances until the greater threat to the country had
been put asunder; others were willing to support the war effort

while persisting in efforts to exact dues too long deferred; there were a few who were unsupportive of America's war effort and thought those who were supportive of that effort foolish; and there were those who were "listlessly loyal," going along because they were unable to decide on an acceptable alternative.[9]

Engulfed in the surge of national unity, some African Americans quickly pledged solidarity with the rest of the nation and condemned the Japanese for launching one of the most "dastardly, cunning and deceptive attacks ever recorded on the infamous pages of human crime." The editorial writers of the *Pittsburgh Courier*, a newspaper noted for its militant advocacy of Negro rights, was quick to declare colored Americans "among the most loyal segments" in the country, "unswerving in their loyalty. "The *Courier* tried to reassure white Americans by proclaiming that there were "no spies, no saboteurs, no Benedict Arnolds" among the ranks of African Americans. At the same time, it tried to entice African Americans to once again take up America's battle standard. Reminding its reader that "this is our native land," the *Courier* pleaded, "Let the German-American fall away from its defense; let the Japanese-Americans desert its ramparts; let the Italian or other American sabotage its vital interests, but let us cling to and protect that which is ours."[10]

The *California Eagle* vowed that African Americans stood "solidly phalanxed," prepared to join in the "titanic struggle to defeat a common enemy." Fearing that the nation's very survival might be at stake, Charlotta Bass, editor and publisher of the *Eagle*, echoing a theme also championed by the American Communist party, advocated a deemphasis of the campaign for the exercise of full citizenship rights. But even the *Eagle* acknowledged that it would be indulging in "self-deception" or "glamorous illusion" to believe that the full measure of freedom would come as a consequence of demonstrated loyalty. But Bass warned, "The Negro problem can no longer dominate our thoughts." National security was at stake and emphasis had to be shifted to the exercise of full citizenship duties, she counselled.[11]

Other members of the black press climbed aboard the war wagon with varying degrees of enthusiasm. The *Amsterdam Star-News* editorialized, "The diabolical treachery of the Japanese attack will find but one clear answer from all Americans. We will show those Japs and Nazis that as one nation indivisible, we fight the battle for democracy. We fight to win!" At the same time, it warned white Americans that it was "no time for superficial distinction based upon skin color" and "no time for subversive race prejudice." Lee J. Martin, a columnist for the *Indianapolis Recorder*, pledged that "there need not be any fear of our loyalty as it has been in the past—we are still 109 per cent American, ready for service to our country despite its short-comings." In the same newspaper, Opal Tandy urged African Americans to support their country and "with the final victory and peace" demand "full rights of complete equality." Carl Murphy of the *Afro-American* newspaper reminded his readers that "America is still a great nation." Lucius Harper, writing for the *Chicago Defender*, titled his piece "We Cannot Look to Japan to Solve Our Problem" and declared that it was "absurd to look to Japan as the racial deliverer of the black man."[12]

Emmett J. Scott, former secretary to Booker T. Washington, writing for the *Indianapolis Recorder*, called the war an opportunity for African Americans to again "put in evidence their democratic faith and their undiminished unity" on behalf of the country. He promised that African Americans would do as they historically had done, "play a willing, winning creditable part." He felt African Americans really had no alternative. "Americanism" was the only "ism" about which African Americans were knowledgable, Scott claimed. In his opinion, of all ethnic groups, only African Americans were "so far above suspicion that the most furtive mind has never charged them with disloyalty, or as lacking in whole-soul devotion to the ideals of Americans."[13]

A government intelligence report classified assertions such as Scott's as "highly stereotyped patriotic statements." Comparable remarks by other prominent African Americans such as Chandler Owen, who served as a consultant to the Office of War Information, and Mary McLeod Bethune, organizer of the National Council of Negro Women and Head of the Office of Minority Affairs in the National Youth Administration, in the same report, were categorized as "atypical positions."[14]

While some prominent African Americans might have agreed to postpone protest activities as a contribution to the national emergency, others believed that the dreams of a better future already had been deferred too long and demanded as a quid pro quo for their services the resolution of racial inequities at home. Regarding war as a great force for social, political, and economic change, a great number of African Americans agreed with the assertion of J. A. Rogers that the war represented the "greatest opportunity" for black people "to consolidate gains in citizenship that might otherwise take a century."[15] Those who shared Rogers' dream hoped that improved status, respect, and appreciation would come through service to the country. It was imperative that black leadership groups find a formula that would have broad appeal.

James G. Thompson, of Wichita, Kansas, in a letter to the editor of the *Pittsburgh Courier*, provided the slogan that symbolized black America's demand for rectification at the end of the war, the "double V" for victory at home, victory abroad. This theme was promoted as a militant but practical demand for redress of grievances at the same time that it was a promise to take up arms again in defense of the nation.[16] With Thompson's letter as a catalyst, the *Courier* emblazoned its masthead with a pair of Vs and began the double V campaign. Other black newspapers quickly adopted this slogan, which offered the illusion of militancy.

Although the Urban League, the NAACP, and the constituencies they represented were willing to persist in the dream of America living up to its promise, nonelite African Americans had grown weary of the unfulfilled pledges of the government to do better. Members of the Ethiopian Pacific Movement, Inc., the Peace Movement of Ethiopia, the Pacific Movement of the Eastern World, the Temple of Islam, the Moorish Science Temple of America, and other groups were unconvinced that military victories over the Japanese would result in any appreciable gains or changes in the status of African Americans in the United States. They preferred to cheer the reports of Japanese triumphs over Allied forces. These groups were composed of people who were dispossessed of any hope that African Americans might have a better future in the United States. They argued that whatever changes might occur as a result of a Japanese takeover of America, black people would be no worse off.

The members of this radical fringe distrusted the intentions of white people and had no confidence in those who postured themselves as black leaders. A dramatic poem that was circulated by the Associated Negro Press summed up the viewpoint of these people rather succinctly:

I know more about Bilbo than I do about Tojo

To me the Black Dragon Society is just a foreign nightmare
but I have been beaten and murdered by the Ku Klux Klan

I know some people want to whip the Japanese for ever daring
to think they are as good as whites

And Hirohito sent work to black men

Japan is the champion of all colored people. Stand ready
to rebel.[17]

Such cynicism, seemingly, was incompatible with the notion of a
double V campaign. The cynics would have to be purged: the black
bourgeoisie disavowed them; the black press crucified them; the
FBI kept them under surveillance; and other government surrogates
jailed them.

Who were these people who posed such a threat to the security of the United States that they called down upon themselves the
combined wrath of both the black and the white power structures?
And of what were they guilty? In terms of origins, composition, and
rhetoric, groups such as the Ethiopian Peace Movement, the Peace
Movement of Ethiopia, and the Temple of Islam shared certain
characteristics. Generally, they were remnants of the Marcus Garvey movement. Upwardly mobile they were not: they had little or
no formal education; many were first-generation migrants from the
South or immigrants from the British West Indies; and they were
generally employed menially, if at all.

Mittie Maude Lena Gordon, founder and president general of
the Chicago-based Peace Movement of Ethiopia confessed that she,
as a black person, felt cheated by the country and misled by the
established leadership of the black community. When asked during
an interrogation by the FBI whether or not she believed African
Americans should go to war in 1942, Gordon replied that her inter-
rogator ought to remember what had been done to African Americans after their contributions in the previous war. It was her recol-
lection that there were "race riots all over the country" and African
Americans "had to fight to live" among their fellow Americans,
and this was after black soldiers had "won the war for them from
1914 to 1918." Having been betrayed once after heroic service to
the nation, why should African Americans want to or be expected
to rush to defend the flag? Gordon could think of no reason why
they should.[18]

In New York, another former Garveyite expressed similar
sympathies and views. Leonard Robert Jordan, a Jamaican, sometimes seaman, sometimes laborer or painter, under FBI questioning
freely admitted his pro-Japanese sympathies. Jordan, who had
worked aboard a Japanese merchant vessel for two years, boasted
that the Japanese would win the war. Japan was a friend of all dark

peoples and would liberate the Negro race and push Europeans and Americans out of Asia and Africa, he crowed. Furthermore, he claimed his willingness to fight for Japan with every drop of his blood without pay, while, at the same time, declaring himself very unwilling to fight for the United States. He would neither fight for this country nor counsel mothers to allow their sons to defend a government that "lynches their son[s] and sold their mother[s]."[19]

Mittie Maud Gordon, after returning disappointed from Marcus Garvey's last hurrah in Jamaica, founded her group on the basis of 400,000 signatures she claimed to have collected in support of Mississippi Senator Theodore Bilbo's fantastic scheme for deporting all African Americans to Liberia. In 1937 Liberia's President Edwin Barclay had indicated a willingness to accept black American immigrants provided they came with one thousand dollars cash, skills in farming or a trade, and the intention of becoming citizens. It was from that time that Mrs. Gordon and her supporters considered themselves citizens of Liberia. Gordon claimed to have branches in Baltimore, Phoenix, Pittsburgh, Gary, St. Louis, Galesburg, Illinois, and Bamboo, Mississippi. Some of the members of these groups were septuagenarians, but the median age was between forty and fifty. They were people tortured by the memory of "what had been done to black folks after the other war." Formerly Baptists and Methodists, the members of the Ethiopian Peace Movement discarded Christianity as a white man's religion and adopted Islam as the true faith of black people.[20]

The trial of Robert Jordan, referred to variously as the "Black Hitler," "Harlem Fuehrer," and "Jap Stooge," became something of a media event even in the white press. The indictment filed in the United States District Court for the Southern District of New York on November 30, 1942, charged Jordan and three associates with making speeches designed to "mislead and corrupt the patriotic, loyal and law abiding colored population of Greater New York and particularly of the community known as Harlem."[21]

For making speeches which might incite "insubordination, disloyalty, mutiny, and refusal of duty" and for "obstructing the recruitment and enlistment service of the United States during wartime," a New York jury, which included three Negroes, found Jordan guilty of conspiracy to commit sedition and violation of the Sedition Act. Judge Clarence G. Galston sentenced Jordan to ten years in prison and levied a fine of ten thousand dollars. Jordan's co-defendants, James Henry Thornhill, Lester Eugene Holness, and the Reverend Ralph Green Best, each received a sentence of eight, seven, and four years, respectively. A white co-defendant, Joseph Hartrey, who was at the time a soldier stationed at Fort Dix, New Jersey, received six years.

In Chicago, Judge William H. Holly ruled that a two-year suspended sentence was adequate punishment for the pro-Japanese activities of the fifty-three-year-old Madame Gordon and her co-defendants. Her sixty-nine-year-old husband, William, due to his age, received three years probation.[22]

Pursuing the twin themes that "the white man's time was up" and "Japan would come and deliver the colored people out of the hands of slaveholders," Gordon, at meetings and in letters, counseled members not to register for the draft or serve in the armed forces. Among the witnesses against her, Chandler Owen, who at the time was a consultant to the Office of War Information, testified about an "infants to old folks" meeting of about three hundred people at which Gordon declared that "on December 7th one billion colored people struck for freedom."[23]

Prior to U.S. entry into World War II, the angry black men and women who cried out against the superordination of whites could be shrugged off as part of the flotsam that could be expected in the backwash of black frustration. But once America went to war, the toleration level for such ballyhoo greatly diminished. The shriller expressions of black discontent, in the minds of white Americans, were regarded as unpatriotic and punishable. The utterances of these more extreme protesters of the status quo generated among government officials fears of race riots because of what was characterized as the "peculiar emotions of the Negro people."[24]

These militant black pro-Japanese groups maintained the basic formula used by Marcus Garvey to cater to the frustrations of those August Meier designated "the slum-shocked urban Negroes." These groups offered identity, self-esteem, upward social mobility, self-improvement, and emotional release. They created "a life meaning out of meaninglessness, self-respect out of poverty."[25] Ultimately, they allowed a sense of community with the greater majority, all of the darker races of the world. Within such groups, a membership of humble circumstances had a forum where they could discuss and elaborate upon issues of an international dimension. The members of these groups imagined themselves privy to information that suggested a restructuring of racial patterns more to their favor, not only within the United States but also on the world scene.

These groups manifested characteristics of the black fundamentalist church, black nationalism, and the civil rights movement that culminated in the 1960s. It was the religious element that gave their meetings a high degree of emotionalism. The groups met on Sunday evenings, preached, prayed, testified, and passed the collection plate, much as they had when still Christians. They replaced Jesus Christ with Allah in their rhetoric but not in their hearts, where they remained fused.

During his interrogation by the FBI, Robert Jordan candidly admitted his belief that, within the black community, support for the war effort should be qualified by the extent to which Negroes were granted basic rights of citizenship. Asked if he encouraged members of his race to support Japan in the war, Jordan replied, "I encourage the members of my race to support any country that is willing to give them a better representation in the Government." He stated clearly which government he thought would treat African Americans fairer: "I know that Japan will give the darker people more freedom and more representation than we are getting now." Asked whether he had made statements to the effect that Japan would give the Negro race the right kind of democracy and liberate the Negro, Jordan answered, "Yes." Having worked in the Japanese merchant marine, Jordan's assertion was bound to carry some weight with those who attended his meetings. In response to another set of questions, Jordan declared unequivocally, "I, Robert Jordan, will not fight against any dark nation on behalf of the so-called democracy!" The FBI agent interrogating Jordan wanted to know whether or not he would refuse to fight against Japan. Jordan was candid: "Yes, I would."[26] Consistent with his theme of non-white unity, Jordan had tried to send a telegram expressing support to Gandhi and Nehru, the leaders of the Indian National Congress, who were at the time launching their last great *satyagraha* campaign to force the British to "Quit India."

FBI informants captured the tone and emotion of the meetings of the Ethiopian Pacific Movement. One of them reported Jordan's reaction to a guest speaker who asserted that the Japanese were no better than the British and merely wished to rule Asia for the benefit of Japan: Jordan jumped up and declared that he did not agree with the presumed representative of Gandhi. He argued that "neither Africa nor India can be saved without the help of Japan and Asia." He accused the Indian speaker of being ungrateful for failing to give the Japanese full credit for saving India, Malaya, Singapore, Hong Kong, Burma, and the Dutch East Indies. "Whenever the name of the Rising Sun is mentioned," Jordan proclaimed, "he and everyone should bow and kiss the flag because the mighty Army and Navy of the little brown man is bringing freedom, liberation and justice to all the darker people of the world."[27]

Jordan maintained that the Japanese were teaching white people to respect the abilities of nonwhites as well as offering liberty to the colored peoples of the world. According to FBI sources, Jordan stated that "the white man laughed at the Japanese, calling them funny names before the Pearl Harbor incident but after they took Singapore, Java and Burma, the white man found out that the Japs were not so stupid as they thought [and] that after taking all of these places the Japs would quit and let the Natives rule their own country in the same way the [N]egroes will rule Africa." According to the report, "Jordan advised the audience that if they were drafted and sent over to fight the Japanese or any of the darker people in Africa or elsewhere that as soon as they met the enemy they should throw down their guns and embrace them as their brothers." Jordan's affinity for the Japanese grew from his belief that subject peoples needed military power if they were to remove the weight of oppression. Thus, in his view, the Japanese represented the best hope for the redemption of the colored peoples of the world. "Without big guns, planes and poison gas," he argued that "the [N]egroes and the East Indians could not hope to fight and defeat the white races and that Japan is the only member of the darker races who possesses these weapons of warfare; therefore, India, Africa and all the darker peoples of the world should join hands with the Japanese."[28]

According to the FBI report, Jordan preferred to regard the Japanese as the senior member of the Axis powers, and therefore he gave still greater weight to the implications of his loyalties. In proclaiming the futility of Allied efforts to fight the Axis powers, Jordan, in a very dramatic speech, claimed that "the Axis is now being directed from Japan under the leadership of Admiral Tojo; that Tojo now gives orders to Hitler."[29] Accuracy aside, Jordan's view of Japan as senior partner in the Axis coalition provided a strong geopolitical argument that encouraged his followers to feel a kindred spirit with the Japanese.

Beyond talking about his experience as a seaman aboard a Japanese merchant ship, Jordan interacted with Japanese in a way that persuaded his followers that a special relationship existed between Negroes and Japanese and convinced the government that he was a real threat to the security of the nation. He invited Japanese to speak at meetings. One of them, Takejiro "Byron" Kikuchi, had been introduced to Jordan in 1934 or 1935 by Fujiyama, a fellow countryman. Fujiyama had owned a Japanese restaurant at 116th Street and Lenox Avenue before returning to Japan. Jordan had frequented his restaurant and another which was owned by A. Kato. Jordan periodically visited the Japan Institute, which was located at 630 Fifth Avenue, and the Japanese news agency on the thirty-sixth floor of the Rockefeller Center Building. At the Japan Institute, which had as its primary purpose the building of goodwill, Jordan became acquainted with Asao Ashida by way of an introduction by Kyuya Abiko, of the Japan Association.

A uniformed soldier attended one of Jordan's meetings, providing the key to his undoing. At this meeting, witnesses testified, Jordan said to "a person wearing the uniform and distinctive insignia of a member of the United States Army and to others, in substance, that [N]egro soldier[s] should not fight for the United States against Japan and the other Axis Powers with which the United States was at war."[30]

Jordan, Gordon, and their followers stimulated the greatest fears when they aimed their barbs at black soldiers. Various government agencies were afraid that the agitation of even small groups in Harlem might prove infectious. Intelligence reports of the FBI stressed the fact that the Ethiopian Pacific Movement speakers expressed "pro-Japanese and anti-Ally sentiments," and a "trend of agitation against race discrimination." Army intelligence observed, "The Japanese sentiment among the colored people in Harlem is becoming more prevalent, and the people seem to be greatly pleased with each Japanese success." This intelligence officer concluded:

> Because of the peculiar emotions of the Negro people, it is considered dangerous to the city to allow Jordan with a following of about 150 sympathizers, to be allowed to continue spreading pro-Japanese sympathies in Harlem, as they are easily excited, and continued Japanese successes might sufficiently arouse their emotions to cause a race riot.

Almost as a postscript, the writer expressed the source of his concern: two regiments of black troops had been assigned to defend the city of New York and two additional regiments of black anti-aircraft troops were scheduled for assignment at Camp Upton, New York.[31]

Although their rhetoric at times contained allusions to Pan Africanism, Jordan and others who would be convicted of seditious activities articulated goals and objectives similar to those espoused by mainstream groups. When pinned down to specifics, they expressed a desire for more freedom and better representation in government; they complained that African Americans were lynched, discriminated against, placed in positions below their qualifications, and thrown out of jobs; they distributed a circular entitled "Why Black Men Are Used Only as Messmen in the U.S. Navy" and even sent a telegram to President Roosevelt appealing to his office to see that Negroes receive equal rights in the government. But the reward that they wanted once America's enemies had been defeated was black rule of Africa, rather than merely the limited reform of American racial custom.[32]

Paradoxically, some of the established leaders in the black community, at the same time that they denounced people such as Jordan as the lunatic fringe, articulated one of their most extreme themes: the war against Japan, in essence, was a race war. Lester B. Granger, of the National Urban League, before the National Conference of Social Work, in May 1942 admitted that the war was "in a certain sense a racial war." Two years later he was arguing the same point that "contempt for 'the dirty little yellow monkeys [sic]' was at the bottom of our Navy's inexcusable unreadiness at Pearl Harbor." Dean Gordon B. Hancock, a writer for the Associated Negro Press, agreed that Pearl Harbor was an outgrowth of prejudice and discrimination. Even the premier politician of Harlem, Adam Clayton Powell, Jr., whose newspaper, *Peoples' Voice*, was consistently and sensationally anti-Japanese, acknowledged that since Japan entered the war color had become an aspect of the conflict that could not be denied.[33]

Another favorite theme of Jordan's with which more established black leaders tended to agree was that the war with Japan was in retaliation for years of discrimination. This view was expressed by people such as P. L. Prattis and George Schuyler, both of the *Pittsburgh Courier*; Roy Wilkins and Walter White, of the NAACP; and A. Philip Randolph, of the Brotherhood of Sleeping Car Porters and Maids. Each of them had made the point that white racism was the cause for the war with Japan.[34]

Leonard Robert Jordan and Mittie Maud Gordon had the same functional value that Malcolm X was to have later during the civil rights movement. On the one hand, they legitimized the more moderately toned leadership. They were the specters of what might be if more African Americans came to feel that they were totally without access to the system. On the other hand, these radicals goaded their more cautious adversaries further along the path of militancy than they, otherwise, might have chosen to go in a time when the nation was at war. As an army private said in praising people of Jordan's persuasion, they were folks who did not "seek to pacify whites" or "pussyfoot."[35]

The most important emotional issue over which seditionists and the elite contended was the black soldier: the seditionist wanted to persuade him that he had no real reason to fight; loyalists wanted him to carry on the tradition of service to the country in times of distress. An aspect of this issue that divided the conservative elite from the government and moved them closer to the radicals was the bigoted treatment of black servicemen. It was an issue that left the elite open to attack and ridicule; they would have to convince the black soldier that there would be real gains made as a result of their sacrifice. The black serviceman, trained in military bases located in the South, commanded by white officers who, generally, held them in contempt, more than anyone else, understood well the ambiguity of the Negro's situation, asked to defend democracy abroad when at home he was unable to protect himself or loved ones from racist assault. Although deprived of the trappings of glory, the black soldier was expected to bear burdens above and beyond the call of duty as a matter of routine.

Instead, black soldiers often revealed themselves closely allied to those who were most cynical about the war. A secret document, written for the army by historian Bell I. Wiley, reported numerous complaints that black recruits were uninterested in military life and the war itself. Among the hundreds of bits of anecdotal evidence were many instances of disaffection and indifference. The commander of a black cavalry brigade, for example, estimated that approximately 95 percent of his troops lacked the desire to fight. The report revealed that the disinterest of African Americans arose from a conviction that the war would do little or nothing to advance their lot; furthermore, African Americans were persuaded that the United States was a white man's country and would continue to be so after the war. The attitudes of southern white officers who referred to black recruits as "boys," "shines," "darkies," and "jigaboos" underscored this conviction.[36]

Many of those who went into the military were representative of the broad center of black life who were neither unswerving patriots nor seditionists. It was for the hearts and minds of this element that the ideologues of the old line activists and of the various cells of Japan-backers vied. Ultimately, many of both antagonistic wings would take the middle path and swell the ranks of those who would come to advocate the double V. Many would choose the military as a better alternative than prison. Once in the military, the double V campaign was a good rationalization for doing what became one's duty. For a small minority, force of argument would count for less than the instinct for survival: once the government placed them in a combat zone, it became a matter of kill or be killed.

Nothing caused as much consternation among African Americans as when Negro soldiers were abused in and around southern posts by white soldiers, white civilians, and white policemen. Between 1941 and 1944, major racial disturbances occurred at Fort Bragg and Camp Davis, North Carolina; Fort Benning and Camp Stewart, Georgia; Fort Dix, New Jersey; Fort Bliss, Texas; Camp Tyson, Tennessee; Camp Claiborne, Louisiana; and Camp Shelby, Mississippi. The pattern of disturbance was fairly uniform: trouble usually began with an act of discrimination or abuse; gossip and rumor heightened tensions; and a minor incident sparked a general outbreak.[37]

The Wiley report acknowledged that the factors leading to racial violence were "numerous and complex." The inadequacy of transportation and recreational facilities, the character of southern law enforcement, conflicting views of the Negro's place in society, and the presence of white military police among black troops were all contributory. Confrontations were perceived as almost inevitable as southern whites resisted what they viewed as the federal government's attempt to use the war as a wedge to open up the society, and African Americans were convinced that it was nonsensical to submit to oppression at home when they were being trained to fight for the four freedoms overseas.[38]

In at least one instance, the attitudes of African Americans regarding the Japanese were important: the racial riot that occurred in June 1943 at Camp Stewart, Georgia, which the Wiley report used as "the profile of a typical outbreak." Soldiers of the 369th Antiaircraft Artillery Regiment, originally from New York, had served in Hawaii where they had been well treated by "the natives and the nonbelligerent Japanese." Confronted by the social conventions of Georgia and the conditions at Camp Stewart, these troops became "disgruntled." According to the report, these men raised the question whether the Japanese would treat them better than white Georgians. In the aftermath of another riot, a platoon commander of the Ninety-second Division who had been involved in suppressing the disturbance told of rock-throwing black troops who yelled, "Get out of here, you white son of a bitch; when we get over we're going to be shooting someone besides the Japs."[39]

The army seemed trapped by its own policy of thrusting African Americans into southern camps as though no incident need have been anticipated as a result. The Wiley report admitted that the policy of the War Department that put young African American men from the North in southern communities was akin to "placing extreme antagonists at each other's throats"; yet it stopped short of criticizing that policy. The reason most African Americans were stationed in the South, Wiley understood, was for "factors of military convenience, including climate."[40] The mood of the black soldier was reflected best, perhaps, in an anecdote attributed to a black recruit at induction: "Just carve on my tombstone; here lies a black man, who died fighting a yellow man to protect a white man."[41]

When his uniform failed to protect him from the barbs of prejudice, black soldiers, in the view of mainstream African Americans, were supposed to keep their anger in check. When a conductor aboard a Richmond-bound train and some Army M.P.s forced several black soldiers to vacate their seats in favor of white passengers, one black Yank, protesting this treatment loudly, exclaimed, "I would not mind fighting if we had anything to fight for. We have no reason to fight the Japanese because they have not done nothing to us." This prompted the *Afro-American* to caution, "Unpatriotic displays won't help correct the injustices heaped upon colored persons. We must learn how to fight and still be patriotic."[42]

As this incident and the riot at Camp Stewart demonstrated, some African Americans used the Japanese as the demons with which they could intimidate whites; the use of the Japanese as their bête noire was one way for African Americans to express their grievances against domestic racism. But it was also a device to which African Americans resorted because they wanted to identify with those colored people who would tolerate no such abuse by whites. They were not conjuring up images of Germans or Italians, Congolese or Ethiopians as a rule.

Even if black soldiers were willing to fight for democracy overseas, this gave black civilians no respite from the war against bigotry in America. Detroit and Harlem became domestic battle zones. Riots and lynchings still occurred frequently across the country. This reality made it difficult for some African Americans who were involved in the war to think of the Japanese as enemies. When a propaganda poster depicting a Japanese soldier with his bayonet poised over a white woman was put up in the Ford Motor Company, which was manufacturing bombers, five black workers left their machines and tore down the poster. Asked why they had destroyed it, one replied, "The Japs are colored people. So are we. We are not fighting colored people. We are fighting for democracy."[43]

The African Americans who went overseas as soldiers could not rest assured that their kin and loved ones would be protected by the constituted law enforcement agencies at home. During riots or lynchings, policemen or sheriffs' deputies were more than likely to be involved in assaults on black people. The *Afro-American* asked editorially two questions that must have troubled much of black America: "How can America condemn the ruthlessness of Japan— America which sprinkled the pavements of her cities with the blood of citizens whose only offense is the color of their skin?" More to the point, it asked, "How can one fight an enemy abroad when he fears for his kinsmen at home, knowing them to be at the mercy of enemies as savage and as brutal as the Germans, Italians, or the Japanese?"[44]

Although no black leader of prominence challenged African Americans to close ranks as Du Bois had done during World War I, the black press, with the urging of the OWI, pursued a policy of advising African Americans to do as they had done historically in times of war, suffer silently but keep on marching. Some African Americans, however, were persuaded that this war more particularly than wars past was not their war. The views of two African American social scientists are instructive here.

Horace Cayton, the noted black sociologist, wrote an incisive analysis of the Negro's disaffection for the war. An important factor, he noted, was the "growing tendency toward psychological identification with other non-white people." As a consequence, any change that brought nonwhite peoples into greater prominence was seen as positive. African Americans, in Cayton's opinion, were "beginning to feel that dark peoples throughout the world will soon be on the 'march.'" According to Cayton, the more "the slogans of democracy" were raised, the lower Negro morale sank. Cayton claimed that a feeling of isolation and alienation was detectable among all classes of Negroes. He also pointed out that few African Americans believed strongly that the war would result in an improved status for African Americans.[45]

J. Saunders Redding, a noted historian, used himself and his family to illustrate the depth of conflict among African Americans as a result of Japan becoming America's enemy. Like Robert Jordan or Mittie Maude Gordon, Redding confessed that when he first listened to the war news "bad news hadn't seemed bad." He admitted "a kind of grim, perverted satisfaction" from hearing that "some non-white men were killing some white men and it might be that the non-white would win." He dreamed that "perhaps in a world conquered and ruled by yellow men, there would be no onus attached to being black."[46]

But upon reflection, Redding decided that any "New Order" invented by the Axis powers would hold nothing for ethnic minorities. He felt that the threat to democracy was grave enough that the Negro's "own private and important war to enlarge freedom here in America" ought to be postponed. The only reason African Americans had to fight, he believed, was in order to make America truly democratic. Despite his own turnabout, Redding admitted, other members of his family remained cynical.[47]

The division within the Redding family was a microcosm of that found in the greater black community; black views were never monolithic. Another example of their varied thinking was the black reaction to the internment of Japanese Americans on the Pacific Coast. The range of views encompassed those who saw an opportunity for black economic advancement at the expense of the Japanese and those who protested a government action that was obviously racially inspired.

When the government first began to round up and incarcerate Japanese agricultural workers, the Los Angeles branch of the National Negro Business League (NNBL) saw it as the "greatest opportunity ever offered by the State of California." Pointing to the virtual monopolization by Japanese of truck farming, commercial fishing, and even a number of domestic positions once dominated by African Americans, the NNBL argued that Americans ought to be free of dependence on produce grown by people from a nation with which the United States was at war. This was also a position taken by actor Clarence Muse at a meeting sponsored by the NAACP.[48]

The removal of the Japanese, in the opinion of members of the NNBL, presented African Americans with a dual opportunity: they could make an important contribution to the national defense and, at the same time, "entrench" themselves "in a manner not previously granted." One state official endorsed the position of the NNBL with the observation, "You don't have to distrust a Negro face in a boat plying in California waters; nor would you need to fear a traitor in our lettuce fields . . . if they were there."[49]

The *California Eagle*, which in the past had tended to flip-flop, at times advising that African Americans emulate the Japanese and at other times complaining that Japanese made progress where African Americans did not, in January told its readers to "continue normal relations in schools, businesses, and in our social relations with the Japanese residents of our communities." To have done otherwise after the Japanese-American Citizens League pledged its loyalty would have violated the principle of fair play as African Americans understood it. But in February an *Eagle* editorial concluded, "If [an agrarian empire] must be lost to [the Japanese], why shouldn't it fall into our hands?"[50]

One individual who was a staunch advocate of the notion that African Americans might ably fill the void left by the removal of Japanese from the fields of agriculture was William Greenwell, president of the Salinas branch of the NAACP. Greenwell, a bootblack who organized the branch in 1939, stated his position succinctly: America could insure against sabotage by placing African Americans in the fields of California; black hands could be "identified, tried and trusted." He believed it dangerous to allow "any Japanese, American born or alien, to handle food stuffs which are for American tables." Greenwell took the position that since African Americans were "100% American" and natural tillers of the soil they were entitled to take the place of the Japanese in the fruit and vegetable gardens. He contacted the national office for support of his scheme. In New York, Adam Clayton Powell shared Greenwell's enthusiasm for sending African Americans to replace the Japanese in the agricultural fields of California. Powell, even before Greenwell's proposal, had complained of the "hordes of Japanese, maintaining the arrogance of their father land . . . virtually throttling California's million-dollar vegetable and produce industry."[51]

The national office of the NAACP was inclined to lend support to Greenwell's scheme. In response to Greenwell's urging, it sent out a release calling for two thousand African Americans to work in the lettuce fields of Salinas and sent Roy Wilkens to California. Despite Greenwell's zeal and optimism, his idea was stillborn. Wilkens, reporting from the field, informed Walter White that farmers along the coast were bringing in Mexicans to replace the Japanese. African Americans, the farmers explained, would not work like either of these other two ethnic groups, "from sun-up to sun-down seven days a week."[52]

Despite his own strong bias against the Japanese, Adam Clayton Powell polled readers of his *Peoples' Voice* in an effort to ascertain their feelings regarding the internment of Japanese and to determine whether or not they thought the president acted within his constitutional authority; Powell got mixed reactions. An elevator operator, cook, and salesman all thought the president's action was proper. They believed respectively that any measure to protect the country was acceptable; no good American had anything to fear from an executive power used to remove them from their domicile; and the power to remove a citizen in order to reach an enemy alien was justifiable. Another respondent made two points which would be heard many times over when the issue of Japanese internment was discussed among African Americans: first, American citizens of Japanese ancestry were uprooted and locked up while Germans and Italians, including noncitizens, went untouched. Second, the respondent charged, the removal of Japanese on the Pacific Coast was racially motivated, and therefore a precedent had been set by which African Americans or any other group out of favor might be similarly abused of constitutional rights.[53]

Harry Paxton Howard, in a critical analysis of the government's policy for *Crisis* magazine, made this same point. "If native-born Americans of Asiatic descent, can be denied all civil rights and civil liberties . . . can be reduced to bondage, deprived of citizenship and property, the same can be done to Afro-American[s]," he warned. Howard, who had spent nineteen years in China and five in Japan, from which he was expelled for radical activities, pointed out the fact that even those Japanese who were categorized as "enemy aliens" had been deemed ineligible for citizenship solely because they were not white. Howard chastised African Americans for lacking sufficient vigilance and protectiveness where the rights of their Asian brothers and sisters were concerned.[54]

One Los Angeles resident, Samuel W. Thompson, describing himself as "a firm believer in NAACP principles and aims since the Niagara Movement," wrote to Walter White urging that the pending thirty-third annual conference of the NAACP be rescheduled for another city as a gesture of protest against the treatment of Japanese-American citizens. Thompson claimed that the evacuation of the Japanese-Americans had "caused a very tensed feeling among the inhabitants [of Los Angeles]." A columnist for the *Los Angeles Tribune* also called upon the premier civil rights organization to take a firm stand on the issue of Japanese internment. "The mass abrogation of the civil liberties of nearly 115,000 people is not to be lightly dismissed by people who know what that means," the writer declared. "Today," he continued, "the once-glorious banner of democracy droops in weather-beaten folds from the flagstaff of expediency. . . . If the [NAACP] is to justify the fighting it made to meet, it must make the first steps toward living up to its name," he implored. In a subsequent column he raised the question that must have troubled other people of good conscience, can we feel that "we did the best we could in this situation?"[55]

Perhaps two black residents of Los Angeles expected too much when they asked the NAACP to take a strong stand on behalf of citizens who were deprived of their constitutional rights merely because of race. When the delegates did convene in Los Angeles, they addressed the issue of Japanese in concentration camps with a resolution: "Be it resolved that we protest vigorously the use of race or color as the sole basis for any arbitrary classification by which the fundamental rights of any group of American citizens is infringed." This particular resolution was preceded by twenty-three others, touching on topics such as "War and National Policy," "the Pacific Charter," "Social Security," "the Red Cross," "Education," "the March on Washington," "the Poll Tax," and "the Double V." The resolution protesting the violations of fellow citizens' civil rights was even preceded by one concerned with wages paid in the Caribbean.[56] To say that the NAACP's protest of the violation of Japanese-American's citizenship rights was muted would be an understatement.

If reports from California were accurate, the tepid response of the NAACP delegates to the plight of Japanese Americans hardly reflected the sentiments of those African Americans who lived close to and among the Japanese. Vincent Tubbs, a reporter for the *Afro-American* newspaper, went to San Francisco after the implementation of the evacuation policy. From that vantage point he reported changes that occurred within the community and within himself because of what was done to Japanese-American citizens. As a result of his sojourn on the West Coast, he said, a "mental metamorphosis" occurred whereby he no longer saw the race problem as strictly a conflict between African Americans and whites. He became more empathetic regarding the predicament of the interned Japanese Americans.

Tubbs attributed his changed awareness to conversations with Caleb Foote, field secretary of the Fellowship of Reconciliation, and the attitudes of many local residents. Foote, a graduate of Harvard and Columbia, worked to relocate American-born Japanese who were being kept in detention camps. Foote stressed that these Americans had been victimized by a violation of human rights, without trial or hearing, solely on account of race. Many African Americans of San Francisco, according to Tubbs, referred to the Japanese as "good friends." It was they who reminded Tubbs that what had been done to Japanese-Americans might just as easily have happened to Negro Americans or any other minority group. Tubbs related how several black people had mentioned that male family members had expressed a reluctance to serve in the army if it would mean facing a former Japanese friend on the field of battle.[57]

Since they generally looked upon the Japanese Americans as people who had gotten a raw deal, African Americans to a considerable degree were not resentful that ex-internees would be returning to their homes, even at times when that might mean the African Americans would have to relocate. A confidential government report had predicted, "The release of Japanese from War Relocation Authority Camps will be the cause of friction and racial clashes when the Japanese arrive back in California." Despite the dire predictions of both the government and the Hearst newspapers, what actually occurred supported Tubbs' findings. The pessimistic predictions were based on the knowledge that great numbers of African Americans had moved into the areas formerly inhabited by the relocated Japanese. What had been Los Angeles' "Little Tokyo" became "Bronzeville." According to *Ebony* magazine, African Americans of Bronzeville "felt a strong brother-bond towards the discriminated-against Japanese." This "miracle in interracial adjustment," in the opinion of Raymond Booth of the Los Angels Council for Civic Unity was attributable to the "magnificent statesman-like attitude of Negroes toward Japanese."[58]

The head of the local Japanese-American Citizens League (JACL), Scotty Tsuchiya, admitted an initial apprehension since the JACL was aware that African Americans occupied their homes and stores, but were pleased to find African Americans friendly, respectful, and sympathetic. Prior to the release of the internees, the Carver Club posed as a debate topic at the Booker T. Community Center in San Francisco "Should the Japanese be returned to the West Coast?" No one was willing to debate the negative side.[59]

A black minister was the first cleric to welcome the returned evacuees and invite them to join his San Francisco church. In Oakland, black neighbors were among the first to welcome back a Nisei dentist and his wife. One returning family reported that the friendliest person they met enroute home had been a black porter on the train. In San Mateo, returnees reported to the WRA that black occupants who had leased their homes had kept them immaculate and had taken remarkable care of their possessions. A number of black families took Japanese into their homes until they could organize their affairs, and black leaders looked for jobs on behalf of their returned neighbors.

One observer thought that the reason African Americans extended themselves was because the Japanese "did not follow the established policy of the dominant group in dealing with Afro-Americans." According to Thelma Thurston Gorham, writing for *Crisis* magazine, "even before the war, Japanese Americans were more kindly disposed toward Negro Americans." Therefore, African Americans, she said, were more likely "to remember former kindnesses and courtesies" than "ponder the question of why he should resent the return of the Japanese." Roi Ottley made essentially the same point: "Relations between Japanese and Negroes on the West Coast were wholly on a personal basis."[60]

Cordial before the evacuation, aware of the grave injustice of that policy, African Americans and Japanese made the wedding of Little Tokyo and Bronzeville representative of the kind of democracy both believed should occur in America. *Ebony* captured the spirit of the occasion: "Blood-tested proof of Bronzeville–Little Tokyo harmony is the First Street Clinic in a Buddhist building. Here all races are given medical treatment at low cost by an interracial staff." Other photographs and captions struck the same themes: "Japanese barber gives haircut to a Negro"; "Shopping together in a Japanese market; Mrs. Kiki Kamimura and Mrs. Amelia Dudley"; "Sticker on restaurants run by Japanese or Negroes in Little Tokyo proclaims tolerance policy"; and "Jolly kids of all races play together at Pilgrim House." One other picture was captioned "Negro and Nisei Vets in American Veterans Committee fight for FEPC." A black Texan, in a letter to the editor, told how much he liked the article and thought that African Americans and Japanese shared a desire "to see democracy practiced in the United States some day."[61]

The reaction of black Californians to the return of Japanese-Americans to their homes helped to persuade more remote, more conservative African Americans to speak out against the wrong that had been perpetrated against an industrious and loyal segment of the population. Saunders Redding labeled the evacuation "a great wrong." "It was discrimination of the rankest kind with little to justify it," he asserted. The *Pittsburgh Courier* declared that there was "never any valid reason for moving . . . American citizens from their homes to concentration camps on the basis of what they MIGHT say or do." The *Courier*, Willard Townsend, a leading union official, and "Confucious," a columnist for the *Michigan Chronicle*, were among those who resurrected the argument that the Japanese had been singled out for a treatment the Italian and German communities were spared, "although numerous spies and traitors were discovered among them." They also made much of the argument that a "bad precedent" had been set.[62]

As it became clearer that bigotry was the sole reason for the incarceration of Japanese, even Adam Clayton Powell's *Peoples' Voice*, which had been very much opposed to the Japanese, changed its tone and ran an article by a resident of Wyoming's Heart Mountain relocation camp. The article suggested that Japanese Americans might return from the camps with "a new feeling [toward African Americans], one founded in mutual suffering from discrimination." "While this is being done, little has been undertaken to ready Negroes to an acceptance of the Nisei," the Harlem newspaper lamented. It complained that little had been printed in black publications about the plight of the Japanese Americans; it did hold up Harry Paxton Howard's article in the *Crisis* as the singular exception.[63]

Despite the disclaimer of the *Peoples' Voice*, other black newspapers had expressed empathy for the Japanese-Americans earlier than Powell's newspaper. Roy Wilkens, in his column in the rival *Amsterdam Star-News*, argued, "The treatment of these people remains one chapter of which America should be thoroughly ashamed, and for which amends should be made." Wilkens concluded, "The fact that we gave them different treatment [from that given Germans and Italians], and a careful examination of the whole situation compels the conclusion that the difference was on account of color."[64]

When the army proposed that separate units be established for American-born Japanese from Hawaii, the *Afro-American* newspaper opposed the idea. "We have not set up special units for Germans or Italians, whether they be foreign born, naturalized or born in America," the *Afro* observed. German and Italian citizens were integrated throughout the armed services, the *Afro* pointed out, and their patriotic offers to serve were regarded as genuine until it could be proved otherwise. The Baltimore newspaper implied rather emphatically that the same should have held true for Japanese-Americans.[65]

The black media, unless perceived interests of African Americans were imperiled, tended to be sympathetic toward the Americans of Japanese ancestry and critical of attempts to discriminate against them. The *Afro* reported that a commander of a unit of the Nisei 442nd Regimental Combat Team criticized the racial discrimination directed against Japanese citizens, while the *Pittsburgh Courier*'s executive editor concentrated on the heroic exploits of the Nisei in Europe. The *Michigan Chronicle* protested when the town of Hood River, Oregon, removed from its "Roll of Honor" the names of sixteen Nisei; the *Nashville Globe* applauded when the national commander of the American Legion told the Hood River post to restore the names.[66]

Negative references to the interned Japanese were rare. In Baltimore the *Afro-American* did complain when it found that teachers in the relocation camps were paid two to seven times the average salary for teachers in southern black schools. Even more upsetting for black Baltimoreans was a proposal to bring Japanese girls from internment camps to cope with a shortage of nurses in the City Hospital and Johns Hopkins Hospital. Dr. Ralph Young, a member of the Welfare Board, and Carl Murphy, editor of the *Afro*, were angry because an earlier proposal that black women be trained to meet the need for nurses had been rejected. The white medical elite argued that "there would be less objection on the part of white patients if they were served by colored Jap nurses than by colored Baltimore women." In arguing against the plan to bring female internees to Baltimore hospitals to fill the void in the nursing ranks, Young and Murphy lumped all Japanese together. Young called the proposal "an insult" to colored people and asked, "Why should the city prefer suspect Japanese to loyal colored nurses?" Murphy claimed to have no objection to using the Japanese-American girls except that it indicated that some white people hated African Americans "more than they do our enemies." The issue was resolved when the Welfare Board disapproved the recommendation because no effort had been made to recruit black nurses.[67]

The African American newspapers, of course, extolled the exploits of black soldiers who engaged the Japanese in combat as part of their patriotic duty, but an interesting facet of the black reportage was that it generally did not include strident condemnation of the Japanese. The black press recorded the black soldiers' impressions of the Japanese based on a combination of military propaganda, face-to-face encounters, and historic images. African American newspaper men at times wrote stereotypical portrayals of the Japanese as "cunning foes." While describing Japanese as "fanatical, tricky, and vicious fighters," however, one Baltimorean seemed to derive perverse pleasure from suggesting that they were "no push-over[s] like the Italians."[68]

More significantly, the black press tended to view the war as a race war, seemed anxious to explain war excesses on the part of Japanese as reactive, and tended to be more condemnatory of atrocities on the part of whites, whether Americans or Europeans. Black editors and columnists seemingly were willing to forgive those who "trespassed against them": within less than two years of war, some began to focus again on issues of racism as aspects of the policies of the government and the white media. Black thinkers began to argue more forcefully a theme which earlier had been associated with the so-called seditionists: American policy toward Japan was racially motivated.

Black writers once again asked why Japan had launched an attack against Pearl Harbor and voiced doubts that it was unprovoked. W. E. B. Du Bois suggested in 1943 that the war with Japan was unnecessary. Alluding to a bill pending in Congress to remove immigration restrictions against the Chinese, Du Bois credited the attack on Pearl Harbor with forcing the United States to "acknowledge the equality of the white and yellow races." He concluded that if the United States similarly had yielded to the Japanese, war would have been unnecessary. The *Nashville Globe*, in a series of editorials, concluded that what had been billed as a "sneak attack" was anything but. The sacrifice in men and materials, the *Globe* charged, was "a case of plotting an incident of such terrible consequences as to force Congress to declare war." Commenting critically on the possession of lands by England, France, and Holland, and the United States' holdings of Hawaii and the Philippines, J. A. Rogers declared, "Had there been no grab of these territories, there could have been no war with Japan—no Pearl Harbor."[69]

More than a few African Americans believed that white Americans had a particularly virulent attitude toward the Japanese when compared to their dislike for European enemies. Marjorie McKenzie, writing for the *Pittsburgh Courier*, made this point: "There is a quality of hate which Americans hold for the Japanese which does not compare with general sentiment about the Germans, even the Nazi leaders." Accusing white writers of tagging the Japanese with all the epithets in the book, Roy Wilkens maintained that it was a favorite habit of patriotic writers" to refer to Japanese as "sub-humans," as if they were animals that ought to be exterminated.[70]

The *Nashville Globe* warned its readers, "We should not go in for name-calling." "Name calling," the *Globe* insisted, "is encouraged by the warmongers on both sides of a conflict, so as to get the best in butchery out of their conscripts, who can see a better reason to kill a fellow-man in protest against his race or color than because of his political or religious views." The use of the terms *yellow bastards, yellow monkeys, little yellow devils,* or anything else with *yellow* affixed were generally deplored by African Americans.[71]

The *Afro-American* similarly maintained that the widespread use of such terms by the average white soldier made it "convincingly clear that the war now being fought is a racial war." The same article explained that "there is not a great deal of hostility between the individual Americans and Germans."[72]

The *Nashville Globe* actually denounced Admiral William "Bull" Halsey as a "WARMONGER and WINDBAG" when he was widely quoted as saying, "The only good Japs are dead Japs." A columnist for the *Michigan Chronicle* also took Halsey to task for remarks about the "beastial Japs." The writer proclaimed that such statements "diminished our respect for him and the navy blue."[73]

While whites generally seemed eager to deny the Japanese the status of "civilized" because of the excesses of war committed by some soldiers of Japan, black analysts seemed much more willing to explain them as reactions to prejudice and discrimination or point out that they were no more bestial than atrocities committed by white people, both soldiers and civilians. As far as African Americans were concerned no one ranked lower on the scale of human evolution than the bigoted white southerner. A. M. Wendell Malliet, writing in the *Amsterdam-Star News*, exclaimed, "The atrocities, insults and humiliations which are being heaped upon white captives by the Japanese are the fruits of the white man's prejudices and race hates." The *Nashville Globe* also blamed "those who by stirring race prejudice have assiduously cultivated the enmity of the Japanese." The *Globe* attributed "the bitter do-or-die spirit" of the Japanese to their fear of enslavement at the hands of the victorious Allies. The victims of prejudicial treatment, in the view of the *Globe*, also assimilated some of the prejudices of their oppressor and acted upon them. Finally, the *Globe* perceived the reality to be that war was a dirty business and it was "sheer nonsense to pretend that you can carry on a war with rules that deserved the stamp 'civilized.'"[74]

African Americans in their commentaries on Japanese atrocities emphasized that there was a seamy side to war which evoked the basest emotions of human nature. When the white *Detroit News* ran an editorial expressing outrage at reports that the Japanese had blown up a hospital ship and killed "innocents by tens of thousands," the *Michigan Chronicle* replied that "Germans and Italians have done some fancy butchering of innocents also." Commenting on reports that Japanese had bombed field hospitals and hospital ships clearly marked with the Red Cross, Roy Wilkens remarked that when the Germans did the same thing in Italy the white media went to considerable lengths to explain how it had been a mistake. In Wilkens' opinion, white Americans were interested in making the issue of atrocities a racial one. Referring to the white American media, he said, "They have said that ONLY Japanese would do things like this. They have implied that WHITE MEN would not do such things."[75]

The black press was just as likely to do as the *Afro-American* and decry comparable acts against humanity perpetrated by white nations, most particularly their own. The *Afro* listed what it perceived to be white crimes against people they considered inferior: the British enslavement of natives of India and Africa; the Italian use of gas against Ethiopians; the German murder and persecution of Jews; the American equipment of overseas units with poison gas; and American race riots, lynchings, and racial segregation. This last category was the one that did the most to shape black attitudes toward war atrocities. As the *Afro* noted, "The test of civilization is not merely how a nation treats its enemies, but also what it does to its own citizens."[76]

When there was an uproar over allegations of extreme misconduct on the part of Japanese soldiers guarding war prisoners, black writers were quick to point out that the hands of Americans also were soaked with the blood of innocents. Besides, the excesses of soldiers at war paled by comparison to the brutalities committed with impunity against unoffensive African Americans in the southern states. The *Michigan Chronicle* compared the militarists of Japan and Germany who whipped their people into "a frenzy of hatred" to those in the South who inflamed mobs "to the point where they are willing to burn a Negro alive and cut off his limbs for keepsakes." In an editorial about the atrocities at Bataan in the Philippines, the *Nashville Globe* suggested that the Japanese had learned their lesson from a Mississippi lynching "where the accused (but never convicted) victims were sent to their deaths by using a blowtorch to burn out their entrails."[77]

One reason black writers possessed a comparatively high tolerance regarding the issue of atrocities was because it had long been rumored that the Japanese treated black prisoners of war differently from the way they dealt with whites; this had been one of the central themes advanced by the seditionists. When Ernest Clarke, a former New York musician who had lived for eight years in East and Southeast Asia, was repatriated, the *Peoples' Voice* ran a headline: "Japs No Color Kin Says Freed Prisoner: Racial Identity Has No Weight with Nipponese."[78]

Clarke had been interned in Hong Kong. The lead to the story was "Brothers-Under-The-Skin? Baloney! No Leniency for Negro Says Internee of Japs." "From the beginning Clarke made one thing clear; as far as the Japs are concerned an American is an American and skin color be damned," the *Voice* reported. The reporter admitted that Clarke had said that as an individual he had been treated "alright." But he denied that the way he was treated was due to his race: "The Japs are not fighting a race war. They are fighting a war for domination." Master Sergeant William Walker, of St. Louis, Missouri, held prisoner in Japan, told how he ducked work "by teaching the Japanese the art of jitter-bugging and how to prepare chitterlings.[79]

The largest number of black POWs were located in the Philippines. There were twenty among the more than two thousand POWs from the Los Banos camp, which was forty-five miles south of Manila. Freed black prisoners told how they were offered better treatment by the Japanese in exchange for cooperation in an anti-white campaign. The ex-POWs told of the same policy at another prison camp, Santo Tomas. One Los Banos internee refused preferential treatment: "I found it impossible to take more than my share of food when so many of my white countrymen, who had treated me as their equal, were hungry."[80]

There was considerable range in the experience of the few African Americans who became prisoners of the Japanese: one family found the Japanese reluctant to imprison them; another man survived the harshest deprivation. Captain Walter A. White, formerly of Everett, Massachusetts, was captured with the last defenders of Corregidor. White had been attached to a quartermaster transportation company with civil service status, but he was activated on December 10, 1941, two weeks before the invasion of Luzon. White's Filipino wife, daughter, and two sons, all of whom were dark-skinned, repeatedly showed American citizenship papers to inquiring Japanese officers, but the Japanese refused to intern them until a few months before the Americans arrived. The *Afro* concluded from this that the Japanese were disinclined to imprison the white family because the Japanese idea of an American was a white skin, a dominating attitude, and a southern accent. Captain Chester B. Sanders was one of six African Americans who survived the Bataan "Death March."[81]

According to the account in the *Afro*, the Japanese were inclined to be less cruel toward the six colored men in the prison camp. But when they tried to extract some information from Captain Sanders they did place him in solitary confinement without a light or a bed. In the camp prisoners were beaten by guards for infractions of the rules. Sanders, however, claimed to have been spared beatings although he admitted to being kicked once. Sanders lost 112 pounds within one year. His wife, who was in the Santo Tomas prison camp from 1941 to 1945, claimed to have suffered many privations and cruelties. She charged that in the last year prisoners had so little to eat that they were actually starving.[82]

The cruel treatment of prisoners was not easy to explain. Noted anthropologist Ruth Benedict, while researching her book on the patterns of Japanese culture, learned from Japanese POWs that they had no code of conduct; they associated surrender with shame and dishonor, and they considered their lives as having been forfeited.[83] The lack of a sanctioned pattern of behavior, in the event of capture, meant that Japanese soldiers had no uniformly approved operational procedure for dealing with people whom they captured. Generally, the care and comfort of POWs rated low priority, but the caliber of treatment might vary according to whether the Japanese command was administered by the army or the navy. Whatever the duress these prisoners experienced, any sympathy on the part of Japanese was bound to be personal and individual.

The *Nashville Globe*, like the Office of War Information, cautioned against hating the enemy too much, but unlike the government, it reminded its readers that Americans had dropped bombs and killed women and children of Japan just as successfully as the Japanese had killed Allied soldiers. The *Pittsburgh Courier* punctuated this point: it told of Americans machine-gunning helpless survivors after sinking thirty ships in the Battle of the Bismarck Sea; it told of American bombers wiping out residential areas, indiscriminately slaughtering men, women, and babies. All of these the *Courier* judged to be atrocities. But the supreme atrocity, in the minds of many, was committed by Americans. "When atomic bombs were dropped over Hiroshima and Nagasaki, killing and wounding hundreds of thousands of helpless people, that was an atrocity," the *Courier* declared.[84]

Some African Americans viewed the use of this technology against the Japanese as vindictive racism. Despite claims to the contrary, the *Afro-American* referred to reports that the nuclear age could have been inaugurated against the Germans and concluded, "We apparently saved our most devastating weapon for the hated yellow men of the Pacific." The *Nashville Globe* saw the use of atomic weaponry as an act of revenge. "In reprisal for the cruelties the Japanese had heaped upon American soldiers," the Tennessee newspaper charged, "our B-29's and lastly, our world-shaking atomic bombs had dished out much more than we had ever received." The *Globe* lamented: "As for the war with Japan, we are very generally ashamed that we employed the destructive atomic bomb, an instrument of death more inhumane than anything ever employed in war, to chalk up our victory. . . . Can we as a Nation hold up our heads with crystal clear conscience after dropping atomic bombs on the Japanese which wiped out hundreds of thousands of human lives?" The Allies, in its opinion, had "trampled their Christian morals under foot." Despite government arguments that millions of American lives were probably saved, the end of the war was hastened, and the Japanese had committed heinous acts, the *Globe* concluded that America had "Lost Plenty, Won Nothing."[85]

The reactions of two of the columnists for the *Pittsburgh Courier* were so irate that the paper included disclaimers with their columns; the views of the writers did not necessarily reflect those of the *Courier*. "The most shocking aspect of the entire fantastic week," according to Marjorie McKenzie, "was the callousness with which the American public accepted the wiping out of several hundred thousand Japanese, many of them civilians, women and children, when two atomic bombs neatly erased Hiroshima and Nagasaki." In her view the American government had ignored its "moral obligations to mankind and civilization" and done "irreparable damage to the very concept of international justice." She judged it "illustrative of our shallow thinking."[86]

No one bristled any more than George Schuyler. Schuyler saw the use of the A-bomb as the device that put the Anglo-Saxons on top. The atomic bomb was a "tremendous power for evil'" as controlled by "second-rate and small-minded men filled with racial arrogance," he fumed. Schuyler condemned, what he termed, the "disgusting drivel from the highest-placed Americans and British about re-educating the Germans and Japanese to 'our-way of life' and nauseating cant about Axis atrocities in a holier-than-thou tone which can only provoke bitter cynical laughter from the intelligent observer." He blamed earlier American reverses on "our boneheaded complacency and sense of white supremacy." Even after Americans got the upper hand and defeated the Japanese, Schuyler claimed, American leaders "showed themselves to be as bad winners as they were bad losers, deliberately misconstruing every act of courtesy on the part of the Japanese."[87]

With the surrender of Japan, some African Americans were anxious to seek reconciliation with the Japanese on the basis of equality. These African Americans, due to their historical affinity for the Japanese, were natural supporters of a liberal policy of occupation. When the inquiring reporter of the *Afro* asked Baltimoreans "do you think our soldiers should fraternize with Japanese women?" All respondents but one answered in the affirmative. The lone negative response was due to the interviewee's objection to mixing "business and pleasure." The others answered affirmatively because they believed that fraternization would result in such worthy goals as "peace and happiness," the selling of "the idea of American democracy," reduction of future dissension," and realization "that there is only one human race."[88]

A month earlier the inquiring reporter had asked whether the emperor of Japan ought to be retained or whether he should be tried as a war criminal. According to the *Afro*, Emperor Hirohito, in the opinion of residents of Washington, Philadelphia, Newark, Richmond, and Baltimore, should be treated the same as other war criminals. Some of the more interesting responses came from Philadelphia. A garage owner advocated, "Fight until the people repudiate [the] ruler who asked senseless sacrifices." Another fellow who had two sons overseas reasoned, "Keep the ruler because he is part of the religion." He did suggest, however, that the emperor's powers be checked. A veteran of the campaigns in the Philippines and New Guinea echoed this point: "Let Japan have its emperor. After all, his powers will be checked since we are going to occupy the country."[89]

The plan to try certain Japanese as war criminals sparked a fresh outburst from George Schuyler. "What must particularly make honest men gag," he wrote, "is the current terrorization and robbery in Japan where the most prominent soldiers, sailors, politicians, and businessmen are being grabbed and tried as war criminals, as if Americans themselves were innocent flowers, guiltless of aggression." If Japanese officers who occasionally beheaded an American soldier or feasted on one "in order to stave off the ravages of hunger" were to be tried, what was to be done with those Americans who manufactured and dropped atomic bombs? he asked. "Our aggressors and war criminals," he concluded, "will die in bed covered with honors." The people Schuyler thought should be punished were officials he labeled "those arrogant brass hats who were simply stupid and incompetent." That they went unpunished he deemed evidence that the country was run by "poor whites whose pose of superiority is laughable."[90]

Accompanying the occupying forces to Japan, the black press sent two representatives, Jerry Tubbs, of the *Afro-American*, and Charles H. Loeb, representing the Negro Newspaper Publishers Association. Of the two, Tubbs' reports reflected his personal anti-Japanese bias and an overreliance on the official handouts given to pool reporters by General Douglas MacArthur's headquarters. Upon his arrival in Japan, Tubbs began to moralize about the evils of fraternization between black soldiers and Japanese women. He claimed that black GIs had "pent up emotions born of years on jungle islands and man's insatiable lust for the touch of a woman's flesh." What particularly upset him was his belief that such desires on the part of soldiers of the occupation forces made them "laughing stocks in the eyes of the Japanese." Tubbs had been informed that the Japanese had been "disciplined by 2,000 years of tradition to have different evaluations." He also had learned that Japanese believed that the easiest way to pacify the American soldier was to give him "a bottle, a geisha girl, and a souvenir." He advised a "hands off policy" for the black soldiers and "some bludgeoning for Japanese." The bludgeoning of the Japanese he recommended as punishment for their betrayal of those they were supposed to have helped with their sloganeering. By this he meant the Koreans, Chinese, Filipinos, Indians, Malays, and Manchurians.[91]

Tubbs, convinced that it was too soon to feel compassion for the Japanese, tended to be hypercritical: the Japanese of occupied Japan stared at Americans, especially black ones in "obvious curiosity"; they counted change in "elementary and very ungrammatical English"; almost all needed "a bath and a change of their aged, tattered and filthy clothing"; most possessed "an almost stifling body odor"; few had shoes, and others wore wooden clogs, which caused them to move "in a toddle that seem to make them stumble instead of walk." Clearly, Tubbs disliked the Japanese. He wrote unflatteringly about Japanese women: they wore pantaloons; few wore makeup; they carried their babies "strapped on their backs just as the so-called uncivilized Africans do." Tubbs wrote that their markets, street vendors, and various other customs almost moved him to write a piece "comparing them [the Japanese] with equatorial Africans, but that he decided wouldn't be fair to the Africans."[92]

Abstract ideas fared better than people in Tubbs' writings. He was somewhat impressed by the concept of *'Bushido'*, which he termed, "the expression of the code of knighthood" which "gave rise to "the spirit of sportsmanship in defeat." Occupation authorities gave credence to this idea that the code of conduct of ancient warriors was the reason for the relative calm of the occupation. Tubbs also credited the Japanese with sparking nationalism among former colonized peoples of Asia. Military authorities told him that the antiwhite wartime propaganda of the Japanese had laid a maze of "intellectual landmines" that caused the Indonesian war for independence. He learned that the hold foreigners once had over Asians would be difficult if not impossible to reestablish.[93]

Charles Loeb sent back a vastly different picture of the Japanese and their reactions to the black troops among the occupation forces. On the same day that the *Afro-American* carried Tubbs' recommendation that African Americans keep their distance, Charles Loeb's column appeared in the *Pittsburgh Courier* revealing that "inhabitants of the Tokyo-Yokohama area are rapidly becoming accustomed to the ebony faces of Negro troops" and "their initial awe and unconcealed curiosity is being replaced by friendly overtures." He wrote of Japanese stevedores in Yokohama, who worked under the supervision of black noncommissioned officers, "exchanging Japanese words and phrases for a collection of pure Harlemese."[94]

Loeb interviewed members of the 4095th Quartermaster Service Company who had visited with several Japanese families. The soldiers told him that they had been welcomed "with the greatest cordiality and extreme politeness." They drank tea and listened to the screechy family phonograph at one home. Two of the recordings were of the Jimmie Lunceford orchestra. "We have encountered not the slightest sign that the Japanese regard us as anything but Americans," a private from Chicago told Loeb. This private and his companions agreed that "such a situation is almost payment for having to stay in this neck of the world when we'd all like to be on the way back home, Jim Crow to the contrary notwithstanding."[95]

Loeb was more tolerant of the social interests of the soldiers than was Tubbs. "Tan Yanks get most friendly reception from natives in rural areas," he found. Soldiers told him of their visits to Japanese homes; the GI took field rations, and the Japanese host provided "scalding hot tea and occasionally a rare bottle of beer or saki." Loeb reported that the military authorities were alarmed at what they perceived to be the promiscuous "fraternization" between the army of occupation and indigenous persons of Japan. Loeb, in his column, even told where the girls could be found.[96]

Both Tubbs and Loeb commented on the aftermath of the war, the bitter poverty, the widespread devastation. Both seemed impressed by the clash of the twentieth century and ancient Japan. One, obviously seduced by the convenience and life-style of the rear-echelon correspondent, saw little value in cultivating personal relationships between African Americans and Japanese. The other went out in the field and found African Americans and Japanese already engaged in peeling away layers of cultural difference, forming friendships that were healthy, normal, and lasting. The war with Japan ended as it had begun with African Americans looking at Japan and seeing different things.

In summary, after Pearl Harbor, in the time of the United State's greatest crisis, not all black Americans took to the warpath pleading for the granting of deferred citizenship rights. Although this ultimately became the response of the greatest number of black Americans, there were significant numbers of African Americans who were unwilling to regard the Japanese as their enemies. In response to segregation, discrimination, and lynchings, even African Americans who were unprepared to desert America could dream of a common consciousness that would bind together the colored peoples of the world; this was a notion actively encouraged by some Japanese.

It was most significant that conferees drawn from representative black leadership groups felt that they were unable to endorse wholeheartedly their nation's involvement in the war with Japan. George Schuyler explained why: the masses were skeptical and cynical regarding the war. Military commanders and OWI polls confirmed this. Amongst African Americans there were some who were persuaded that they would not be any worse off under the suzerainty of the Japanese; many of these people cheered reports of Japanese victories.

Black leaders denounced this radical element. Yet, at the same time, these leaders articulated some of the same themes as the radicals: Japan's attack on Pearl Harbor was in retaliation for past injustice and discrimination; the war against Japan was a race war.

Horace Cayton in his analysis of black attitudes toward the Japanese had articulated the view that African Americans had a psychological identification with the Japanese that allowed them to empathize with the plight of the Japanese, whether they were incarcerated U.S. citizens or those who warred against the United States. Thus, with the end of the war, many African Americans emerged ready and eager for reconciliation with the Japanese.

⊠⊠⊠⊠⊠

SEVEN

SHOCKWAVES
OUT OF JAPAN

I n September 1986 former Prime Minister Yasuhiro Nakasone
told members of his ruling Liberal Democratic party that the
presence of African Americans, Puerto Ricans, and Mexicans
was responsible for a decline in "American intelligence levels."
Two years later, Michio Watanabe accused blacks of being congen-
itally unconcerned about paying off debts. Then in September 1990,
Seiroku Kajiyama, at that time the justice minister, attributed the
flight of shoppers and business people from Shinjuku, an area of
Tokyo, to an increase in prostitution. He claimed that this was
comparable to the exodus of whites from cities in the United States
due to increasing numbers of blacks moving into certain neighborhoods. This chorus of antiblack rhetoric usually associated with
the most conservative of white Americans when uttered by prominent Japanese officials struck black communities of the United
States like an earthquake followed by a succession of aftershocks.
As a result, African American opinion regarding Japan split as never
before: some came to view Japan as a land of racists; others visited
and found it to be a land of cordiality, challenge, and great opportunity.

American newspapers duly reported the various faux pas committed by the Japanese politicians; discriminatory business prac-

tices of Japanese companies operating in the United States, the perpetuation of stereotypical black images as motifs on everything from beach towels to handbags, discrimination of immigrant laborers, mainly Iranians and Pakistanis, and indigeneous minorities in Japan. The *New York Times*, although not known for its coverage of the ancient sport of sumo, even reported an alleged remark by Konishiki, the huge Hawaiian-born sumo wrestler, that his failure to gain the topmost rank of *yokozuna* was because he was not Japanese.[1]

These revelations, coming as they did in seemingly rapid succession, struck African American communities of the United States like an earthquake followed by a series of aftershocks. With the changed circumstances of both themselves and the Japanese following World War II, African Americans paid much less attention to Japan than they had.

The reasons for their paying reduced attention to Japan are not difficult to understand. First, African American interest in international relations often has been shaped by the racial milieu at home. Thus, the attention span of African Americans has been episodic. Second, black coverage of Japan reflected the degree to which African Americans were preoccupied with agitation for their own equality of rights and opportunity in the United States. Finally, Japan had lost the war in a dramatic and devastating way.

In the era of segregation, a few African Americans dreamed of a foreign power that would emerge as the "savior of the colored races." Following the civil rights movement era African Americans did not look for a foreign savior to rescue them from the morass of the American racial system. When compared to the attention they paid to Japan between 1905 and 1945, African Americans virtually ignored the Japanese until Nakasone caught their attention, and once they looked again across the Pacific, African Americans tended to view the Japanese negatively and stereotypically because that was the way they were viewed by Americans generally.

Before Nakasone bestirred them, one major source of information regarding Japan was the reminiscences of black soldiers who had been stationed there. Many African American writers seemed especially pleased to relate instances when the Japanese showed an interest in or fascination with aspects of black culture. Actually, this theme predated the end of the war and continued long after it. Even during the 1940s, black ex-POWs told of their efforts to introduce Japanese to jazz, boogie woogie, and "chittlins." In the 1950s, *Ebony* magazine ran several articles about blacks in

Japan. One story was an account of an enlisted man who could "live like a king" as a member of the U.S. Army in Japan. In stories such as this, writers presented African Americans as benevolent and the Japanese as initially curious and distant but finally won over to accept the tanned Yanks as warm, fun-loving human beings.

One article focused on the irresponsibility of some black GIs. It was a story about a Japanese mother who was abandoned when her lover returned to the States. Alone, dying of tuberculosis, and impoverished, she was forced to give up her daughter to the Saunders Home for adoption. The series ended on a happier note when a black Samaritan from California, upon reading of the plight of the forlorn mother, decided to send her a portion of his retirement check.

There were stories about African Americans who went to Japan as celebrities or gained celebrity status after arrival as entertainers, musicians, television personalities, or sports figures. Don Newcombe, pitcher for the Brooklyn Dodgers, the third black player on their roster, went to play in Japan.

One hot topic was intermarriage between African Americans and Japanese. Of particular interest were the circumstances of the children of such relationships. African Americans often were distressed to learn that the offspring of such affairs faced a life of discrimination.

In the 1960s, *Ebony* carried an article about the popularity of Afro hair styles, the dashiki, and soul music. Of course, these cultural trends appealed largely to successive generations of Japan's youth. Most recently, in music, rappers and reggae have captured the attention of a great many Japanese young people. Concerts attract unbelievably large crowds, prompting one promoter to refer to Japan as "the money-store." Some might just as easily refer to Japan as "the tanning salon." More fashion-conscious than healthwise, many Japanese youngsters spend long hours and much money trying to get a deep tan that they think necessary to match their "hip-hop" look, braids, fades, or dredlocks.

In the 1950s, Mabel and Hugh Smythe, an academic couple who taught and did research in Japan, wrote more scholarly articles about Japanese society and cultural practices. Among the issues that captured their attention, the Smythes found the prejudice, discrimination, and even segregation of the *Burakumin*, Ainu, and Koreans as irrational and intractable as the system of racial subordination in their own country. In the 1990s John Russell, an anthropologist from Harvard and Harlem, not only researches popular attitudes in Japan but also shares his findings with the Japanese in their own language.

The images of Japanese held by most African Americans are less likely the result of GI reminiscence and a few articles that once appeared in the black media. Hollywood and a largely white media are more likely to be the sources of African American images of Japanese. The same media that is largely responsible for projecting a negative image of African Americans abroad also casts Japanese in a negative way. Today, Hollywood often portrays Japanese in the role of villain. Japanese villainy stirred emotions in the highly popular "kiddie movie," *Teenage Mutant Ninja Turtles*. In two movies that starred Dolph Lungren, *High Plains Drifter* and *The Punisher*, and one with Michael Douglas, *Black Rain*, Japanese criminals were so menacing that mafia types were portrayed as innocuous by comparison. Who can forget the scene where the *yakuza* bad guy walks into a New York restaurant, in the middle of the day, and calmly cuts the throat of an adversary who is sitting at a table with members of the mafia? In *Kinjite*, a movie that starred Charles Bronson, a Japanese businessman was preoccupied with adultery, kinky sex, and pedophilia. In *Rising Sun*, Wesley Snipes and Sean Connery matched wits with Japanese businessmen who believed conducting business was the same as fighting a war. In that movie, businessmen and *yakuza*, the so-called Japanese mafia, were indistinguishable. A television pilot, *Raven*, in June 1992 tried to resurrect the most sinister imagery that struck fear in the hearts of whites of the 1930s and 1940s. The plot called for Black Dragon Society ninja warriors to team with *yakuza*. In their attempts to defeat this loathsome combination both in *Raven* and in the *Punisher*, the heroes had to team with mafia bosses. Hollywood is even more harsh on African Americans, producing many more movies that portray them as heavies.

High government officials often speak of the relationship between the United States and Japan as the most important bilateral relationship in the world; however, the media attention Japan receives belies that assessment. The general coverage of Japan in the American media pays less attention to the many areas of economic cooperation and mutual interest. Attention to culture and society is so superficial that Japan is still caricatured as a land of economic giants and kimono-wearing geisha. The president of the American Journalism Foundation, as recently as May 1997, warned that "ordinary Americans hear nothing about those areas of mutually reinforcing partnership of shared U.S. and Japanese interests."[2]

Bombarded with anti-Japanese propaganda, without the counterpoints once offered by Du Bois, Cayton, Johnson, and others, African Americans are quite as liable to accept the image of Japanese as people intent on "giving us the business."[3] Although Nakasone, Watanabe, and Kajiyama were not the first Japanese to speak disparagingly of African Americans, previously blacks were less inclined to view the personal statements of politicians as representative of the attitudes of all Japanese. On the one hand, due to their own experiences with politicians in the United States, African Americans tended to see the statements of politicians as very individualistic; on the other hand, African Americans regarded the Japanese as allies in the struggle against white supremacy.

Today, in the African American community of the United States there is considerable hostility toward Japanese. The Joint Center for Political and Economic Studies, America's sole African American think tank, in April 1991 issued the results of a survey designed to find out the attitudes black Americans had regarding Japanese and issues affecting U.S.-Japan relations. The survey was designed to answer the questions: What opinions do blacks have about Japanese? Do white and black Americans hold the same opinions about Japanese? On what subjects might they differ?

More black Americans than white Americans described their attitudes toward Japanese as "very favorable," but 25 percent of the African American respondents viewed Japanese negatively. Fully 47 percent of them believed that Japanese companies were more discriminatory toward African Americans than American companies.

Even without the pedagogical essays by people such as Du Bois, African Americans remain more reluctant than white Americans to view Japanese negatively. According to a second survey conducted by the Joint Center in 1992, blacks indicated a desire to get to know the Japanese and felt that if Japanese were to learn more about them relations would improve.

Contemporary black leaders have a different agenda than leaders of the past, and they insist that Japanese leaders be more sophisticated about matters of race. Two of the driving forces behind the effort to hold Japan accountable for the utterances of its politicians have been former California representative Mervyn Dymally and Albert Nellum, of the Washington-based Black Business Council. They have been particularly interested in trying to encourage Japanese to be more amenable to establishing entrepreneurial ties with African Americans. Dymally, while chairman of the Congressional Black Caucus (CBC), issued an eleven-point code of conduct urging Japanese companies to hire, promote, and do more business with black Americans and other minorities. According to one analyst, in order to bring real pressure to bear on Japanese businesses, Dymally needed to fan protectionist sentiment or tie his issue to one that had wide bipartisan support. Dymally called on blacks to select American products over those made in Japan to protest what he termed "Japanese insensitivity to black Americans." He said that he spoke for a National Black Leadership Summit, which included the Congressional Black Caucus, the NAACP, the Southern Christian Leadership Conference, the Urban League, and the Black Business Council. Both the National Urban League and the CBC threatened to lead a boycott of Japanese goods because of the slurs. Although he realized flirting with protectionism would benefit neither his black constituents nor Japanese, Dymally and his allies continued this tactic through mere frustration. "After almost two years, we feel somewhat betrayed," Albert Nellum lamented. "We asked Japan for more US jobs, business partnerships, Japanese investment dollars, and import auto franchises. Instead, we've been talked, tea-cupped and bowed to death." The unfavorable views of these respondents were at odds with what had been a strong tendency for African Americans historically to see Japanese in a much more positive light. Even during World War II, support for Japan in the black media was such that the government contemplated censoring what it called an "agitational press," and a survey conducted by the Office of War Information determined that nearly one half the respondents believed that victory by Japan would not be so bad.[4]

What caused this significant change in black opinion regarding the Japanese? First, simply speaking, times had changed; there were improvements in domestic circumstances. With these domestic changes, the fortunes of blacks improved remarkably. The changed circumstances of African Americans did not bode well for continued interest in Japan as a counterfoil to white racism. As they came to believe their condition was improving in the United States, African Americans identified with their white fellow citizens more resolutely. Believing the system more responsive than in the past, African Americans found less need to look abroad for allies in their struggle for equality. Understanding that today, more than in the past, most Americans do share the notion that equality of opportunity is a birthright of all citizens, African Americans became more willing to look at Japan from the point of view of its relationship with the United States rather than in terms of its impact on a re-ordering of racial hegemony in the world. The improved status of African Americans in the United States, the internment of the system of segregation, and the relative decline of overt racism all contributed to making African Americans more distant from the Japanese. The civil rights movement of the 1960s was particularly important: prejudice and discrimination within their own country became less blatant, and more job opportunities opened up. Particularly with their inclusion in the labor movement, more people were removed from the poverty lists and moved into the ranks of the middle class. Those who went unaffected by these improvements in status became candidates for the Nation of Islam or other black nationalist groups. Most African Americans, however, saw less need to seek overseas allies in the struggle against domestic discrimination. With a reduction in the racial animosities that had divided them from white Americans, African Americans were more inclined to respond to events as Americans.

Furthermore, the circumstances that once allowed African Americans to identify with Japanese became less apparent. Few people were likely to see Japanese as underdogs in the world community. The resurgence and superpower status of Japan as an economic competitor allowed few African Americans to see their circumstances as in any way analogous to that of the Japanese. Also, African American leaders were disinclined to forgive and forget the blunders of Japanese politicians, partially because they viewed them as arrogant and overbearing. When the role of the media is so fundamentally important to the shaping of African American attitudes toward Japan, the demise of the black press is particularly lamentable.

Black entrepreneurs like their white counterparts sought more economic opportunities with the Japanese. Some imagined the antiblack comments of leading Japanese politicians and actions of major business organizations could be used as a crowbar to extract certain economic concessions. This strategy prompted broad cooperation among representative groups of African Americans. Members of the Congressional Black Caucus joined with the National Association for the Advancement of Colored People, the National Urban Leaue, the Southern Christian Leadership Conference, and the Black Business Council of Washington, D.C., in denouncing Japanese racism.

At the same time, representatives of African American interests, elected and self-appointed, advised the Japanese that doing business with black American consumers made good business sense. They pointed out the tremendous buying power of African American consumers. They reminded Japanese officials that black consumers have a high propensity to buy the kinds of consumer-oriented products for which the Japanese are noted. Drawing upon their domestic experience in fighting for access, black leaders also threatened to push for a boycott of Japanese goods unless certain demands were met. Automobile franchises, personal loans, and employment and hiring practices of Japanese companies operating in the United States were areas targeted as in need of particular improvement.

A study by University of Michigan researchers Robert E. Cole and Donald R. Deskins, Jr., showed that Japanese car manufacturers and suppliers located most of their new American plants far away from African American population centers and hired blacks at rates well below their representation in the local populations. In Ohio, Honda employed African Americans at the ridiculously low rate of 5.1 percent. Although the two academics hesitated, saying that their data did not establish intent to discriminate because of the complexity of the factors involved, Cole and Deskins did conclude that a range of anecdotal data suggested that the Japanese auto manufacturers had a "taste for discrimination."[5]

Japanese bankers in California seemed to have just as healthy an appetite for discrimination. Community advocacy groups accused the five largest Japanese-owned banks in California of virtually ignoring the credit needs of low-income African Americans and Hispanics in 1990. Mitsui, Mitsubishi, Sanwa, Sumitomo, and the Bank of Tokyo violated community reinvestment laws that required banks to meet the credit needs of surrounding communities. Low-income African Americans and Hispanics received just twenty-eight home loans, totaling $1.3 million, from the five Japanese banks, while the domestic-owned Bank of America made 708 such loans during the same period. In 1990 the five Japanese banks made a total of 68 loans to African Americans, 224 to Hispanics, and 513 to Asian Americans. The Bank of Tokyo made 547 of these loans. Mitsui made no loans to African Americans. African Americans received 2 from Mitsubishi, 1 from Sanwa, and 2 from Sumitomo. By contrast, the Bank of America made 13,000 or twenty-two times the number of loans to minorities.[6]

Japanese bankers and businessmen evidently did not realize that African Americans were among the most loyal purchasers of Japanese-made automobiles, televisions, videorecorders, Walkmans, VCRs, and other consumer goods for which Japanese are famous. Considering how important a clientele for Japanese consumer products they were, African Americans had a right to expect the kind of cordiality and respect Japanese routinely bestow on their customers at home. Somehow, in the United States, Japanese had difficulty relating to African American customers. For the most part, Japanese retailers did not advertise in black-owned media, recruit on the campuses of historically black colleges and universities, or use black businesses in any major way. Consequently, a group of black businessmen, in October 1986, paid $68,000 to run a full-page ad in major daily newspapers around the country. They pointed out that although African Americans spent $7 billion buying Japanese goods and services, little profit from those sales benefited black distributers, sales representatives, media, educational institutions, communities, or businesses. Andrew Young and Tom Bradley were among those frustrated with seeming intransigence on the part of Japanese political and business leaders.

In a way, Japanese business people who seek to emulate conservative models of American business practices relative to dealing with minorities are, to use a Lyndon Johnson expression, "caught between a rock and a hard place." First, American business practices relative to minorities have been undergoing change. Second, enforcement agencies seem more aggressive in making Japanese companies toe the line where American law is concerned. Finally, minorities will not meekly allow foreigners to get away with practices that they find odious in American companies. Japanese companies that have faced sex or race bias lawsuits include Sumitomo Corporation of America, C Itoh and Company, Nikko Securities International, Honda of America, Nissan Motor Corporation, and Toyota Motor Sales USA.

In 1991, Rep. Tom Lantos(D-CA) chaired hearings of the House Government Operations Committee in Washington and Seattle to investigate complaints of sexual and racial bias. Lantos believed that there appeared to be a pattern of discriminatory employment practices unique to Japanese companies in the United States. He also observed that the bulk of the top managerial positions at Japanese companies are reserved for Japanese nationals who come and go on a rotating basis from Japan, usually for two or three years. Lantos' hearings revealed that the Itoh Company made little effort to recruit, hire, or promote minorities. Taking affirmative action in an effort to employ a diverse work force was obviously an alien concept for some Japanese companies. In San Francisco, a white former vice-president and manager of the San Diego branch of the Dai-Ichi Kangyo Bank testified regarding that bank's hiring policy. He said that a Japanese senior executive instructed him that a proper profile for a loan officer position meant no women or blacks.[7]

This pattern of discrimination was confirmed by another white former assistant vice-president at the Sanwa Bank of California. A black woman was hired as a telecommunications systems engineer at Sanwa. When she was introduced to a Japanese executive, he refused to shake her hand and left the room. Asked about his behavior, the Japanese executive mumbled, "Black woman, black woman" and shook his head.[8]

Pearl McCoy, a black woman fired after eighteen months as an assistant vice president in charge of data processing deposits for Sanwa Bank of California, said her Japanese manager told her "the reason blacks couldn't get ahead was because we were lazy." McCoy testified to working between twelve and fourteen-hour days and three weekends a month. After going sixteen months without a vacation, she was criticized for taking the two weeks due her.[9]

Annette Darnes, a vice-president and regional credit administrator for the San Francisco Bay area for the Japanese-owned Union Bank, admitted that even in the relatively happy atmosphere she enjoyed, there was need for improvement. "We need more women and minorities," she admitted. Considering that Oakland is a largely black city, she concluded that in the majority of positions blacks were underrepresented. Additionally, the manager of the branch was a white female. She observed, "There are more black males in American-owned banks."[10]

Even a person of Darnes' obvious ability encountered problems at a personal level dealing with Japanese bankers. "I was hired by a Japanese," related Darnes, "I report directly to him. I'm responsible for eleven branches. About half have Japanese managers. I do my job very well. The fact that I am a black female is not a problem." She did concede, however, that promotions might have been slower. "I have always had to work longer and wait longer, but things always came."[11]

Darnes commented on Japanese banking in America in general: Wells Fargo had a black executive vice-president, but, she said, "I don't think any Japanese bank does." She believed that Japanese did not particularly care about American workers. When the Japanese talk about lifetime employment, she concluded, "It's for the Japanese, not for us." When they need a top executive, they send a

person over from Japan. She pointed out that Mitsui had a particularly poor record when it came to promotion of women and minorities. She accused them of being uninterested in addressing affirmative action matters.[12]

Mitsui also got bad marks from Clyde Johnson, president of
the Los Angeles-based Black Employees Association. The organization had filed administrative charges against Mitsui Manufacturers'
Bank with the Federal Reserve Bank. There had been complaints
against Mitsui for terminating employees merely for being late.
According to Johnson, Japanese banks in California had no history
of hiring blacks at decision-making levels. Moreover, they hired far
fewer tellers than other banks in California.[13]

Aided sometimes by other victims, black Americans have
been aggressive in fighting the discriminatory practices of some
companies. Considering the percentage of blacks in the population,
three Honda Ohio plants had employed them at the ridiculously
low rate of 5.1 percent. As a result of a class action suit, Honda was
forced to pay $6 million to blacks and women who had been denied
jobs at the company between 1983 and 1986. These events caused
one author to write an article suggesting that racism might have
been "made in Japan."[14]

African Americans, wanting changes in Japanese business attitudes and practices, have viewed the enforcement of laws, statutes,
and regulations for doing business in the United States as one of the
best ways to affect Japanese policy decisions. One black vice-president with the Xerox corporation felt that Japanese should want to
mend fences with America's minorities purely out of economic
self-interest. He alluded to the potential buying power of minority
Americans in the year 2000, which has been estimated at between
$400 billion and $1 trillion.[15]

Another black businessman claimed that if they want to do
business with African-Americans in the future, Japanese will need
to develop new models. Until now, he asserted, Japanese businessmen have been content to use models already in place in the United
States, models that included few minorities. The Japanese business
community relied on interpreters of the American business culture
who, historically, have been unfriendly towards minorities.

The image of Japanese as racists was sharpened by reports that
Buraku, the ethnic Korean minority, and Ainu still face discrimination in employment and marriage. There were reports of racial
intolerance and xenophobia faced by tens of thousands of other
Asians and some Africans who arrived in Japan seeking the dirty

and dangerous jobs at the lower echelons of the Japanese economy. More recently, descendants of Japanese who emigrated to Peru or Brazil, who are culturally either Peruvians or Brazilians, sometimes have found that the cultural gap acts as a barrier to full acceptance in Japan.

Before Nelson Mandella became president of South Africa, a steady rise in Japanese trade with the apartheid regime, an issue that had been of considerable symbolic importance to black Americans, deepened black frustrations. Many of the Japanese firms acquired operations that had been divested by U.S. companies. These divestures occurred only after considerable pressures had been applied by anti-apartheid lobbyists. Thus, the result found American business people and minorities both angry and allied in opposition to the Japanese.

Some American newspapers carried the story of the existence of an internal police report that singled out Pakistanis for contempt. The document contained statements such as the following: "It is absolutely necessary to wash your hands after questioning or detaining Pakistani suspects because many of them suffer from contagious skin diseases." It warned, "Since they have a unique body odor, the detention and interrogation room will stink." The document went further to characterize Pakistanis as people who get mad when they are fed pork without being told and tend to "lie under the name of Allah" during interrogation.[16]

A spate of anti-Semitic books, the display of grotesque black mannequins and Sambo toys in Tokyo stores, and a rise in trade with the white minority government of South Africa all reinforced the image of Japanese intolerance. Some African Americans living in Japan have complained that Japanese refused to rent them houses or apartments or seemed reluctant to sit next to them on buses. One reason Japanese used to give was that foreigners were *batakusai*, smelled like butter.

But are Americans correct when they accuse the Japanese of being racists? Most African Americans who have spent any time in Japan would reply that the answer is not a simple "yes," particularly when they compare living in Japan with living in the United States. The Japanese definitely are not racists in the sense that most Americans understand the word. Certainly, among Japanese there is no virulent hatred of African Americans. There is not the kind of animosity that one sees daily in the United States. Those who have lived and worked in Japan for any appreciable amount of time talk of how much their expertise is appreciated by Japanese; they tell of being given opportunities that they could not dream of in their own country; they speak of the day-to-day cordiality and respect that they experience.

In the abstract, most Japanese have not met nor do they think much about African Americans, until they hear about an event like the Los Angeles riots. Whatever image they have of African Americans is largely the product of the American media. The image of African Americans among Japanese is favorable enough that Africans—whether they are from Cameroon, Sierra Leone, Nigeria, Zaire, or any other country on the continent—readily identify themselves as African Americans. So in Japan, some American blacks identify themselves as Africans, and some Africans identify themselves as Americans. White people seem to have more difficulty dealing with the Japanese and their way of categorizing people.

For Japanese, there are Japanese, and there are *gaikokujin*. *Gaikokujin* is literally translated as "people from outside the country." They are all people who are not listed in someone's family register as Japanese. The term can be used to describe even Japanese who are not from Tokyo. Some Koreans who have been living in Japan for several generations are *gaikokujin* or *gaijin*. For Japanese, the term includes all other peoples of the planet. Some people who were ethnic Japanese who went away, for example, to Manchuria, and tried to return after being away from Japan fifty years found that they were no longer regarded as Japanese unless they could find a relative willing to accept responsibility for them.

Years ago foreigners in Japan were usually accosted by children calling them "*gaijin, gaijin*." These children were not prejudiced; they were making a statement obvious to all: the person so accosted was perceptibly not Japanese. Even babies strapped to their mothers' backs have "stared" at the only black face in the crowd. Japanese can and do love and marry *gaijin*, but neither love nor marriage alters one's *gaijin* status. There are some Japanese who have no desire to associate with *gaijin*. One fellow from Australia told how an elderly Japanese man flying Japan Air Lines complained to the stewardess that he was being forced to sit next to a *gaijin*. The stewardess apologized as they are prone to do when they have committed some social error and changed the old man's seating. There was the politician who said that every time he shook hands with a black person, he felt he got a little black.[17] People of this mentality are few. Most Japanese tend to be curious about foreigners, but they are often shy about making contact. This is especially so if they feel that their English is inadequate (they rarely expect foreigners to be fluent in Japanese).

Mutual misunderstanding is the crux of the problem between African Americans and Japanese. Under the stimuli of antiblack remarks, African Americans understandably became incensed. Both African American and nonblack writers criticized the Japanese for having racist attitudes. Marcus Mabry, an associate editor at *Newsweek* magazine in Washington, D.C., writing in the *Black Collegian* called Japan a "famously racist society." He asserted that "the remarks of Japanese leaders reflect an anti-Black sentiment that permeates much of their society." Mabry argues, "Its position as an economic superpower makes Japan's racism all the more dangerous—and all the more destructive for African American economic well-being."[18]

Michael H. Cottman breezed through Japan as a part of the contingent that accompanied former New York Mayor David Dinkins to Japan and wrote a piece for *Newsday* magazine. It was carried in the *Japan Times* titled "Blacks Face Image Problem." Cottman's article illustrated the image problem facing the Japanese. He implied that Japanese were racists and said explicitly that the only images of blacks in Japan were "odious."[19]

In 1991, Michael Berger, chief of the *San Francisco Chronicle*'s Asia Bureau, wrote an article in which he asked whether the Japanese are racists. Many of those best qualified to answer the question—African Americans living in Japan—he reported, had conflicting emotions running the gamut from bitter to heart-warming. The over-all theme of the piece was that African Americans living in Japan felt at home. Individuals whom he interviewed claimed Japanese racism was real, but neither absolute nor simple. They felt that it was tempered by very real opportunity. Berger reported that one reason many blacks choose to stay in Japan is because of their perception of continuing racial problems in the United States. He interviewed people such as Robert Jefferson, who left a multiracial suburb of Philadelphia as an enlisted man in the air force. His former landlady, a Japanese woman, who told him that he was the first black person she had ever known, came to treat him like her son. Jefferson, on the basis of his experience, concluded that Japanese prejudice was largely due to ignorance. Very few Japanese have had any personal contact with black people, he realized. Canadian-born J. R. Dash also refused to make sweeping indictments. "I've met too many kind people here to believe that it's just a racist country," she said. Dash believes that ordinary

Japanese are more advanced than their leaders.[20] Regge Life, an African American film-maker, recorded similar testimonials in *Struggle and Success—The African-American Experience in Japan*, his highly acclaimed TV documentary about long-time African American residents in Japan.

Juan Williams, a columnist for the *Washington Post*, who received a fellowship from the Japan Society, an American organization dedicated to improving relations between Japan and the United States, had a chance to explore racial and ethnic issues for ten weeks in Japan. Interviewing whites, blacks, Asians, and minority groups indigenous to Japan, Williams claimed, "A portrait of the Japanese—and the way most of them relate to people who are not Japanese—began to emerge." He interviewed people who told him, "Those who have lived here a long time are ambivalent about Japan, but not negative." Declaring, "In Japan, we have gotten away from the race issue as an everyday issue," one respondent asserted, "We do feel free of race." The same individual pointed out that the negative image Japanese may have of African Americans is not based on personal experiences but on feeds from the white U.S. media. Another interviewee reported that she had no negative stories to tell. Her experiences, she claimed, were as a foreigner and thus comparable to that of other non-Japanese, including whites.[21]

Williams learned that Koreans born in Japan are regarded as Korean nationals by the Japanese government and have no political rights unless they apply for citizenship and submit to accept a Japanese name. He wrote about the *burakumin*, people relegated to the bottom of the caste system of the sixteenth century and still discriminated against. Williams was told that 150 or more Japanese companies used a book—a location register—to help them avoid hiring *burakumin*. He went to Hokkaido, the northernmost island, to talk with Ainu who are struggling to keep their language from dying out. He visited with an illegal Pakistani worker who lives a surreptitious life and bears discriminatory treatment to make money in Japan.[22]

Within Japanese society, various groups that are ethnic Japanese suffer from discrimination, not least of which are women. The top politicians and bureaucrats of Japan are overwhelmingly male. Many men believe women should work only until they have children. Companies routinely discriminate against women in hiring and promotion and set quotas for male and female hires. Periods of recession were especially bad for women who want to work. During the current recession, it was reported in the media that major companies announced that they would hire a lower percentage of women, the assumption being men as potential heads of households needed jobs more. While overall unemployment reached a postwar high of 3.4 percent, among women aged fifteen to twenty-four the figure is 7.4 percent, or more than double the average. In a company that claimed to have a good environment for women, a 28-year-old former employee revealed that at the initial orientation female workers were told that they had to report earlier than their male colleagues in order to clean all the desks in the office.

Japanese who as children were left behind in Manchuria, in practical terms, lose their Japanese citizenship unless a relative comes forward to serve as a guarantor. Hisako Kumai, sixty-three, who was born to Japanese parents and is fluent in the Japanese language, sought to return to Japan to live out her remaining years. She was raised by an aunt in Hiroshima. The primary school she went to has a record of her attendance, but because she has no family register in Japan—her father who was living in the United States neglected to have her birth registered at the Japanese consulate—the Japanese government classified her as a stateless person. She is one of many who are ethnically Japanese, but may be denied the right to live out their sunset years in Japan.

Peruvians and Brazilians who are of Japanese ancestry also have complained of discrimination. Ethnic Japanese who were invited by the Japanese government as a way of addressing the need for workers found that they were disliked because they were regarded as too culturally different. Women born in what is considered the unluckiest year of the Japanese zodiac also face discrimination. Woman born in the Fiery Horse Year, known as Hinoeuma in Japanese, a sixty-year cycle, are considered strong-willed and occasionally violent. Traditionally, they were said to be doomed to a loveless, single life, as Japanese men avoided marrying a woman with so much bad luck or a strong will.

Compared to the discrimination various groups face in Japanese society, the experiences of African Americans in Japan are not so bad. Compared to the discrimination they face in America, blacks find Japan much more compatible. The peripatetic Reverend Jesse Jackson has traveled to Japan to lecture authorities on the grievances that concern a significant number of African Americans. At the Foreign Correspondents' Club of Japan, Jackson accused the Japanese of insensitivity toward minorities. He then called upon Japanese companies to do more business with American minority-owned companies. He ticked off the statistics of black buying power. According to Jackson, at the time, blacks bought 9 percent of the videocassette recorders; 10 percent of the cameras, stereo equipment, and microwave ovens; and 12 percent of the automobiles sold in the United States. He also urged Japan to pull out of South Africa. Furthermore, at a rally in Hibiya Park, he also called attention to the continued plight of Japan's indigenous minorities.[23]

Other African Americans lashed back at the Japanese. Garland Thompson, a columnist with the *Baltimore Morning Sun* asked "whether success has drained the color from the Nippon soul." Furthermore, he observed rightly that Japan's economic power depends on people's willingness to buy and not on the existential glories of Japanese culture. The truth of this observation was illustrated by an informal survey conducted by the NAACP in October 1990, which found that two-thirds of the respondents favored boycotting Japanese products. Benjamin Hooks, the executive director of the NAACP, declared, "The voice of African Americans clearly proclaims that they have had enough insults from Japanese officials . . . and they are at the point where they are favorably disposed toward making their feelings known with their dollars."[24]

Urban League president John Jacob, speaking at a convention at Cobo Hall in Detroit, announced that he had joined with twenty-three members of the CBC in calling for an investigation of employment and business practices of Japanese firms operating in the United States. They were particularly concerned about the equal opportunity efforts made by these companies and whether lenders discriminate against blacks. The CBC also discussed drafting a bill to require minority hiring quotas at all plants owned by foreign countries receiving American military aid. Earl Graves, publisher of *Black Enterprise*, a magazine dedicated to the black entrepreneurial spirit, stated the issue simply enough that even the unsophisticated could understand: "We already import enough products from Japan, we don't need to import racism."[25]

African Americans were not alone in criticizing Japanese business practices. Proclaiming, "Prejudice is common in Japan and it reaches into high places," Carol Schwalberg enumerated practices that made Japanese look bad in America. She began by telling why Japanese bigotry was of such concern to most African-Americans: now that the Japanese have exported part of their banking, commercial and manufacturing operations to the US, Japanese-owned firms provide about 300,000 jobs. Drawing on Takeshi Yabe's *Japanese Companies Discriminate* (1991), she pointed out that the largest Japanese-owned firms in the United States have paid at least

$12 million since January 1988 to settle civil rights lawsuits. In 1990, the U.S. Equal Opportunity Employment Commission filed documents showing that Interplace and Recruit Company, two employment agencies partly owned by Japanese firms, used code words to identify workers by race, sex, and age, and regularly avoided referring workers in certain categories. Their operations were shut down by court order.[26]

Fortunately, some individuals and groups recognized the need for direct communication between black Americans and Japanese. The Joint Center for Political and Economic Studies, the distinguished black think tank in Washington, D.C., once operated a United States–Japan Project, in its effort to build bridges of understanding between African Americans and Japanese. The Japan Society also acknowledged the need to address the issue of race in Japan. It co-hosted with the Joint Center a series of symposia and public forums on the subject in 1991. Kathryn D. Leary, a telecommunications entrepreneur in New York, began to publish a monthly newsletter *Japan Watch*. Leary hoped to provide resource information on Japan and the Pacific Rim that might prove of particular interest to black subscribers.

One of the highlights of the New York symposium was the address made by William H. Gray III, former majority whip of the U.S. House of Representatives and current president and chief executive officer of the United Negro College Fund. Gray alluded to the "shock," "unbelievable feeling of despair," and "outrage" so many blacks felt at learning of affronts such as Nakasone's gaff, Sambo dolls, and discriminatory hiring practices. More optimistically, however, he spoke of the need for the development of a plan to encourage grassroots level contact and expressed the hope that Japanese and African Americans might cooperate regarding certain key issues—such as South Africa and foreign aid. Gray's suggestion of more exchange programs as an aspect of grass roots contact, especially between historically black colleges and universities (HBCUs) and Japanese universities, had already begun. Clark Atlanta University, Dillard University, Johnson C. Smith University, Morehouse College, Xavier University, Hampton University, and Spelman College all sought to establish some kind of exchange programs.

Today, the African Americans who come to Japan are coming in different capacities than previously. No longer are they merely military, athletes, or entertainers; more are coming as professors, university students, business people, lawyers, and diplomats. They will allow the Japanese to see African Americans operating in non-stereotypical capacities.

Some of these people will make a significant contribution to African American and Japanese relations by pointing out some of the ambivalence. They may help Japanese to become more sensitive to issues important to nonwhites. At the same time, they may do what Du Bois and others did in the past, that is, help homebound African Americans to see Japanese as more than economic animals.

Anthropologist John Russell has tried to help Japanese to understand that stereotypical representations of blacks found in Japanese comic books, on television shows, and in other popular media are first, offensive, and second, no longer to escape notice. Russell, who now teaches as a member of the faculty at Gifu University in Japan, wrote a book informing the Japanese how offensive are the stereotypical images of black people found in the popular culture.

Two participants at the New York symposium related their personal reactions to Japan after brief visits. Leary, the communications consultant, went to Japan with her daughter. In an article written for *Essence* magazine, she admitted that she went to Japan with trepidation but returned with a strongly positive impression of the Japanese.[27]

A president of one of the historically black universities, who spent time in Japan as a recipient of a Japan Society Leadership Fellowship, declared that sojourn to be three of the best months of his life. He spoke of his trips into the countryside, unescorted and incognito. He had nothing but high praise for the cordiality of the people he met. A black law professor who specializes in Japanese constitutional law spoke of similar jaunts and similar reactions. He said that he made it a point to go with his family to out-of-the-way places. Other than natural curiosity, he and his family had no negative encounters. On the contrary, he said that he felt a greater sense of personal safety for himself, his wife, and two daughters in Japan than in the United States.

Comparing their experience in Japan to what they had known in white corporate America or even in academia, several black professionals expressed the view that Japanese show greater respect for their professional competence. This perception of Japan as a land of opportunity was strong enough among some black Americans that they decided to make it their home. The image of Japan as a country where a black person can live a good life is one quite at variance with the picture of Japan widely held in black America. On May 15,

1993, NHK's BS-1 aired Regge Life's "Struggle and Success—the African American Experience in Japan." The people featured in the film were all long-time residents who found Japan to be a land of cordiality, challenge, and opportunity.

Russell summed up the reason some African-Americans could live in Japan for more than thirty years. They were people who saw "Japan as full of opportunity" and viewed its racism as "no worse and less virulent than that of the United States," he pointed out.

Although Japan is considered a male chauvinist country, particularly when considering the underemployment of women, African American women also have found challenge and opportunity enough to make a home there. Karen Hill-Anton has a column, "Crossing Cultures," in the *Japan Times*, in which she writes of the daily casual life experiences that she and her children have in a small village, and it is clear that her neighbors have accepted them as members of the community, with the rights, privileges, and obligations that that entails.

Teresa Williams, who once taught at the Showa Women's University and Tsuda College, in the magazine *African Commentary*, explained why she thought some blacks were attracted to life in Japan: they form an immense attachment to the "Japanese way of getting things done" and the "Japanese aesthetic."[28]

In Japan, some blacks and Japanese work to promote better understanding and more positive relations as members of the Japan African Descendants American Friendship Association(JAFA) or the Japan Institute for Globalism (JAIG).[29] The former group was founded by African Americans and its membership tends to be mostly black. JAIG is a Japanese organization. Whereas JAFA functioned primarily as a mutual support group, JAIG is more educational. The two groups tend to support the other's programs. Their is some overlap in membership; at one time the president of JAIG was a vice-president of JAFA.

In the final analysis, Japanese firms that antagonize black consumers do themselves a serious disservice, precisely because African American consumers have a high propensity to buy the kinds of products for which the Japanese manufacturers are noted, goods of high quality that sell at affordable prices. Politicians who step on their tongues embarrass not only themselves but also the people they presume to represent. Some Japanese companies now understand that a social conscience can benefit corporate interest. Conceivably, the politicians also will realize that the cost benefits from learning tolerance will proliferate. Images derived from negative encounters over hiring and employment practices are difficult to eradicate and costly.

As we move into the twenty-first century, Japan will assume a position of real leadership in the international arena, so Japanese must be able to work in harmony with peoples from all over the globe. Therefore, the recurring spasms of intolerance must be eliminated.

Percy Luney became interested in Japan because he saw that Japanese in Africa were much more sensitive to the cultures, needs, and aspirations of Africans than Americans or Europeans. As Luney witnessed, the Japanese are quite able to adapt to the social environment in which they find themselves operating. Adaptability is a necessary prerequisite for people aspiring to be tradesmen to the world. In an interview with Juan Williams, Nakasone admitted that he and some of his colleagues had embarrassed themselves because of their ignorance of racial matters.[30] Except for unrepentant conservatives, Japanese in high places will work to avoid future embarrassments.

⌘⌘⌘⌘

EPILOGUE

Between 1900 and 1945, African American views of the Japanese went through a series of stages: before 1904, there was little awareness of the Japanese except to see them as remote, somewhat exotic, and progressive people; during the Russo-Japanese War, blacks came to focus on the Japanese as colored people who might overthrow white hegemony, demonstrating the fallacy of notions of white superiority; from 1906 to 1919, virulent racist attacks underscored the reality that blacks and Japanese were fellow victims of racism in America; during the 1920s and 1930s, important blacks observed, empathized, and reached out to the Japanese as partners in the struggle to overturn white dominance; many Japanese seemed to reciprocate; when war broke out between Japan and the United States, some blacks unhesitatingly closed ranks with white Americans, and other black Americans pondered whether or not to acquiesce to an anti-Japanese sentiment during this critical period.

Some scholars have studied African American interests regarding Jews, Jamaicans, Haitians, Liberians, Ethiopians, and Africans generally. This study moves into virgin territory in its focus on the attitudes of African Americans toward the Japanese; it breaks new ground in the attention it pays to views expressed by certain lower class blacks who ran afoul of the FBI and the American national security apparatus. By doing so, they also became objects of ridicule, disdain, and embarrassment as far as their leadership class was concerned.

Within the broad range of black opinion, the Japanese enjoyed favorable reviews with a consistency that is somewhat surprising, considering the great divide that separated elites from nonelites, radicals from conservatives, northerners from southerners, urbanites from their country cousins, black nationalists from integrationists. In a way, African American infatuation with the Japanese and their accomplishments was both rational and logical; many blacks thought Japan's success had important meaning for the racial struggle in the United States. From the period of the Russo-Japanese War, the struggles of the Japanese in the arena of international politics underscored the notion that the fight against racism was but a facet of a worldwide movement. From this time, African American commentators cheered the Japanese as a brown people. Different black intellectuals could point to the achievements of the Japanese to support themes either of protest or of accomodation. But the African American elite overwhelmingly respected the Japanese for standing up to white aggression. In doing so, the elite helped shape the thinking of a segment of the black population who would cling even more tenaciously to the image of the Japanese as fighters against white hegemony. The most alienated blacks remained pro-Japanese after most of the bourgeois elite who wrote or talked about the subject judiciously backed away from the logic of their rhetoric. While middle-class types reaffirmed their loyalty, members of the lower strata of the black community applauded Pearl Harbor and other reports of Japanese victories.

Interestingly, those blacks usually identified as having the strongest attachment for Africa—the most alienated from American society, those with little voice within the black subculture—were inclined to see Japan as an even more "realistic" focus for their aspirations. Japan was nonwhite, strong, competitive with the other powers, not hobbled by white imperialism or colonialism, and had already humbled one of the great powers of Europe.

The support Japan enjoyed among African Americans was so broad and so strong that during the period of America's greatest crisis there was divided opinion in the black community regarding whether or not blacks should even support their country's involvement in World War II. Black leaders understood that among the black masses there was a strong sense that Japanese were colored people who were also being victimized by white racism. OWI polls supported the view that blacks were indifferent toward the war, but the surveys also revealed that many of those who were indifferent were members of the black middle class. The black elite shared with the masses the suspicion that the war was at root a matter of race, that Pearl Harbor was a retaliatory strike for past injustices.

Yet the extent to which some African Americans opposed fighting the Japanese was allowed to fade into memory. The most ordinary and alienated members of the black community were dismissed as lunatics for thinking that America would never grant them equality of opportunity and that perhaps they ought to cast their lot with the equally despised Japanese. The middle class or aspiring elite continued to dream that someday, somehow they would be integrated into white society and granted full citizenship rights. After Japan's defeat, leaders of black America wanted to forget how tenuous their hold was on the allegiance of the masses, and they wanted white Americans to remember only a record of black loyalty in the wars of America's past.

Robert Jordan epitomized those people who were so alienated from the mainstream of American society that they were unresponsive to the exhortations and cajolery of the black leadership. These were people who continued to march to Garvey's cadences, not those of the NAACP or National Urban League.

A contemporary of Elijah Muhammad, Jordan might be viewed even more as the spiritual forebear of Malcolm X: both were voices of what Peter Goldman has called "that estranged backstreet black community" in Harlem; each used demagoguery as a legitimate means of struggle against white America; each embraced his African past while identifying with the dark majority of the world; each rhetorically endorsed armed struggle as a legitimate weapon of liberation; both challenged the established leadership claiming the allegiance of "a ghetto lumpenproletariat" that the middle-class leaders talked about and around but never reached. Both sought international help in forcing America to redress black people's grievances. In Jordan's day, Japan seemed the best hope for achieving this; Malcolm X sought assistance from the United Nations and the Organization of African Unity.[1]

The black elite was very successful in expurgating the Jordan story from the chronicles of history. This has been a recurring phenomenon: the voices of black radicalism reach a decibel count at which they become obtrusive; in response, the moderate elite with the support of the white establishment rallies to dampen the clamor because they consider it the reasonable thing to do, much as they did on August 28, 1963, at the "second March on Washington" when John Lewis, of the Student Non-violent Coordinating Committee, proposed making a caustic critique of the Kennedy administration's record on civil rights.

The relationship between the black elite and the masses has been complex. Although they rejected what they perceived to be the extreme positions of people such as Jordan, Mittie Maud Gordon, or Elijah Muhammad, the black elite had helped shape these opinions by their espousal of the positiveness of Japan's rise to world power status. It was the members of the elite who interpreted Japan's position in the realm of international politics, articulated what the rise of Japan meant for race relations, and told blacks how they ought to feel about the Japanese.

The story of African American views of the Japanese between 1900 and 1945 was not merely a tale of sycophantic adoration. Some blacks were critical of what they perceived to be the race chauvinism of the Japanese; especially when there were the occasional negative references to blacks, African Americans complained of brown men aping whites. Many condemned the oppression of the Koreans and the massacre of Chinese. A few perceived the racial equality issue raised by Japan before the League of Nations in 1919 as solely a concern for the equal treatment of Japanese.

Blacks also were not devoid of certain self-serving interests as when some of them attempted to mount a campaign to introduce black migrant farmers into California as replacements for the Americans of Japanese descent who had been interned in American-style concentration camps. The NAACP, the premier organization dedicated to the advocacy and the preservation of civil rights, chose to stand aloof during this period when the constitutional rights of Japanese-Americans were grossly violated.

Despite the occasional disparaging remark, black perceptions of the Japanese were much more positive than negative. Where the Japanese were concerned blacks seemed to display an abiding interest. When looking at the Japanese functioning in the international arena, blacks generally reached conclusions based on their perceptions as to how events related to the issue of race.

In the 1930s Yasuichi Hikida, a sojourner in black America, observed that African Americans and Japanese had distorted views of each other because each group received its information about the other through the filter of a white media. Hikida's observation is as valid today as it was then.

Yet none of these changes needed to cause blacks to look at Japanese in an unfavorable light. Japanese politicians, business men operating in the United States, and Japanese retailers in Japan helped to accomplish this. The remarks of three prominent Japanese politicians were most significant in persuading black Americans that Japanese generally were racists. Nakasone, Watanabe, and Kajiyama made remarks that were widely regarded as evidence of Japanese racism. Anthropologist John Russell suggests that the Japanese perception of blacks has been "heavily influenced by Western values and racial paradigms, imported along with Dutch learning and Western science." I suspect that an association with twelve years of Republican administrations had more to do with shaping the prejudiced views that some Japanese politicians expressed regarding black Americans and other minorities than the period in Japanese history characterized by their learning from the Dutch.

Certain traditional attitudes toward indigeneous minority groups within Japan and a strong belief in the homogeneity of the Japanese people might have contributed to the way significant numbers of politicians and business people view minorities in the United States. But in the final analysis, Americans have been the most important influence on the development of Japanese attitudes toward American minorities. With the inauguration of Richard Nixon as president of the United States, the executive branch of the American government moved away from policies that appeared to address the particular needs of a large segment of the black population, as Nixon pursued a "southern strategy" in his effort to break the Democrats' lock on the most conservative and most antiblack region of the American electorate. Presidents Ronald Reagan and George Bush continued to appeal to the most conservative instincts of Americans when drafting policies.

In my view, these developments in the American body politic were much more important than the Rangaku period in Japanese history in shaping discriminatory policies of Japanese companies operating in the United States toward minorities and women. There is no doubt that in Japan indigenous minorities and women know discrimination. Yet, if Professor Luney's observations in Africa are accurate, Japanese are able and willing to adapt to the environment in which they find themselves. They are evidently interested in operating in Africa. The Japanese government was among the first to recognize the new Democratic Republic of the Congo. During the same period that Jesse Jackson berated the

Japanese for not divesting in white-ruled South Africa, Jerry Matsila, as the representative of the African National Congress, lived in Japan raising money from private Japanese groups for his cause. Worried about future relations between Japanese and black South Africans in the inevitable post-apartheid period, Nakasone and Oliver Tambo, president of the ANC, had arranged to have a resident representative of the ANC in Japan.

While criticizing the infelicities of the Japanese, John Russell also has denounced the American media for its holier than thou attitude. The media praised itself for overcoming prejudice and discrimination and praised the multiethnicity of American society. Yet the images of African Americans emanating from the American media had to leave Japanese as well as other foreigners with the impression that black Americans are indolent, licentious, and felonious welfare cheats.

Negative images of African Americans in the American media may be the single most important reason for the image of African Americans projected abroad. Ishmael Reed, chairman of the media committee of PEN Oakland, a branch of the international writers' group that fights censorship, analyzed the content of prime time network news and concluded that it relentlessly presents negative news coverage of African Americans and Hispanic Americans. He asserts, "More often than not, they associate black and Hispanic people exclusively with drugs, crime, unwed parenthood, welfare, homelessness, child abuse, and rape. The American media tends to ignore the fact that the majority of people involved in such circumstances are white.

The Black Entertainment News network found that television news links drugs with blacks 50 percent of the time, while only 32 percent of the drug stories focus on whites; yet a poll by *USA Today* showed that only 15 percent of the drug users in America are black, and 70 percent are white. When the American press is guilty of such antiblack reporting, anyone can understand why people in Japan might believe that most black or Hispanic Americans are either entertainers, athletes, or criminals.

Hollywood has contributed significantly with movies like *New Jack City, Boys 'n the Hood, Juice,* and other movies that depict African Americans in roles that enhance the stereotype of blacks as criminals, athletes, or entertainers. The number of quality films about the African American experience are pitifully too few.

John Dower and Ron Takaki have each written very important

books illustrating how race was an important issue in the prosecution of the war against Japan and in the decision to drop the most diabolical weapon of mass destruction conceived by supposedly rational men. Clearly, there was a need for people who thought differently regarding the race issue. Had Du Bois, Johnson, Schuyler, or some of the others who could see merit in positions taken by Japan been included in the decision-making process of the American government, actions taken by the United States at critical junctures conceivably might have been ameliorated. In other words, a greater concern for conflict resolution and less cowboy machismo on the American side possibly could have encouraged a less uncompromising attitude on the side of the Japanese. On both sides, as Dower points out, prejudice and racial stereotypes often distorted intentions and capabilities until "race hate fed atrocities" and the conflict became a "war without mercy."[2]

After the war, the American propaganda machine went into high gear to justify use of weapons of mass destruction against the largely civilian populations of Hiroshima and Nagasaki. The myths made in America cast Americans as good guys defending democracy and Japanese as evil fanatics led by a mad military-industrial complex. Under this interpretation the Japanese were so fanatical that combat-hardened American troops would be seriously threatened by women, children, and old folks armed with bamboo spears.

Too often Americans have believed that a chasm of difference separated them from Japanese. In some ways, however, the Americans and Japanese were much alike. Both believed they had a manifest destiny to expand into contiguous regions, even at the expense of their neighbors; both shared a certain cultural arrogance that grew out of confidence in their military might; both were imbibed with a distorted sense of mission. Both allowed their prejudices to outpace good sense. An important difference is that the introduction of the nuclear age at their expense and the gift of a "Peace Constitution" persuaded most Japanese that peace is preferable to war and in America Pentagon people and patriots, even after the end of the cold war, persuasively continue to push for bigger and better weapons systems.

Yet even Japanese, partially as a result of the tenor of the occupation, accepted the American interpretation as did other Asians newly freed of their erstwhile liberators. Japanese claimed that they had invaded their neighbors with the intent of forcing out their European and American masters. Colored peoples joining together to expel white hegemony from Asia was a persuasive message emanating from Japan and finding resonance as far away as Harlem in the 1930s and 1940s. But a military machine was not the best delivery vehicle. The choice of message bearers, samurai romantics and the sons of Japanese farmers and fishermen who lacked appreciation for the integrity of other cultures and sensitivity for the nationalistic aspirations of other Asian peoples, was perhaps the biggest single mistake the Japanese made.

Historically, where Japan was concerned, African Americans were disinclined to share the attitudes generally held by white Americans. When his country went to war against Japan, Du Bois, one of the most learned men of his generation, lacked enthusiasm due to his belief that Japan was a colored nation and color was a root cause of the war. Du Bois accused the Europeans and Americans of greater transgressions against the countries of Asia and credited Japan for freeing its neighbors of white domination. He had prophesied that under the leadership of Japan and black Americans the vast majority of humanity would rise up to end racial prejudice, imperialism, economic subjugation, and religious hypocrisy. Du Bois' dream became the dream of countless thousands of black Americans. They accepted Japan's claims of a sphere of influence in East Asia.

Should what African Americans think of them concern the Japanese? Of course, I believe that the answer is yes. My view is that both groups can only benefit from better understanding. First of all, despite the negative reviews that they may get in the American media, African Americans have a well-deserved reputation for being in the forefront of progressive thinking regarding race. Historically, they have been significant in the shaping of American democracy, insisting that it be inclusive; they were in the forefront of the fight for the ideals of civil and human rights; they have advocated an appreciation for ethnic diversity, the foundation for a truly multicultural society, and led the fight for progressive social policies.

From another perspective, the most popular political figure in America today is an African American who refused to run for president or accept the nomination for vice-president on a Republican ticket. The fact that Bob Dole as presidential candidate of the more conservative of the two major political parties in the United States earnestly wanted Colin Powell, the first black head of the Joint Chiefs to share his ticket means that the day is approaching when a black American may very well sit in the White House. Certainly, African Americans will be more included in the upper echelons of

American decision making. Besides, within the next century, some demographers are predicting that white Americans may very well become a minority. Furthermore, black Americans are already major consumers of Japanese products.

Thus, the Japanese already have good reasons for wanting to maintain amicable relations with African Americans. In the 1920s and 1930s Yasuichi Hikida became something of a fixture in Harlem and Naka Nakane organized African Americans of the Midwest. They were rather effective in their efforts to build bridges to black America. Today, Seiho Tajiri attempt a similar thing as he tries to teach black farmers to grow soybeans for making tofu, a major source of vegetable protein for Japanese.

Seemingly, the forging of a mutually beneficial relationship between Japanese and African Americans has a better chance of realization in this period when African American participation in the body politic is greater than ever before. Unlike the time when Du Bois wrote trying to persuade black Americans that they had common interests with Japanese, however, today there is an absence of a vigorous black press to support this point of view. The black press has fallen victim to integration. Black journalists now work for the major white media. Often they become assimilated and do not share the myth of colored unity of their predecessors; they have replaced it with the myth of Afrocentricity. Immersed in a white and often hostile environment, ironically, they claim an identity with a supportive black culture that frees them to identify with the interests and attitudes of their white counterparts where Japan is concerned. If whites are hostile to Japan and Japan is judged racist, than black reporters or journalists working for white media can be comfortable articulating anti-Japanese positions.

Kathryn Leary, who has visited Japan fifteen times, told me recently of an encounter she had with a black acquaintance who writes for the Associated Press. At a chance meeting, they were talking, and when she said that she was on her way to Japan, the reporter asked her why did she want to go to that racist country, that place with the Sambo dolls. In an effort to help him to acquire a more balanced view she took him a copy of Regge Life's film about African Americans living in Japan; she suggested other people that he could talk with who were knowledgeable about conditions in Japan and sat for a two-hour interview. After all of her efforts to help this writer to bring some balance to his view of Japan, the reporter chose to write an article quoting her out of context in a way that ignored everything but his own negative preconception.[3]

Reporters who really want to be informative about Japanese would do well to remember that the people of Japan have throughout their history been adaptable. They ought to understand as well that social attitudes are not immutable. The pace of change can be swift or slow, depending on the variables at work. To understand this, one only has to look at sumo, probably the most tradition-bound of Japanese sports. Today, of the two *yokozuna*, the highest rank, one, Akebono, was born Chadwick Rowan and raised in Hawaii. Another Hawaiian, known to Japanese and other sumo fans as Musashimaru (Fiamalu Penitani), holds the second highest rank of *ozeki*. Two other Hawaiians persevered to the top of this ancient sport. Konishiki (Salevaa Atisanoe) held the rank of Ozeki longer than anyone else. The former Takamiyama (Jesse Kuhaulua) became Azumazeki Oyakata (Azumazeki stable master or sumo coach). Wherever a sumo wrestler might have originated, once he makes it to the upper division profit and popularity are his reward. There are other young Hawaiian aspirants. One of the newest sensations is from Mongolia. Another wrestler, formerly known as Sentoryu, or "fighting dragon," a play on the name of his hometown, St. Louis, is an African American.

Others who live in Japan in different capacities also find acceptance. No others must submit to anything like the stringent, even feudal protocols required of a sumo wrestler. But Japanese often do insist on doing things their way, and sometimes that will include actions that non-Japanese will understand as discriminatory. If African Americans and Japanese are to come to know each other and move beyond stereotypes, Hikida believed, they must interact directly. This is still an important need. Although they often have acted otherwise, American leaders have stated that the U.S.-Japan relationship is the most vital bilateral partnership in the world. On the premis that this is so, African Americans can no longer permit white people to be the sole interpreters of the American experience. Today blacks must communicate directly with the Japanese and explain the meaning and substance of black aspirations.

Historically, African Americans saw Japanese as "brown brothers" because of their perception that both faced discrimination in an overwhelmingly white-dominated environment. When they looked at Japan in the world scene, African Americans saw them playing against a stacked deck. They were not equals among equals, although they displayed the paraphernalia of power.

In some ways, the circumstances of the Japanese are not so different even today. When Mitsubishi bought controlling interest in Rockefeller Center and Sony acquired Columbia Pictures, a great many white Americans reacted as if they had been deprived of national icons. "Japan Invades Hollywood!" shrieked the cover of *Newsweek* magazine, in a way reminiscent of the old-style yellow journalism of the Hearst newspapers. When Canadian, British, Australian, or Dutch entrepreneurs bought pieces of the American dream there were no comparable outcries. There were no laments in the American media when Pathe Communications Corporation of Italy purchased MGM/United Artists or Robert Murdoch, an Australian, bought 20th Century Fox. When the Japanese purchasers subsequently had to sell their pieces of Americana at a loss, or otherwise seemed to be stumbling, those same white Americans who had felt robbed sighed relief.

Yet coming to America may prove to be very beneficial to Japanese corporations more than monetarily. From having to pay large financial settlements to aggrieved Americans, certain Japanese, who pursued discriminatory policies and echoed the conservative, short-sighted rhetoric of American "right-wingers," learned that a corporate culture that allowed business people to play loose with employees' feelings was not exportable. They learned also that intolerance was not to be tolerated and bigotry was bad for business. In the process, Japanese businesses gained much in negative publicity and paid or lost millions that could have been better invested in securing the goodwill and loyalty of a significant segment of the American population. The repercussions obligate Japanese firms to prove that they are good corporate neighbors.

A bridge to understanding between African Americans and Japanese will be of mutual benefit to both sides. African Americans have a well-deserved reputation for loyalty to those who give them respect and fairness. If more astute, rather than following the Republicans rhetoric, the Japanese would do better to look at the numbers of African Americans who support the Democrats.

Proactive policies on the part of Japanese, in time, will override the generally negative image. Today there are more black congressmen and congresswomen than ever before. Rather than taking cues from the most conservative opinion makers, if Japanese officials and business people were to pursue policies beneficial to African American politicians and their constituencies that would be a powerful way of winning friends and influencing people. Programs that would help build up the infrastructure of the inner cities—such as economic development zones—would benefit black congressmen and congresswomen and Japan at the same time by providing jobs, restoring dignity to a people, and producing happy consumers while rehabilitating the reputations of certain Japanese-owned companies.

The prospects for improved relations between African Americans and Japanese are good. There is already considerable evidence that various sectors in Japan and Japanese affiliates overseas are making adjustments, some less reluctantly than others. The Ministry of Foreign Affairs and the Japan Federation of Economic Organization (Keidanren) are working to encourage international corporate responsibility. Major Japanese Corporations actively seek to provide more than products. In 1989, Japanese business interests established the Council for Better Corporate Citizenship as a way of fostering better international understanding in an age of increased global economic activity. The CBCC encourages businessmen to become "grassroots ambassadors." By this they mean that it should be policy for members to get involved in the activities of the community in which they work. The president of the Hitachi Foundation, Delwin Roy, speaking for his organization, says that conduct in the area of minority concerns increasingly has been put "squarely in front of the Hitachi Group's chief executives."[4] The trend in this direction will only increase.

Often in the past, American historians have interpreted the war against the Axis powers as a "right or good war" that the American people supported unquestionably and with near unanimity, with the possible exception of peace activists and a few "hyphenated" Americans. African Americans had been portrayed as steadfast on the side of democracy, lacking divided loyalties. By their inability to deliver a statement of unreserved and whole-hearted support, representative leadership groups of African Americans admitted that loyalties indeed were divided, and racism was the wedge.

Historians have played down or ignored the disquiet, ambiguity, and even rage that plagued black communities during World War II. Disillusionment among African Americans, however, antedated Vietnam; the anger and vehemence of expression associated with the likes of Malcolm X, Muhammad Ali, or Louis Farrakhan was preceded by nearly a century of articulated anguish and frustration. Today, the models of approbation may be Islam or Afrocentricism, but in an earlier period, for tens of thousands of disenchanted African Americans, the Japanese were the exemplars of what it meant to be nonwhite and proud.

In our own time, a wave of antipathy has arisen between African Americans and Asians, and most people have forgotten about the positive relationship between blacks and the Japanese. They have forgotten (as have some politicians in Japan) that the Japanese were once regarded as oppressed "brown" brothers, because they too were victims of prejudice. Elijah Muhammad served as a direct link between that past and the present. He taught that the so-called Negro was the original Asiatic man, and when he needed help establishing his fledgling entrepreneurial efforts he sought and got help from Seiho Tajiri.

The Japanese helped to stimulate the rise of an ideology of race that persisted into the postwar era; it was an ideology with an accent on protest over accommodation. For all of those at the bottom of society's rung, Japanese were models of militancy and accomplishment. They encouraged the notion that African Americans were a minority in America, but members of the majority in the world. In the 1930s, the Communist party of the United States was worried about the competitiveness of Japan's appeal enough that the Negro Commission of the National Committee put out a pamphlet titled *Is Japan the Champion of the Colored Races?* challenging the assertion. After making the claim that peace-loving people around the world were aghast over the Japanese military machine's conquest of China, the black representative of communism wrote, "But the deepest disillusionment is felt by the millions of colored peoples in America, Africa and Asia who once regarded seriously Japan's claim to leadership of the colored world."[5]

As African American history, I hope this study serves as a flicker of light which suggests further need for illumination of the shadows where the greater masses of black Americans have been relegated. In those shadows, the interplay between elite and nonelite, the extent to which so-called leaders settled for a fraction of what they had a right to demand ought to become clearer. Of course, it is important to study those who articulated the perceived grievances of blacks and took the lead in trying to advance their status in this country, but there is as great a need to try to understand the dreams, aspirations, depths of despair, and alienation of those in whose name the presumed leaders were supposed to have acted. Only in this way can historians accurately gauge the success or failure of the black leadership class. I also hope it will serve to demonstrate the need for further investigation of the international consciousness of African Americans.

NOTES

PREFACE

1. David E. Sanger, "Sumo Star Charges Racism," *New York Times*, April 22, 1992; Sanger, "American Sumo Star Denies accusing the Japanese of Racism," *NYT*, April 24, 1992. In an interview with the Japanese press Konishiki denied saying that his failure to get promoted to *yokozuna* was because of racism. Lora Sharnoff, the author of *Grand Sumo*, perhaps, the best book on the sport in English, says that Konishiki was misquoted. Telephone interview, June 1995.

2. Sheila Johnson, *The Japanese Through American Eyes* (Tokyo, New York, and London: Kodansha International, 1988); originally printed as *American Attitudes Toward Japan, 1941–1975* (Washington: American Enterprise Institute for Public Policy Research, 1975); translated as *Amerika-jin no Nihon-kan* (Tokyo: Simul Press, 1986).

3. G. James Fleming, "Compensatory Characteristics of the Negro Press," G. James Fleming Papers, Soper Library, Morgan State University, Baltimore, Maryland; Gunnar Myrdal, *An American Dilemma* 2 vols. (New York, Toronto, London: McGraw-Hill Book Company, 1964), 2:911, 921.

4. Ibid.

5. Frederick Douglass commented on the negative reception given the delegation in Philadelphia, one of the cities where some of the citizens hurled the epithet *nigger* at the Japanese. *Douglass' Monthly* (July 1860).

6. *Chicago Defender*, September 3, 1921; April 19, 1924.

INTRODUCTION

1. Elliot Rudwick, *W. E. B. Du Bois: Propagandist of the Negro Protest* (New York: Antheneum Press, 1969, 318; David L. Lewis, *When Harlem Was in Vogue* (New York: Oxford: Oxford University Press, 1979), 6: W. E. B. Du Bois, "Atlanta University," in Kelly Miller, Hollis Burke Frissell, Roscoe Conkling Bruce, W. G. Frost, and J. G. Merrill, *From Servitude to Service* (Boston: American Unitarian Association, 1904), 153; reprint New York: Negro Universities Press, Arno Press, 1969). Du Bois often set forth this theme in his writings about Japan's role in international politics. See "The African Roots of War," *Atlantic Monthly* (May 1915): 707–14; *Philadelphia Tribune*, October 22, 1931; Herbert Aptheker, ed., *The Correspondence of W. E. B. Du Bois*, 3 vols. (Amherst: University of Massachusetts Press, 1973–78), 2:147; *Phylon* 1 (1940): 175–92.

2. In 1977, while I was in Japan, attending the Inter-University Center for Japanese Language Studies, two articles appeared that were germane to my topic: David J. Hellwig, "Afro-American Reactions to the Japanese and the Anti-Japanese Movement, 1906–1924," *Phylon* 38 (1977): 93–104; Arnold Shankman, "'Asiatic Ogre' or 'Desirable Citizen'? The Image of Japanese Americans in the Afro-American Press, 1867–1933," *Pacific Historical Review* 46 (1977):567–87. While the Hellwig article is a fair treatment of the period he chose to discuss, the Shankman effort is marred by a number of factual inaccuracies. For example, Shankman asserts that the first mention of Japanese in the black press occurs in 1867, that mention of Japanese-Americans virtually disappeared in 1933 as there was lessened fear of economic competition, and that the image of the Japanese after 1941 was that of "a sinister enemy." Even his interpretation of how the expression *Asiatic Ogre* was used distorts the author's meaning. I am indebted to Roger Daniels for calling these two articles to my attention.

3. Leonard Robert Jordan, interrogation held at the office of the Federal Bureau of Investigation, 607 U.S. Court House, Foley Square, New York, February 16, 1942, Investigative Case Files re: Ethiopian Pacific Movement, Inc., Internal Security-J, Sedition, FBI Files 100-15291 (hereafter cited as EPM/FBI).

4. Charles A. Siepman to Sherman H. Dryer, June 8, 1942, Office of Facts and Figures, Office of War Information, RG208, Entry 5, Box 3, Decimal file 002.11, Washington National Record Center, Suitland, Maryland (hereafter cited WNRC).

5. Letter from "Negroes of Birmingham," August 4, 1919, "Negro Subversion," Security Classified Correspondence, RG 165, Entry 65, file 10218-356, National Archives, Washington, D.C. (hereafter cited NA).

6. "Japanese Plan for Use of American Negroes for Subversive and Espionage Purposes," Memo of Colonel C. H. Mason, July 9,1941, Security Correspondence, RG 165, Entry 65, Box 329, file 1766-z-699, NA.

7. "Japan's Race Propaganda," *Radio Reports of the Far East #58* November 10, 1944, Records of the Foreign Broadcast Service, RG 262, Entry 34, Box 4, WNRC.

8. George A. Barnes to Ulric Bell, memo March 12, 1942, "Suggestions to Encourage Negro Morale," Records of OWI, Decimal File of the Director, 1941–1942, RG 208, Entry 5, Box 3, NRC.

9. Annual Report, Hollywood Office, Bureau of Motion Pictures, Domestic Branch, OWI, RG 208, Entry 566, Box 3510.

10. Carlton Moss to Archibald MacLeish, 2-4230, OWI, Director's folder 002.1.

11. Carlton Moss to Philip Wiley, March 21, 1942, OWI, folder 002.11.

12. Moss to MacLeish.

13. *Negro Soldier* is available on videotape at the National Archives. For a more detailed analysis of the making of *Negro Soldier*, see Tom Cripps's *Making Movies Black*.

14. *Marching On* is available at the University of Illinois, Champaign-Urbana.

15. "Trends in Hollywood Pictures," May 24, 1943, OWI, RG 208; *BAA*, October 30, 1943.

16. *BAA*, October 30, 1943.

17. Ibid., November 13, 1943.

18. Ibid.

19. Siepman to Dryer.

CHAPTER 1

1. *Portland (OR) New Age*, June 30, 1900 (imperial decree); *Chicago Broad Ax*, October 5, 1901 (sumo wrestlers); *Kansas City (MO) Rising Son*, May 22, 1903 (bonsai); *CBA*, May 3, 1902 (carpentry); December 7, 1901

(fire fighters' tattoos); *Washington (DC) Bee,* March 5, 1904 (blackened teeth); *Cleveland Gazette,* February 2, 1901 (labels on kids); *CBA,* November 8, 1902 (pickled plums); *St. Paul (MN) Afro-American Advance,* June 16, 1900 (paper toys); *WB,* August 6, 1904 (liars' punishment); *PNA,* June 30, 1900 (crickets); *CBA,* July 7, 1900 (fishing); *CG,* August 17, 1901 (horseshoes).

2. *Indianapolis World,* April 2, 1904 (carpenter tools); *PNA,* May 7, 1904 (reading); *CBA,* October 5, 1901 (funeral attire); *KCRS,* May 22, 1903 (best room).

3. *IW,* October 8, 1904.

4. *PNA,* April 14, 1900; March 21, 1903.

5. *WB,* April 16, 1904; *CG,* December 21, 1901; *CBA,* July 11, 1901; May 20, 1905.

6. *PNA,* May 21, 1904; *KCRS,* November 11, 1904; *IW,* March 5, 1904.

7. *IF,* October 1, 1904; *IW,* March 19, 1904.

8. *CBA,* August 31, 1901; September 26, 1903; June 21, 1902; April 9, 1904.

9. *CBA,* July 7, 1900; *IW,* June 16, 1900; *Savannah Tribune,* 29, 1900.

10. *PNA,* September 22, 1900; *ST,* December 29, 1900.

11. *Denver Statesman,* January 27, 1900; Josephine E. Holmes, "A Study of Education's Triumphs," *Colored American Magazine* 14(January 1908): 38; Josephine Silone Yates, "The Twentieth Century Negro—His Opportunities for Success," *CAM* 11 (October 1906): 227.

12. "Tomorrow in the East," *Voice* 4 (October 1907): 349.

13. *PNA,* May 5, 1906; *Alexander's Magazine,* January 15, 1907; March 29, 1902; *Baltimore Afro-American Ledger,* November 30, 1901.

14. Dudley C. Plummer, "A Colored Man's Dream," *CAM* 14(October 1908): 530; *BAAL,* November 30, 1901; *CBA,* March 29, 1902.

15. *PNA,* July 21, 1900; *St. Paul-Minneapolis Afro-American Advance,* June 16, 1900; *ST,* February 16, 1901.

16. *CBA,* August 25, 1900; Nicholas H. Campbell, "The Negro in the Navy," *Colored American Magazine* 6 (May–June 1903): 412.

17. *CBA,* June 16, 1900; August 25, 1900.

18. *CBA,* September 1, 1900.

19. *Indianapolis Freeman*, June 16, 1900.

20. Ibid.

21. *IF*, July 28, 1900.

22. *New York Age*, June 22, 1902.

23. *Boston Guardian*, December 20, 1902.

24. Ibid.

25. *WB*, September 2, 1905.

26. *IW*, April 1, 1905; *St. Louis Post Dispatch*, March 9, 1904, cited in *Indianapolis Recorder*, March, 1904.

27. *NYA*, March 12, 1904.

28. Ibid.

29. *IF*, January 7, 1905.

30. *ST*, October 20, 1900 (Wide Awakes); February 24, 1900(Home and Foreign Missionary Club); February 23, 1901 (West End, Young Adelphia Aid); BG, November 22, 1902 (Crispus Tabernacle, Love and Charity); July 4, 1903 (Silver Cross); *CBA*, April 4, 1903 (Phyllis Wheatley); *ST*, February 25, March 4, 1905 ("Japs" vs. "Russians"); African Americans tended to use the term *Japs* as an expression of familiarity, much as they would use *Yanks*; Kelly Miller, professor and dean at Howard University, learned from a former student that Japanese found the word offensive.

31. *KCRS*, November 11, 1904.

32. *CBA*, December 9, 1905.

33. *ST*, May 20, 1905; *IF*, July 14, 1900.

34. *IW*, February 6, 1904; *WB*, September 17, 1904; *IF*, July 14, 1900.

35. *WB*, September 24, 1904; *KCRS*, August 19, 1904. Even today whites, who take up residence in Japan, are more likely than blacks to take umbrage due to a slight directed at them as gaijin.

36. *WB*, September 24, 1904.

CHAPTER 2

1. *St. Louis Palladium*, September 9, 1905.

2. "The Effects of Togo's Victory Upon the Warfare Between the Races," *Colored American Magazine* 9 (July 1905): 348.

3. Du Bois, "Atlanta University," 197; Du Bois, *Dusk of Dawn: AnEssay Toward an Autobiography of a Race Concept* (New York: Schocken Books, 1968), 232. While the Japanese victory over the Russians might have stirred "Japanophobia" among whites, it made Du Bois an enduring "Japanophile."

4. *Portland (Oregon) New Age*, June 11, 1904; October 22, 1904; *Indianapolis Freeman*, June 4, 1904; January 7,1905; June 24, 1905; *New York Age*, January 19, 1905; "Togo's Victory," 347, 348; David McJon, "The Miracle of Modern Times," *Alexander's Magazine* 6 (August 15, 1905): 37.

5. Mary Church Terrell, "Taking Things for Granted," n.d., Terrell-Papers, Speeches and Writing File, Library of Congress, Washington, D.C.; *SLP*, October 28, 1905.

6. August Meier, *Negro Thought in America, 1880–1915: Racial Ideologies in the Age of Booker T. Washington* (Ann Arbor: University of Michigan Press, 1963), 239–40 n. 310.

7. *NYA*, June 22, 1905.

8. Ibid., July 13, 1905.

9. *Washington Bee*, February 13, 1904; September 3, 1904.

10. *NYA*, June 8, 1905; *SLP*, October 15, 1904.

11. *Voice of the Negro* 1 (November 1904): 523; *IF*, October 1, 1904; October 8, 1904; May 7, 1904.

12. *CAM* 9 (July 1905): 348; *IF*, July 8, 1905.

13. *Chicago Broad Ax*, April 22, 1905; November 28, 1914.

14. *WB*, September 2, 1905; *CBA*, April 22, 1905; *Kansas City Rising Son*, August 25, 1905; *IF*, June 4, 1904.

15. *Indianapolis World*, May 14, 1904; April 1, 1905.

16. *NYA*, July 13, 1905; *Voice of the Negro*, April 1, 1905.

17. *PNA*, July 26; *IW*, August 6, 1904.

18. *IW*, April 9 (behind Japan); April 30 (fireless shells/dredges); May 21 (Corkosumato); June 4, 1904 (damming the Yalu River).

19. *IF*, April 2, 1904.

20. *CBA*, March 25; April 15 (both Taylor's remark about atheism and Miller's reply); April 22, 1905.

21. *WB*, August 6, 1904.

22. *KCRS*, May 6, 1904; *NYA*, June 8, 1905.

23. Thomas J. Clement, "Athletics in the American Army," *CAM* 8 (January 1905): 21; *PNA*, January 14, 1905; *IW*, March 5, 1904; February 4, 1905; March 4, 1905; *WB*, November 25, 1905; "Togo's Victory," 348.

24. "Togo's Victory," 347.

25. *NYA*, July 13, 1905.

26. *IF*, January 27, 1900.

27. Ibid., December 28, 1905; Richard T. Greener to Department of State, Report from Consul (Vladivostok), May 15, 1906, Microfilm Publications M486, NA.

28. *WB*, February 13, 1904; "The War in the East," *VN* 2 (January 1905): 658.

29. *NYA*, July 13, 1905.

30. *IF*, February 20, 1904; *IW*, February 27, 1904.

31. Joseph G. Bryant, "The War in the Far East," *CAM* 9 (March 1905): 133–35.

32. *Savannah Tribune*, April 2, 9, 16, 1904; May 7, 1904.

33. *IF*, September 2, 1905.

34. *NYA*, June 22, 1905; *IW*, October 28, 1905; *NYA*, August 10, 1905.

35. *CBA*, December 30, 1905; *CAM* 9 (October 1905): 532; *CBA*, September 30, 1905.

36. Seth M. Scheiner, "President Theodore Roosevelt and the Negro," *Journal of Negro History* 47 (July 1962): 169–82, cited by Melvin Steinfield, *Our Racist Presidents: From Washington to Nixon* (San Ramon, CA: Consensus Publishers, Inc., 1972), 210, 212; George Sinkler, *The Racial Attitudes of American Presidents: From Abraham Lincoln to Theodore Roosevelt* (Garden City, NY: Doubleday and Company, Inc., 1971), 328.

37. Shumpei Okamoto, *The Japanese Oligarchy and the Russo-Japanese War* (New York and London: Columbia University Press, 1970), 124–25.

38. *NYA*, September 14, 1905; "Japan's Great Victory," *AM* 6 (September 15, 1905): 46.

39. *IF*, September 2, 1905; *SLP*, September 2, 1905; On this same date the *Savannah Tribune* reported that Japanese envoys, although they did not want to be quoted, felt that they had gotten their primary objectives.

40. Okamoto, 152–54.

41. *IW,* September 9, 1905; *CAM* 9 (October 1905):532.

42. "From the Great White Nation of the West," *CAM* 9 (November 1905): 596.

43. *IF,* January 13, 1906.

44. *Seattle Republican,* March 17, 1905; *IF,* February 18,1905.

45. *Indianapolis Recorder,* June 17, 1905; *IF,* June 10, 1905; *IW,* June 10, 1905.

46. *Topeka Star Ledger,* February 13, 1904; *PNA,* July 9, 1904.

47. *PNA,* January 9, 1904; *IW,* January 9, 1904; February 13, 1904.

48. *Pittsburgh Courier,* March 20, 1937.

49. *IW,* December 3, 1904.

50. *NYA,* January 19, 1905; June 8, 1905; These themes were also pursued in *CAM* 7 (July 1904): 466; Joseph G. Bryant, "The War in the Far East," *CAM* 9 (March 1905): 135; *IF,* June 4, 1904; January 7, 1905; "Modern Miracle," 37; *ST,* February 11, 1905; Du Bois, "Atlanta University," 197.

CHAPTER 3

1. *Indianapolis World,* May 10, 17, 24, June 7, July 12, 1913; Roger Daniels, *The Politics of Prejudice* (New York: Atheneum, 1973), 36.

2. *Indianapolis Freeman,* November 10, 1906; "Japan and San Francisco Discrimination," *Colored American Magazine* 11 (November 1906): 285; *New York Age,* May 30, 1907; "The Controversy with Japan," *Voice* 4 (March 1907): 33; *Nashville Globe,* July 19, 1907; *NYA,* April 1, 1909; *Portland New Age,* February 16, 1907.

3. "Japan and San Francisco Discrimination," *CAM* 11 (November 1906): 285; *NYA,* May 30, 1907; "The Controversy with Japan," 33; *NG,* July 19, 1907; *NYA,* April 1, 1909; *PNA,* February 16, 1907.

4. *NYA,* February 7, 1907; March 21, 1907.

5. *NYA,* April 1, 1909; December 13, 1906; NG, February 19, 1909.

6. "The California Muddle," *CAM* 12 (March 1907): 168; NG, July 19, 1907; *NYA,* April 1, 1909.

7. *NG,* July 19, 1907; *Washington Bee,* March 2, 1907; *NYA,* December 13, 1906; January 17, 1907; *Cleveland Gazette,* July 3, 1909.

8. *Chicago Broad Ax*, May 24, 1913; *WB*, May 10, 1913; "California Muddle," 169.

9. *IF*, December 15, 1906.

10. Ibid., December 8, 1906.

11. *CG*, December 8, 1906.

12. *IF*, December 15, 1906; Ida Wells-Barnett, "Lynching Our National Crime," William Loren Katz, ed., *Proceedings of the National Negro Conference, 1909* (New York: Arno Press and *New York Times*, 1969).

13. *NG*, May 17, 1907; February 19, 1909.

14. *NYA*, April 4, 1907.

15. Ibid., November 1, 1906; April 4, 1907.

16. *NG*, May 31, 1907; July 19, 1907; *PNA*, September 15, 1906; October 13, 1906.

17. *WB*, March 2, 1907; *NG*, July 19, 1907; February 12, 1909.

18. *Chicago Defender*, April 26, 1913.

19. *Philadelphia Tribune*, September 26, 1914; *WB*, January 31, 1914.

20. *Savannah Tribune*, January 22, 1915. Six years later the *Tribune* featured on its front page an Associated Negro Press release about an Episcopalian pastor in Boston who declared that in the event of war between the United States and Japan African Americans would side with Japan. *Baltimore Afro-American*, September 29, 1917.

21. *IF*, June 7, 1913.

22. *IW*, May 10, 17, 1913.

23. *PNA*, October 20, November 17, December 1, 15, 22, 1906. The *Age* was obviously anxious that the model of Japanese standing up against white bullies get as wide a circulation as possible.

24. Ibid., December 22, 1906.

25. *Los Angeles California Eagle*, July 4, August 29, October 3, 1914.

26. Ibid., October 25, 1919; February 26, 1916; February 28, 1914.

27. Ibid., May 13, 1916.

28. Ibid., January 29, 1916.

29. Ibid., September 5, 12, 1914; September 4, 1915.

30. *NYA*, July 12, 1919.

31. *ST*, March 6, 1915; *NYA*, March 16, 1918; *PT*, June 9, 1917; *LACE*, January 29, 1916; *CD*, November 21, 1914.

CHAPTER 4

1. *Chicago Broad Ax*, January 4, 1919; *Philadelphia Tribune*, January 18, 1919; April 26, 1919.

2. The National Colored Congress for World Democracy met in Washington, D.C., under the auspices of the National Equal Rights League and adopted a resolution calling for the establishment of a world court to adjudicate "every denial or violation of justice, humanity, and democracy." It further called for the end of all race or class discrimination and "the abolition of autocracy of race Colored persons faced everywhere." In an effort to gain wider acceptance among representative groups, the original petition was watered down to read: "Real democracy for the world being the avowed war aim of nations establishing the League of Nations, the high contracting parties agree to vouchsafe to their citizens respectively full liberty, rights of democracy and protection of life without restriction of distinction based on race, color, or previous condition." Of the original committee selected to present the petition to the Japanese, only three, Walker, Wells Barnett, and Trotter, attended the meeting at the Waldorf. *CBA*, January 4, April 26, 1919; *PT*, January 18, 1919.

3. *Chicago Whip*, July 9, 1919; Stephen Fox, *The Guardian of Boston: William Monroe Trotter* (New York: Atheneum, 1971), 221–30.

4. "Japan and the Far East," *Messenger* 2 (July 1918): 22.

5. *New York Age*, March 29, 1919.

6. *Baltimore Afro-American*, April 11, 1919; *Atlanta Independent* April 5, 1919.

7. *NYA*, November 20, 1918; *Cleveland Advocate*, November 30, 1918; "Reconstruction," *Crisis* 17 (January 1919): 130.

8. *PT*, August 2, 1919; *Chicago Defender*, June 7, 1919; *NYA*, November 30, 1918; *BAA*, May 2, 1919.

9. *NYA*, May 24, 1919.

10. *Savannah Tribune*, January 26, 1918; *NYA*, May 24, 1919; *PT*, July 24, 1919; October 22, 1921.

11. Peter Gilbert, ed., *The Selected Writings of John Edward Bruce: Militant Black Journalist* (New York: Arno Press and *New York Times*, 1971), 99.

12. *NYA*, December 24, 1921.

13. *CD*, May 26, 1928.

14. *PT*, November 10, 1921; *ST*, November 10, 24, 1921.

15. *ST*, December 1, 1921; January 5, 1922.

16. Ibid., January 5, 1922.

17. *NYA*, July 23, 1921.

18. Ibid., August 6, October 29, November 5, December 24, 1921; February 18, 1922.

19. Ibid., July 23, 1921.

20. *PT*, August 4, 1927.

21. Emory S. Bogardus, *The New Sociological Research* (Los Angeles: Jesse Ray Miller, 1926), 234.

22. Bogardus, 234, 235, 237; *PT*, August 4, 1927.

23. *CD*, September 8, 1923.

24. Ibid., September 15, 1923; *ST*, September 13, 1923.

25. "Negro Peoples of the World Send Their Sympathy to Japan," "The Appalling Disaster That Struck Japan," Editorial: "Grief-Stricken Japan," *Negro World*, September 15, 1923; "Negroes Show Their Sympathy for the Japanese," *Negro World*, 22, 1923.

26. Marcus Garvey, "What Japan Says," *NW*, June 21, 1924.

27. Editorial: "The Black Man's Philosophy," *NW*, March 3, 1923; editorial: "Japanese People Greatly Offended by the Exclusion Act," *NW*, June 7, 1924; Marcus Garvey, "Japan Developed by Itself," *NW*, February 24, 1923.

28. "Hon. W. L. Sherrill Thrills Charleston," *NW*, June 14, 1924; T. Thomas Fortune, "Some Dream Hours in Glorious Japan," *NW*, June 14, 1924; Fortune, "Race Problem the Same Everywhere," *NW*, May 31, 1924. Fortune waxed and waned in his appreciation of the Japanese. In January 1924 he wrote, "When I was to the Far East, in China, Japan and the Philippines, it seemed to me that the atmosphere was surcharged with a dense and soggy spirit life. . . . I think it was the dead spirits of the dead of ages that made the atmosphere dense and soggy." *NW*, January 26, 1924. Later,

in June he reminisced, "Indeed, I seemed to be very much at home in Japan and readily adapted myself to the country and the people and their ways." *NW*, June 14, 1924. A Garvey editorial seemed to support a scheme to have African American agricultural workers replace the Japanese driven from California. See editorial: "Japanese Farmers Settle in Brazil," *NW*, June 21, 1924.

29. *NW*, June 7, 1924.

30. *CD*, June 28, 1924; October 11, 1924.

31. *Oakland (CA) Sunshine*, February 25, 1922 (silk, Nadaokaco); January 5, 1915 (dentist); September 25, 1915 (Mikado); October 23, 1915 (shoemaker).

32. *PT*, July 16, 1921.

33. *Los Angeles California Eagle*, June 24,1921.

34. Claude McKay, "Soviet Russia and the Negro," *Crisis* (December 1923): 64.

35. *LACE*, January 7, 1921.

36. Ibid.

37. *PT*, April 26, 1920.

38. *CD*, September 17, 1921; *ST*, March 9, 1922.

39. *CD*, September 17, 1921; *Atlanta Independent*, July 7, 1921.

40. Booker T. Washington, *Up from Slavery* (New York: Doubleday, 1901; Bantam Books, 1963), 108–9; idem, *Putting the Most into Life* (New York, Thomas Y. Crowell, 1906), 33.

41. *PT*, October 16, 1920.

42. *BAA*, January 18, 1924; *ST*, January 1, 1925.

43. *ST*, January 1, 1925.

44. *PT*, May 9, 1929.

45. Ibid., July 18, 1925.

46. Kelly Miller, *The Everlasting Stain* (Washington, D.C.: Associated Publishers, 1924), 167.

47. *CD*, October 7, 1922.

48. Ibid.

49. Miller, 168; *PT*, December 8, 1927.

CHAPTER 5

1. *Philadelphia Tribune*, October 29, 1931.

2. Ibid.; *Baltimore Afro-American*, January 15, 1938.

3. *BAA*, November 19, 1931.

4. *Chicago Defender*, February 6, 1932.

5. *Pittsburgh Courier*, October 24, 1936; *PT*, February 14, 1935.

6. *CD*, August 31, 1935. Miller had hit on the reason that the Japanese government, although sentimentally attached to Ethiopia, having signed a Treaty of Friendship and Commerce in 1927, sided with Italy in the war between Ethiopia and Italy. The Japanese government recognized the annexation of Ethiopia in exchange for Italy's rubber stamp on the creation of Manchukuo.

7. *Indianapolis Recorder*, September 26, 1936; *CD*, July 13, 1935.

8. *IR*, September 14, 1935; Ibid.; *PC*, October 24, 1936.

9. Marius B. Jansen, *The Japanese and Sun Yat-sen* (Stanford: Stanford University Press, 1954), 35–27.

10. *PT*, June 27, 1935; John Hope Franklin, *From Slavery to Freedom: A History of Negro Americans* 5th ed. (New York: Alfred A. Knopf, Inc., 1980), 422; John Hope Franklin and Alfred A. Moss, Jr., *From Slavery to Freedom*, 6th ed. (New York, London, Tokyo et al.: McGraw-Hill, Inc., 1988), 385. As in the African American communities of the United States, Japanese raised funds for the defense of the African kingdom and set up organizations. While the *Pittsburgh Courier* sent J. A. Rogers to cover the war, many Japanese correspondents were dispatched.

11. John Edgar Hoover, memorandum for the Attorney General, February 19, 1942, FBI Files.

12. I have been unable to find corroboration for Jordans claim of an affiliation with the Kokuryukai. In 1978 I sought to ascertain whether or not it was true and visited the Tokyo headquarters of the group that claims direct descent. The people that I met and talked with expressed surprise at the suggestion that there might have been such an affiliation. They had not heard of it. Looking through extant copies of the Kokuryukai magazines also revealed no mention of African Americans. In the biography of Ryohei Uchida, he did claim a central role in drumming up support for Japan putting before the Paris conference the proposal for racial equality. Moreover, he specifically denied that opposition to racial prejudice was merely for the sake of benefiting Japanese. *Kokushi Uchida Ryoheiden* (biography of Ryohei Uchida, patriot) (Tokyo: Ganshobo, 1967), 582, 583.

13. *CD,* July 13, 1935.

14. *IR,* August 24, 1935; *BAA,* August 29, 1936.

15. *BAA,* August 29, 1936.

16. Ibid.

17. Ibid.

18. *John Edgar Hoover* to L. M. C. Smith, Chief, Special Defense Unit, memorandum, December 18, 1941, FBI file 65–562–82.

19. "Naka Nakane, with aliases, Subversive Activities," report of [agent name deleted], March 20, 1940, Detroit file 62–709.

20. Edward J. Ennis, Director, Alien Enemy Control Unit, to J. Edgar Hoover, memorandum, July 10, 1942, FBI file 146-13-2-43-18. Pearl Takahashi visited her husband numerous times while he was exiled in Canada and was a frequent visitor after Nakane was incarcerated for illegally entering the country and trying to bribe a federal officer. But she was also the one who reported his whereabouts, probably in a fit of jealousy because of his cohabitation with a twenty-six year old secretary. Later, when he was seventy, sickly, and nearly blind, she petitioned to have him pardoned so that they could spend their last years together.

21. Detroit file 62–709.

22. Ernest Allen, Jr., "When Japan Was Champion of the Darker Races: Satokata Takahashi and the Flowering of Black Messianic Nationalism," *The Black Scholar* 24 (Winter 1994): 27, 28. I am indebted to Ernest Allen for his articles.

23. Ibid.

24. Detroit files.

25. Ibid.; because both drew such mass support, some FBI agents speculated that there was a connection between Nakane and Father Divine. What the agents failed to understand was that both appealed to a great many people who sought solace from their dismal realities.

26. Ernest Allen, "Waiting for Tojo: The Pro-Japan Vigil of Black Missourians, 1932–1943," *Gateway Heritage* (Fall 1995): 40; Allen, "Champion of the Darker Races," 25.

27. *IR,* March 11, 1933.

28. Walter White to James Weldon Johnson, September 25, 1933, James Weldon Johnson Papers, series 1, folder 542, Yale University Beinecke Library, New Haven, Connecticut (hereafter cited as JWJ).

29. Yasuichi Hikida to W. E. B. Du Bois, April 24, 1936, W. E. B. Du Bois Papers, reel 45, frame 1046, University of Massachusetts Library (Amherst), Microfilm Edition (hereafter cited as WEBD); Hikida to Johnson, October 11, 11935, JWJ, folder 206; Hikida to Du Bois, ibid.

30. Ibid., frame 1040.

31. U.S. War Department, Headquarters Third Service Company, Army, memo in re: Ethiopian Pacific Movement, February 11, 1943.

32. *IR*, September 7, 1935.

33. Ibid.

34. Ibid.

35. *PC*, October 30, 1937.

36. Ibid., October 9, 1937.

37. *New York Age*, October 24, 1937.

38. *PT*, February 18, 1932.

39. Ibid.

40. *PC*, March 20, 1937.

41. Ibid., February 13, 1937.

42. Ibid.

43. Ibid., February 20, 1937.

44. Ibid.

45. Ibid.

46. Ibid., March 13, 1937.

47. Had Du Bois been able to read the Japanese news accounts of his visit, he might have been surprised that they were welcoming him as "the father of the Negro." In at least two newspapers he was reported as "the father of the Indian." The latter paternity was apparently the result of a shipboard press conference at which Du Bois expressed interest in the aboriginal Ainu peoples whom he likened to Native Americans. See *Tokyo Asahi*, August 30; *Osaka Mainichi Shimbun*, December 2–6; *Tokyo Nichi Nichi Shimbun*, November 18; December 3, 11, 12, 1936.

48. *PC*, March 27, 1937.

49. Ibid., March 13, 1937.

50. Ibid., October 23, 1937; September 25, 1937.

51. Ibid., February 20, 1937; March 27, 1937; September 25, 1937. Du Bois had articulated the theme of China's submission to white aggression and Japan's resistance as the root cause for the enmity between the two countries before visiting East Asia. See *Philadelphia Tribune*, October 22, 1931; November 19, 1931.

52. *PC*, February 27, 1937.

53. Aptheker, 2, 185.

54. Du Bois to Robert L. Vann, May 25, 1936, WEBD, Reel 46, frame 540; from Vann, May 27, 1936 46/541; from C. J. Tagashira, November 21, 1936, 46/729; to Hikida, April 1, 1936, 45/1041.

CHAPTER 6

1. Gunnar Myrdal, *An American Dilemma: The Negro Problem and Modern Democracy* (New York, Toronto, London: McGraw-Hill Book Company, 1964), 1007.

2. Roi Ottley, *New World A-Coming* (Boston: Houghton Mifflin Company, 1943), 328. Both Ottley and Myrdal badly under-reported the numbers of African Americans who held pro-Japan sympathies. See Allen, "Waiting for Tojo" and "Champion of the Darker Races."

3. Siepmann to Dryer.

4. Horace R. Cayton, *Long Old Road* (Seattle and London: University of Washington Press, 1970), 271–76.

5. "Report of the Conference of National Organizations," January 10, 1942, National Urban League Archives (hereafter cited NUL), Library of Congress, Washington, D.C.

6. *PC*, January 10, 1942.

7. "Report of CNO," NUL.

8. George S. Schuyler, "Views and Reviews," *PC*, January 31, 1942.

9. Ibid., December 13, 1941.

10. Ibid.

11. *PC*, December 13, 1941; *LACE*, December 11, 1941.

12. *New York Amsterdam Star-News*, December 13, 1941; Lee J. Martin , "Remember Pearl Harbor!" *IR*, December 20, 1941; Carl Murphy,

"America—A Great Country," *BAA*, December 27, 1941; Lucius C. Harper, "We Cannot Look to Japan to Solve Our Problem," *CD*, December 27, 1941.

13. Emmett J. Scott, "Our Country Is at War," *IR*, December 27, 1941.

14. "Negro Organization and the War Effort," Special Service Division Report #3, 28 April 1942, Bureau of Intelligence, Records of Office of Government Reports, RG 44, Entry 171, Box 1843, WNRC.

15. *PC*, December 20, 1941.

16. Ibid., January 31, 1942; the double V was first emblazoned on the masthead on February 7, 1942.

17. Frank Marshall Davis, "War Quiz for America," *Crisis* 51 (April 1944): 144, 122; January 31, 1942.

18. Brief for Petitioner, exhibit, United States v. Gordon, 138 F. (2d) 174 (CCA 7) cert. den. 320 US 816. The profiles on the subjects of this discussion were drawn from the trial transcripts and interviews conducted by the FBI. Gordon's petition and transcript is in the National Archives. I have in my possession other transcripts, some of which were acquired by me under the Freedom of Information and Privacy Act.

19. Brief for Petitioner, exhibit, United States of America v. Gordon, 138 F. (2d) 174 (CCA 7) cert. den. 320 US 816 (hereafter cited as Gordon transcripts).

20. Report of Marion E. Torrens, March 31, 1942, Jordan Interview, EPM/FBI.

21. *Daily Worker*, December 17, 1942; *Detroit News*, October 9, 1944; *New York Daily Mirror*, March 9, 11, September 15, December 31, 1942; January 15, 1943; *New York Daily News*, February 20, 1942; *New York Herald Tribune*, December 19, 23, 1942; February 16, 1943; *New York Journal American*, February 20, 1942; *New York Times*, September 16, December 23, 29, 30, 31, 1942, January 15, 1943; *Oregon Journal*, January 1, 1943; *Washington Evening Star*, December 13, 1942; *Washington Times Herald*, December 18, 1942; United States v. Leonard Robert Jordan, alias Robert O. Jordan, C 113–264/C 113–40, US District Court for the Southern District of New York, New York.

22. Gordon transcripts.

23. Testimony of Chandler Owen, Gordon transcripts.

24. M. W. Acers to Director, March 31, 1942, EPM/FBI.

25. August Meier and Elliott M. Rudwick, *From Plantation to Ghetto: An Interpretive History of American Negroes* (New York: Hill and Wang, 1966), 203.

26. "Investigations Concerning Internal Security-J and Sedition," Interrogation of Jordan, March 31, 1942; Gordon petition and transcript; indictments of Jordan and Gordon, EPM/FBI.

27. Report of FBI informant, untitled, undated, EPM/FBI.

28. Ibid.

29. Ibid.

30. F. G. Tillman to F. L. Welch, Memorandum, May 31, 1943, EPM/FBI.

31. M. W. Acers to Director, FBI, March 31, 1942, EPM/FBI.

32. "Why Black Men Are Used Only as Messmen in the U.S. Navy," circular, undated; Ethiopian Pacific Movement, Inc. to President Roosevelt, December 15, 1941. They even asked specifically that African Americans be permitted to enlist in the United States Marine Corps.

33. *IR*, March 28, 1942; Lester B. Granger, "The Problem of Minorities in War Time," an address before the National Conference of Social Work, May 14, 1942; Granger, "Can We Win Racial Peace?" speech at City Club of Rochester, March 25, 1944, NUL; *New York Peoples' Voice*, August 29, 1942.

34. P. L. Prattis, "Anti-Japanese Agitation Looks Like Left-Handed Effort to Whet Up War-like Spirit in United States," *PC*, December 6, 1941; *PC*, September 29, 1945; *ASN*, December 20, 1941; *Los Angeles Tribune*, July 20, 1942.

35. *BAA*, December 5, 1942.

36. Bell I. Wiley, "The Training of Negro Troops," study #36, Historical Section, Army Ground Forces, Reference Collection, Box 292, #4057, NA.

37. Ibid., 52.

38. Ibid., 52, 53.

39. Ibid., 50, 40.

40. Ibid., 55. In his report, Wiley points out that it was not just the northern black who became intolerant of southern social conventions: at Camp Stewart, over half the troops were black southerners who had their views changed by contact with northerners and duty in a more convivial

Canadian environment. Likewise, the southern white officer, who looked upon African Americans condescendingly, was joined by his northern counterpart; after a time, African Americans were unable to differentiate between the white officer of the South and that of the North.

41. Horace Cayton, "Fighting for White Folks?" *Nation* 155 (September 1942): 268.

42. *BAA*, October 2, 16, 1943.

43. C. M. Vandeburg to Elmer Davis, re Negro Problem in Detroit September 19, 1942, OWI, RG 208, Entry 1, Box 8, folder titled "Racial Relations 1942–43."

44. *BAA*, July 10, 1943.

45. Cayton, 268.

46. J. Saunders Redding, "A Negro Looks at This War," *American Mercury* 55 (November 1942): 585.

47. Ibid., 586.

48. Tom Cripps, interview at Morgan State University, Baltimore, Maryland, September 1985.

49. *LACE*, December 18, 1941.

50. Ibid. January 1, 1942; February 12, 1942.

51. Letter, William Greenwell to Walter White, March 14, 1942, NAACP Archives, Library of Congress, Washington, D.C. (hereafter cited NAACP); *Peoples' Voice* (New York), February 21, 1942.

52. "Job Opportunities," news release, March 27, 1942; Letter, Roy Wilkens to White, December 8, 1942, NAACP.

53. *PV*, March 7, 1942.

54. Harry Paxton Howard, "Americans in Concentration Camps," *Crisis* (September 1942): 281–84, 301–2.

55. Letter, Samuel W. Thompson to Walter White, March 25, 1942, "Reflections in a Crackt Mirror," *Los Angeles Tribune*, July 13, 20, 1942, clipping, NAACP, Box 254/1/2.

56. "Report of the 33rd Annual Conference of the NAACP," July 14–19, 1942, NAACP, Box 254/1.

57. Vincent Tubbs, "How Japs Were Chased Out of Their West Coast Homes," *BAA*, April 24, 1943; June 5, 1943.

58. "Possible Friction between Japanese and Negroes in the Ninth Service Command Intelligence Division," December 13, 1944, Confidential Report, A.S.F. Domestic and Counter-Intelligence Branch, War Department, RG 319, Entry 47, Box 380, WNRC; "The Race War That Flopped: Little Tokyo and Bronzeville Upset Predictions of Negro-Nisei Battle," *Ebony* (July 1946): 3–8.

59. "Race War That Flopped," Thelma Thurston Gorham, "Negroes and Japanese Evacuees," *Crisis* 52 (November 1945): 315.

60. Negroes and Japanese Evacuees; Ottley, 331.

61. "Race War That Flopped," 8; Donald L. LeBlanc, Letter to the Editor, *Ebony* (October 1946): 50.

62. Redding, "A Second Look," *BAA*, January 6, 1945; *PC*, August 11, 1945; Willard S. Townsend, "One American Problem and a Possible Solution," in Rayford W. Logan, ed., *What the Negro Wants* (Chapel Hill, 1944), 171; *Michigan Chronicle*, January 13, 1945.

63. *PV*, December 16, 1944.

64. Roy Wilkens, "The Watchtower," *ASN*, July 17, 1943.

65. *BAA*, May 15, 1943.

66. Ibid., September 22, 1945; *PC*, August 18, 1945; *MC*, May 5, 1945; *NG*, February 23, 1945.

67. *BAA*, May 8, 1943; June 12, 1943; June 19, 1943.

68. *LACE*, October 8, 1942; *BAA*, June 26, 1943.

69. W. E. B. Du Bois, "As the Crow Flies," *ASN*, October 23, 1943; *NG*, July 28, 1944; August 24, 1945; November 30, 1945; December 1945; *PC*, September 15, 1945.

70. *PC*, August 25, 1945; Wilkens, "On War-Time Hysteria," *ASN*, November 13, 1943.

71. *NG*, December 8, 1944.

72. *BAA*, July 28, 1945.

73. *NG*, October 5, 1945; *MC*, March 3, 1945.

74. *ASN*, February 12, 1944; *NG*, February 18, 1944; January 26, 1945; November 16, 1945; April 27, 1945.

75. *MC*, May 29, 1943; June 224, 1944.

76. *BAA*, October 16, 1943.

77. *MC*, February 5, 1944; *NG*, February 4, 1944.

78. *PV*, December 11, 1943.

79. Ibid.; *PC*, October 13, 1945.

80. *BAA*, March 3, 1945.

81. Ibid., March 10, 1945; August 4, 1945.

82. *BAA*, May 5, 1945.

83. Ruth Benedict, *The Chrysanthemum and the Sword: Patterns of Japanese Culture* (New York and Scarborough, Ontario: New American Library, 1946), 38–41.

84. *NG*, April 27, 1945; *PC*, September 15, 1945.

85. *BAA*, August 18, 1945; *NG*, August 17, 1945; November 16, 1945; November 23, 1945.

86. *PC*, August 18, 1945.

87. Ibid.

88. *BAA*, September 15, 1945.

89. Ibid., August 18, 1945.

90. *PC*, December 15, 1945.

91. *BAA*, October 13, 1945.

92. Ibid.

93. Ibid., December 8, 1945.

94. *PC*, October 13, 1945.

95. Ibid.

96. Ibid.

CHAPTER 7

1. David E. Sanger, "Sumo Star Charges Racism in Japan," *New York Times*, April 22, 1992; "American Sumo Star Denies Accusing the Japanese of Racism," *NYT*, April 24, 1992. In an interview with the Japanese press Konishiki denied saying that his failure to get promoted to *yokozuna* was because of racism. Lora Sharnoff, the author of *Grand Sumo*, perhaps, the best book on the sport in English, says that Konishiki was misquoted. Telephone interview, June 1995.

2. Jonathan Clarke, "U.S. Media Close Vital Window on Japan," *Japan Times*, May 8, 1997.

3. Lionel C. Barrow Jr., "The Japanese: Are They Giving Us 'the Business'?" *Crisis* (April 1988): 16–21.

4. *Detroit Free Press*, October 30, 1988; Siepman to Dryer, June 8, 1942, Office of Facts and Figures, OWI, WNRC.

5. Robert Cole and Donald Deskins, "Racial Factors in the Employment Patterns of Japanese Auto Firms in America," *California Management Review* (Fall 1988).

6. *Los Angeles Times*, January 20, 1992; "Japanese-Owned Companies," *Crisis* (April–May 1992): 39.

7. Ibid.

8. Ibid.

9. Ibid.

10. Ibid.

11. Ibid.

12. Ibid.

13. Walton Brown, "Racism: Made in Japan," *Business and Society Review* (Summer 1988): 49–51.

14. Racial Attitudesin U.S.-Japan Relations, a symposium at the Japan Society, New York City, December 2, 1991.

15. Ibid.

16. Steven R. Weisman, "Fellow Asians, Yes but Where's the Fellowship?" *New York Times*, January 3, 1990.

17. *Asahi Shimbun*, March 20, 1993; *Japan Times*, March 20, 1993.

18. Marcus Mabry, "Dealing with the Juggernaut: Japan Sells Black America Short, But Recovery May Be on the Way," *The Black Collegian* (January/February 1992): 32.

19. Michael H. Cottman, "Blacks Face Image Problem," *Japan Times*, March 4, 1993. The same article appeared in another magazine, "Racism in Japan: Negative Images of Blacks Fuel Friction and Misunderstanding," *Emerge* (July/August 1993). The first person he quoted said that Japanese had been told nothing about blacks and in bookstores there were no books

about African American history, and almost none about African American literature. The interviewee obviously was unaware that John Hope Franklin's *Race and History* had just been translated. Moreover, Du Bois' *Souls of Black Folks*, Franklin's *From Slavery to Freedom*; and the works of Langston Hughes, Ralph Ellison, Imamu Baraka, Alice Walker, Tony Morrison, and many others have been translated into Japanese. The first book translated into Japanese dealing with the experience of African Americans was *Uncle Tom's Cabin*. Later, left-wing thinkers regarded African American literature highly as social protest literature.

20. Michael Berger, "Blacks at Home in Japan," *San Francisco Chronicle*, February 24, 1991.

21. Juan Williams, "Race and Japan: A Cross-Cultural Journey," *Washington Post*, January 5, 1992.

22. Ibid. Although they face some of the same problems as racial minorities in the United States, almost two-thirds of *burakumin* say in opinion polls that they have never encountered discrimination, and the *buraku* or neighborhoods are no longer slums. Yet, among *burakumin* social problems still abound: the average income is 60 percent the national average; alcoholism is disproportionately high; the number of single-parent households is twice as high as in the nation as a whole; 5 percent are on welfare, seven times the overall rate; a thirty-five-year-old study found that *buraku* children had lower IQs than their non-*buraku* peers; truancy, which in 1960 was twelve times as high as in the nation as a whole, has declined to where it is now merely twice as high.

23. *Jet*, January 12, 1987, 28–32; *Washington Post*, December 10, 1986.

24. *Baltimore Morning Sun*, October 4, 1990; *Baltimore Evening Sun*, October 22, 1990.

25. *Detroit Free Press*, August 3, 1988.

26. Schwalberg, 38.

27. Kathryn D. Leary, "Taking on Tokyo," *Essence* (October 1991): 76.

28. Teresa Williams, "The Japanese and Blacks: Which Direction for the 1990s?" *African Commentary* (May 1990):27.

29. JAFA was founded as the Japan Afro-American Friendship Association and JAIG was originally founded as the Japan African American Society.

30. Percy Luney, tape recording, Durham, NC, June 1991; Juan Williams, "Race and Japan," 27.

Epilogue

1. John Hope Franklin and August Meier, ed., *Black Leaders of the Twentieth Century* (Urbana, Chicago, London: University of Illinois Press, 1982), 306–18.

2. John W. Dower, *War without Mercy* (New York: Pantheon Books, 1986), 11.

3. Kathryn Leary, interview by author, Tokyo, Japan, August 11, 1996.

4. Letter, Delwin A. Roy to author, September 21, 1992.

5. Theodore Bassett et al., *Is Japan the Champion of the Colored Races?* (New York: Workers Library Publishers, Inc., 1938). Although the authors were listed as Bassett, A. W. Berry, Cyril Briggs, James W. Ford, and Harry Haywood, historian Ernest Allen says that Haywood was the actual author. Telephone interview, October 5, 1995.

☒☒☒☒

INDEX